mm

BOSTON MOB

Also by Marc Songini

The Lost Fleet

BOSTON MOB

The Rise and Fall of the New England Mob and Its Most Notorious Killer

MARC SONGINI

ST. MARTIN'S PRESS ≋ NEW YORK

BOSTON MOB. Copyright © 2014 by Marc Songini. All rights reserved. Printed in the United States of America. For information, address St. Martin's Press, 175 Fifth Avenue, New York, N.Y. 10010.

www.stmartins.com

Designed by Steven Seighman

Library of Congress Cataloging-in-Publication Data is available upon request

ISBN 978-0-312-37363-4 (hardcover)
ISBN 978-1-250-02131-1 (e-book)

St. Martin's Press books may be purchased for educational, business, or promotional use. For information on bulk purchases, please contact Macmillan Corporate and Premium Sales Department at 1-800-221-7945, extension 5442, or write specialmarkets@macmillan.com.

First Edition: July 2014

10 9 8 7 6 5 4 3 2 1

To Cian, my wonderful and best buddy—hoping he will choose the straight path, even when it's not the easiest one.

CONTENTS

But thou, O God, shalt bring them down into the pit of destruction: bloody and deceitful men shall not live out half their days

—PSALM 55

They were killing people at bus stops, walking in their house and killing them, walking in nightclubs and killing them. People were found in backs of trunks with their heads sawed off. People were found in suitcases, dissected. Guys were found floating in the river. There was a lot of hits in Boston and all different types of hits. . . .

—JOSEPH BARBOZA

BOSTON MOB

INTRODUCTION

It was winter 2002 in Washington, D.C., many years after the bloodbath. How many had died so prematurely? Sixty people? Eighty? The estimates varied. Some people had just vanished without a trace, making the count difficult.

Most players were off the field now. Their names had already appeared in the "Irish sporting pages"—that is, the obituaries. The McLaughlins, Bernie and Punchy, were memories, so were all three Bennetts, and Jimmy the Bear, the craziest of them all—as well as Buddy McLean, the toughest, perhaps. The top Mafiosi were long gone, or in jail: Raymond Patriarca, Larry Baione, Jerry Angiulo, and others.

And there, before a largely impotent congressional panel, stood the ancient gnomelike FBI agent, H. Paul Rico. His hair was silver, his skin tanned from the Florida sun. His sickening heart was rapidly making him a ghost, and he had many secrets to take with him. On that winter day in Washington, there was blood in the water, old and bad—and the representatives wanted to hand the public a victim. The congressmen even had feared Rico would go the usual route of gangsters, and take the Fifth. But he didn't.

Then the assembled representatives ineptly tried to force the ancient lawman to incriminate himself. But the ever-canny Rico couched all his answers to take any responsibility away from himself or the sacred bureau. That was how the system worked. To be fair, Rico did what the public, the president, and the FBI had asked him to do. The bureau was central in all this, surviving everything. But Rico's former Department of Justice bosses, J. Edgar Hoover and Robert Kennedy, were already ghosts—and tarnished ones, at that. Yet, so was their onetime enemy, the Mafia.

So on this day, even a mere U.S. congressman could dare throw accusations at an FBI special agent. The congressman even bemoaned the fate of a small-time crook, Joseph "the Horse" Salvati. Rico's efforts meant that Salvati had done a lot of time for a matter that, at most, he'd only been slightly connected to.

"You don't care," the congressman charged Rico. "Does it bother you that this man was in jail for thirty years?"

"It would probably be a nice movie or something," Rico responded.

The congressman eventually asked: "Do you have any remorse?"

"Remorse for what?"

"For the fact that you played a role in this."

"I believe the role I played was the role I should have played. . . . That's it. I cannot—"

"So you don't really care much and you don't really have any remorse. Is that true?"

Rico sneered. "Would you like tears or something?"

"Pardon me?"

"What do you want, tears?"

PROLOGUE

"Smile, I miss you so much with such a constant ache of loneliness & love . . . they can't break the one constant train of thought & image I have . . . you, you, you!"

So Joseph Barboza Baron wrote with his elegant penmanship to a far-off woman he barely knew. But he was familiar with letter romance, having once conducted such a courtship for years, with his first wife. Indeed, Joe did write tender letters, even if he was, in the words of one observer, "one of the most dangerous psychopaths in the history of the Commonwealth of Massachusetts." Perhaps more noteworthy than the tone of the letter was the location where Joe was penning it. It was a place even he, admittedly, was surprised to be: the "historical territorial prison" of Deer Lodge, Montana. Given the New England branch of La Cosa Nostra had put a $300,000 open contract on his massive head, he signed his letters "Joe Bentley." By now, it was November 1972, and he was forty, a self-described "Portugee from New Bedford" with a crime record of Torah length. Joe's careers included those of thief, arsonist, extortionist, boxer, assassin, strong-arm man, cook, and public relations specialist. Currently married to a second (and unhappy) wife,

Joe had two children (acknowledged, at least) and faced years of jail. On release, beckoning to Joe was an existence that would be nasty, abrupt, and brutish—rather like Joe himself.

Already, Joe had measured out half of his life behind bars for a cornucopia of misdemeanors and felonies. One novelty of his current sentence (besides the out-of-state penal venues) was that it was Joe's first for murder—and a particularly sloppy killing at that. In public, he'd shot a business partner in the head in front of two eyewitnesses, including the victim's wife. Joe had even bragged that, after laying the partner's body to rest, he then laid the man's wife. Still, no surprises there. An all-but-certified sociopath, Joe "the Animal" Barboza had a way of generating unsavory tales. There was the story of how he beat a taxi driver to death with a tire iron. . . . Joe himself boasted he shot a onetime friend at point-blank range—then brushed pieces of the victim's skull and brains out of his own thick hair. He also bragged about the near-fatal stabbing of a nineteen-year-old over a five-dollars interest payment. He stuck an eighteen-year-old girl in the thigh because of her uncle's debt. Personally, he tallied his crimes at a Herculean seventy-five stabbings, five hundred beatings, and twenty murders.

And the Animal possessed near-mechanical speed and precision. "When it came to killing, I always thought he was more of a device than an animal," said North End gangster Willie Fopiano. "Yet, Joe 'the Device' Barboza didn't have the same ring." But Joe was so magnetic and charming that his victims never knew they were in danger. He might be drinking or schmoozing with a target, and then a gun or a knife could appear in the next instant. As Willie explained: "He was perfect for a war."

A mere disagreement with Joe could earn bodily harm and even death. He demonstrated a "capacity for revenge that makes Caligula look like a benevolent saint," said underworld colleague William Geraway.

By now, parked in the garage, as it were, Joe occupied his mind with his fiancée, along with various outlandish schemes. Joe gushed teenage sentiments into his letters, claiming he read one of his beloved's epistles no less than eight times. During one Christmas—a holiday that he, as a Jew, didn't observe—he wrote, "Of course I want you more then anything in life, not only on Xmas but all year around even more then Maple Walnut ice cream!"

Joe's betrothed, "Green Eyes," was a five-foot-four-inch, 170-pound thirtysomething San Francisco redhead who could rebuild Corvettes. He told, imaginatively, of his pleasure in seeing and reaching the happiness he'd brought alive in her. Joe knew she'd been hurt in the past, like he had been. The Animal kept asking himself, Was this girl for real? The answer was yes: Joe asked her "Where were you when I was growing up and needed you!"

Joe's lady friend was a "patient and reasonable person," who actually believed she had tamed the Animal. He seemed to have a deep appeal for her, as for his other girlfriends. After all, "Barboza fascinated women," as a writer who knew him explained. Green Eyes believed they could build a peaceful life in hiding. They had initially met, in a sense, when she was typing up the manuscript to his unimaginatively named book, *Barboza*. Perhaps the romance with Green Eyes flourished because she hadn't seen him. "I have a very expressive face when I talk & like a lot of Bostonians I use my hands a lot talking," he told her. His appearance was generally unforgettable—the big upper body on small legs—but he possessed a physique useful for receiving and dispensing pain. People couldn't take their eyes off him. His "big ugly head," as he called it, sprouted straight from his broad shoulders—some fellow gangsters called him "No Neck." Under his thick curly black hair was a face with a "Neanderthal look . . . a genuine, tough hoodlum look," as one U.S. marshal noted. It was an "ugly mug," as Joe admitted.

His mouth bristled with healthy strong choppers—of these, the crown jewels were two very large pointed teeth, not quite human, resembling fangs. They fit Joe's head well, given he had "an under

bite like a barracuda." Once, during a brawl at a Nantasket amusement park, a large, strong brawler caught Joe in a tight bear hug.
With one hand, Joe pulled the brawler's face toward his; then he
clamped his formidable teeth into his opponent's cheek. With the
other hand, Joe pushed the man's chin. "The meat on his cheek
started to rip away," said the Animal. "He screamed and let go." After
spitting out the flesh and blood, Joe summarily had knocked his opponent out and then fled from the arriving police. Rinsing his mouth
out repeatedly with Coke didn't let Joe get rid of the taste of blood.

And, Geraway noted, even Joe's palms were odd—they were
padded, not creased, with two vertical and two horizontal lines
crossing them. The texture and contours were "just as though I were
looking at the paw of an animal," said Geraway. "Joe was pretty
unusual, the bastard." Then there was his resonant baritone voice,
which, through years of smoking, sounded like fine sandpaper on
wood. And Joe could speak with methodical calm, something useful to threaten victims.

Given Joe's long and high-profile criminal career, he'd been
uncommonly fortunate. He'd survived a series of Boston gang wars
and assassinations that had killed at least scores of criminals—as
well as women and innocent bystanders who'd been cursed with a
bad sense of place and timing. Even some of the worst gangsters
found these wars distasteful and frightening. Not so much Joe. He
claimed to be an ace with twenty kills, and allegedly said murder-
ing someone "was like fucking Marilyn Monroe." Neither Joe nor
his best friend and partner Vincent James "the Bear" Flemmi
would win any popularity contests with their underworld rivals
and colleagues. As Joe said in a letter to Green Eyes: "By all per-
centages I should have been dead 10 years ago . . . [there were]
more than six attempts made on my life. But destiny had it written
that I was to meet [you] and we have met. . . ."

As a government witness, Joe had crushed the once-invulnerable
dons of New England in a few months of testimony. He also avoided

an eighty-four-year prison sentence in Massachusetts. But later, while doing time in a California prison, he'd blown his own cover by testifying before Congress about mob influence in sports. Joe's expertise in this subject was limited to terrorizing deadbeat jockeys, and clubbing a bookmaker at a racetrack with a banister. During his testimony, Joe had even slandered Frank Sinatra, now royally and publicly pissed.

After that, the Golden State authorities had fobbed Joe off on Montana, for his own safety. But as he admitted to his paramour he'd lost a lot of bitterness and hate, and had been experiencing the healthy "emotion of the wisdom of life." She'd given him the will to live—the Animal now claimed he wanted to share his life and future with her.

Joe was strong and healthy in body—he might live awhile yet, if no one killed him. And he expected *Barboza* to outsell even *The Godfather*. It would make him rich enough to pursue his literary career and remarry grandly. But first, he needed parole—which he believed was in his grasp. After all, he'd only killed an inconsequential biker—and he had strong friends in government.

Joe and his woman were like one person, he boasted: A to B; neither one any good without the other. "My Classy Baby, if I was on the other side of the world you know I will get back to you nothing can stop that, because we have a whole lot of living together to do." He signed that letter, "Eternally yours, Joe."

THE PORTUGEE FROM NEW BEDFORD

"In New Bedford, fathers, they say, give whales for dowers to their daughters, and portion off their nieces with a few porpoises a-piece."
    —Herman Melville, *Moby-Dick*

On September 20, 1932, was born the infant destined to mutate into "one of the worst men on the face of the earth." Joseph Barboza Jr. spent his first years in the small coastal city of New Bedford. This once-legendary former whaling port nestled on a North Atlantic peninsula. But Joe had selected an inopportune time to join this city's oppressed and hard-toiling population. Eight decades before his arrival, the city was "perhaps the dearest place to live in, in all New England," Herman Melville claimed. "It is a land of oil, true enough: but not like Canaan; a land, also, of corn and wine . . . nowhere in all America will you find more patrician-like houses; parks and gardens more opulent, than in New Bedford."

Had Joe been born a hundred years prior, his savagery and viciousness would hardly have drawn attention in a whaleship's forecastle. There had been legal opportunities back then for fierce, bold men like him. However, before Joe arrived, the whalers' staple game, the sperm and bowhead leviathans, grew very scarce. The Civil War and a run of Arctic disasters pared down New Bedford's once-famous whaling fleet. In 1924, New Bedford's last whaler of note, the *Wanderer*, had smashed into the shallows off Cuttyhunk

Island during a gale. That had clearly marked the death and burial of Yankee whaling.

By the 1930s, New Bedford's smart money had relocated into unheroic and unglamorous industries, such as textiles or railroads. Graceful ships' masts went out; smokestacks replaced them. With muscle, blood, spindles, smoke, grime, and decaying grandeur to sustain it, New Bedford persisted in a second (or third) life. Its ugly factories crowded the skyline, and its dirty and overflowing tenements competed for space with the fine houses, banks, ship-yards, and church spires of a prior era. In short, the onetime "City of Light" was like any other New England factory metropolis on the slide down.

At the time of Joe's birth, the white leviathan sinking New Bedford was the Depression. In 1932, a local textile baron kindly loaned a desperate New Bedford $100,000 so it could make its payroll. But this was akin to applying a bandage to an incurable sore. Needless to say, a New Bedford working family's life was then very harsh, only slightly better than a slave's. Factory wages barely sustained life, and malnutrition and poverty killed off more chil-dren in New Bedford than in almost any other U.S. city. A favored child learned the useful skill of weaving from a parent, without pay. Hopefully, the apprentice lasted until age fourteen, when he started working legally and repaying the investment made in him.

The second Barboza child, Joe was about as isolated as one can get. In tiny compartmentalized New Bedford, the Portuguese man-aged to stand apart, clannish, with a separate tongue and unique flavor of Roman Catholicism. In that little hardscrabble commu-nity, Joseph Barboza Sr. managed an uneasy truce with his wife, Palmeda "Patty" Camile, with whom, for a while, he raised five children. Barboza eked out a subsistence living, and sometimes less, as a milkman and factory worker. For cash, he also boxed, proving "one of the best little 160-pounders" from the region. But Barboza was also a convicted petty criminal, with a taste for women and drink, and not exactly monogamous. He was also a wifebeater, and once scattered Patty's front teeth with a blow.

In the long-suffering manner of the time, Patty pretended he was faithful. But the domestic misery was as contagious as measles. "The house we lived in was more of sorrow than of happiness," as Joe later noted. "We were constantly on welfare." One day, Joe came home and found his mother unconscious, with the gas jet on. Patty survived, but her mate abandoned the family completely.

Once, Patty ordered Joe to beg for his father to return home. While Patty waited on the street, the boy found Joseph Sr. outside in a yard with a woman he'd "shacked up" with.

"Get out of here, you little bastard," his father said.

"The punk broke my heart," the future career criminal admitted. Crying, Joe turned and ran down the street to his mother. Having a change of heart, Joseph Sr. drove after him and found him with his mother.

"He will never forget this," Patty told her husband. Joe wept all the way home. Although Barboza bought Joe a pigeon, he didn't return to the family flat.

Minus the family breadwinner, Patty also worked as a waitress and even shoplifted, for which she was arrested. Shunned by her husband, for solace, Patty clung to Joe and his brother—who were then running "wild." Joe felt she used him as bait to keep something, any little bit, of her husband.

Joe never forgot his extreme poverty, nor how his mother had suffered through it. This unhappy childhood packed him with enough explosive rage for a lifetime. Aware he was a shuttlecock between his parents, Joe took to freely roaming the streets with other urchins. There, as he put it, "I had a better type of love." And if his father ignored him, at least he could command the attention of New Bedford. Thus, Joe drifted steadily into wild waters. He started smoking at age seven; at fourteen, police arrested him, apparently for damaging an electronic streetcar signal.

Lacking a stable family at home, Joe created another type of family by forming a gang. Joe's criminal apprenticeship moved from shoplifting to burglary. During the day, Joe's crew would go window-shopping, and then return later to steal whatever items the members had coveted. In 1945, the police arrested Joe for breaking and entering, and at age fourteen, Joe graduated to the Lyman Reform School, a "hellhole" of constant brutality. Orderlies beat Joe and the other residents with belts and pick handles. But the house specialty on the pain menu was the "hot foot," where orderlies struck the naked arch. To survive, Joe made himself the brawling champion of Lyman, getting into three hundred fights.

When released, he began to box in the ring.

"He was tough and strong," noted a New Bedford boxing fan, "a real crowd pleaser who could take an opponent out with one punch—if he could hit him." Few boxers wanted to mix with Joe, who was all attack without much defense. In one notable fight in a Boston arena, a lanky black middleweight knocked Joe down twice, but won by decision. "Actually, it was a hell of a fight; the guy beat Barboza only because he was the better sharpshooter and made his punches count," a fan recalled years later. Against very good fighters, Joe had little chance at all. The incarcerated boxing great (and fellow psychopath) Bobby Quinn sparred in jail with young Joe. "I used to beat him till my hands hurt," he recalled.

The state tried again to rehabilitate Joe, this time by sending him to a vocational school. After a woodworking teacher insulted him, Joe rallied his gang to trash the classroom at night. Newspapers claimed someone had hurled a pie at a wall, and a writer dubbed the crew the "Cream Pie Bandits." With the seventeen-year-old South End resident as their leader, the bandits allegedly broke into two hundred cars in six months. In December 1949, the gang launched a veritable petty reign of terror, entering unoccupied houses, restaurants, businessess, and cars and stealing anything it could spend, enjoy, or sell. The takes generally didn't top ten or twenty dollars apiece, and the goods included a necklace, socks, cigarettes, lighters, caulking tools, and, possibly, even Christmas trees. Before New Year's Day, police arrested Joe, the ringleader, and another thief. In court without counsel, Joe and his colleague, the only two bandits of adult age, pled guilty to all counts.

To mark Joe's holiday season, a judge sentenced him to five years and a day in the Massachusetts Reformatory in Concord. This cut short his formal education at grade eight and put his fight career on hold. Concord existed to reform juvenile delinquents. Its record was reliable: 80 percent of its graduates committed more crimes. There, in the town of the prophets of freedom, Thoreau and Emerson, Joe worked as a penal slave in a weaving mill. Later, he graduated to the dining room, where he remained—until, during a brawl, he broke an older inmate's jaw in two places with a left hook. For that, Joe went to solitary, then to the boiler room to shovel coal and stoke an ever-growing rage. "Being a convict sure is a lowly state & they don't let you forget it!" as he once observed.

In January 1951, Joe transferred to the relatively bucolic Norfolk County Prison, which functioned like a rehabilitation center. There, he boxed as a middleweight, knocking older men out routinely, he later boasted. Such a good thing couldn't last, and in September 1951, high on paint thinner, he challenged the guards to come and get him. After a two-hour stalemate, no longer intoxicated, Joe negotiated peace terms. This finalized the nineteen-year-old Animal's contract in life. The authorities (presciently) determined him beyond rehabilitation. Back to Concord Joe went.

Now Joe joined with a ring of enterprising guards, who, for a premium, did business with the inmates, and even took their bets. Their commodities included steaks and other fine food and drugs, including "goofballs," or tranquilizers, and Benzedrine ("bennies"). Working on his undergraduate's degree in criminal science, Joe apprenticed with a wayward "screw" or guard, who demonstrated the tricks of smuggling. The enterprising Joe began dealing in bennies, liquor, knives, and food with other inmates.

The warden, sensing Joe might be a good leader of bad men, offered him the chance to work the prison farm—if he behaved. Joe repaid this trust by leading a prison riot, and back to solitary (and bread and water) he went. Later, finally allowed back on the farm, Joe enjoyed something like an idyllic life. He drove a team of horses, which he "dug"; surreptitiously swam in the nearby reservoir; and watched TV nightly. From the prison henhouse, he stole chickens for a fellow convict to fry.

Joe had just cracked the second decade of his life when his personality set. He was pretty much—mentally, morally, and physically—the man he'd remain as an adult. As he grew, something in his genetic code misfired, aesthetically and morally, at least. Once, he'd been a slender and clean-cut teenager. But during his jail years, he metamorphosed into a grotesque caveman. He topped off at maybe five feet ten inches, a distance containing a massive torso that included a forty-six-inch chest and thirty-five-inch waist. But the legs remained relatively short and stubby, and didn't quite appear to fit symmetrically with the upper body they supported.

The burly Joe weighed 185 pounds, and his big padded hands were matched by feet that required a size-ten shoe. A mole dotted his right cheek above the massive jaw, while over his small sleepy brown eyes, long eyebrows fluttered. His profile was almost a flat vertical line from his forehead to the jutting Hapsburg-sized chin. He had JOE tattooed on his right forearm, and BORN TO LOSE and 1932 (his birth year) on the right biceps. A pair of boxing gloves and a scar adorned the left biceps. To perfect the appearance, he carried himself with a swagger. As one knowing reporter claimed, "he could have passed for just another cheap punk who hung out on New Bedford street corners and picked up a buck here or there running numbers."

As far as morals, he believed all men will do whatever they want until they are caught violating the law. Therefore, Joe formed a compromise with himself—publicly, he'd appear to be good, while privately, he'd break the rules. And he was often caught. He made the headlines at age twenty-one, when drunk on Concord home brew and goofballs, he led a seven-man escape. His make-shift gang beat several guards, and took one of their cars—an ancient and unreliable machine that died in the middle of Route 27. Joe and four companions reached a nearby gas station, which they robbed. While stealing a car, Joe hit its owner hard enough to fracture his cheekbone, and nearly blinded him in one eye. The crude escape made page 1, and the law sought the fugitives everywhere in New England. Instead of hiding, on July 14, Joe and two other escapees visited a Revere Beach barroom before boarding a bus to East Boston. During a stop at the busy Orient Heights MTA station, three policemen, their guns drawn, boarded the bus. After Joe and his cohorts surrendered peaceably, the police showed them off like landed prize fish, posing the manacled trio for a news photographer.

Back in Concord, Joe visited solitary, exchanging choice words with a guard before striking him with a table. Six more guards descended on Joe to hogtie him. They then hustled him into a dungeon for ten days to live on bread and water. Despite promises of light punishment, he refused to squeal on the ring of corrupt screws he'd partnered with. Sometimes, during his solitary stretches, he staged conversations with himself to avoid going completely crazy.

In May 1954, Joe's Revere vacation resulted in a decade-plus sentence in Charlestown State Prison. The "gray monster" was little more than a series of huge granite slab walls that encased the state's worst men. Dust from the nearby railroad coal yards perpetually covered its surfaces. The cells had no running water, so an inmate defecated in a bucket in his cell. The facility did have one touch of modernity: the state's electricity-powered murder seat. A convict on his way to do time here could briefly catch a glimpse of the Bunker Hill obelisk and the masts of the U.S.S. *Constitution*. Then, he passed through the gates and joined his new family, which included the hardest killers, thieves, rapists, and psychopaths in the Commonwealth. For the infraction of not smiling at a guard, a convict could do solitary—which meant pitch blackness on bread and water. Yet by 1955, at age twenty-two, ever the leader of bad men, Joe headed the inmate council at the "ancient Bastille."

Perhaps sensing leadership potential, the authorities tried to decipher this wayward Bay State ward. In 1956, one doctor noted Joe's "features make him look less bright than he actually is; his I.Q. is of the order of 90–100 and he has the intellectual ability to do well in a moderately skilled occupation." But a later report noted Joe's "sociopathic personality disturbance" and concluded there was "always a great possibility of further anti social behavior in the future."

2

AN ANIMAL IS BORN

"Bubbles, you can believe I never bow to anyone! Never have all my life! Gone to some nightmares . . . to never bow down. . . ."

—Joe Barboza, in a letter

A new home soon beckoned to the budding Animal. In 1955, Walpole Prison opened its gates as the new Harvard University of the criminal class of Massachusetts. Nine million dollars had bought a chalk-white alien-looking rectangle containing a jail, administrative building, and ball field. Twenty-foot walls bristling with coils of razor wire connected the eight outer towers. Anything beyond that would fry on the electric fence surrounding the facility.

"In the joint [Walpole] you live in a space a little bigger than your average closet," said the North End thief Willie Fopiano. "And you sleep just a few feet from your toilet. After lights out, a guard beams a flashlight on you every hour. If he doesn't see some flesh in the bed, he opens the cell and shakes you awake. If that happens too many times they haul you off to solitary. Every day you're ordered around, by shouts of guards or squawks of loudspeakers. It takes a long time to adjust to all that."

Frequently in solitary but needing to communicate, young Joe learned to write poetry as a diversion—and possibly to maintain a dialogue with himself. A jailhouse Walt Whitman, his earnestness almost compensated for a lack of style. In his poem, "City of

Forgotten Men," Joe portrayed himself as one of 500 men locked inside "dark gray stone." The years were coming and going, and they were all creating dreams in the sky.

> *"We only pray that we never again*
> *Return to the city of forgotten men."*

That same year, 1958, Joe at last made parole. Leaving Walpole, in July he married Philomena, a "fine, fine" East Boston divorcée and mother of four. She was sixteen years his senior—but with her, Joe had enjoyed an eight-years-long letter romance. For money, he briefly worked the fish pier and the ring—but, by September, a failed break-in returned Joe to the ever-waiting Walpole.

Back inside, one "weasel" of a kitchen worker annoyed Joe enough to merit a sucker punch. Joe laid the man out cold, so that he required a spinal tap. The warden then exiled Joe from the kitchen to work outside. This helped Joe relaunch his various lending and gaming enterprises. Soon, he'd assembled a bankroll worth hundreds to buy food through a screw.

He ventured into the surrounding woods for meetings, and sometimes donned a sports coat and drove to restaurants. He swam or fished, bred rabbits, and indulged in what eventually became his lifelong passion for cooking. In 1960, with the help of his boxing manager, Joe again made parole. Before he left Walpole, Joe handed his bookmaking and shylocking operations to Vincent James Flemmi—always just "the Bear" to Joe—and other favored convicts.

Once out, for reasons unclear, he also filed divorce papers against Philomena. She didn't contest them and died a few years later of a "bad heart," as Joe said. Focusing on his career, Joe reentered the ring—a boxing magazine featured him as a prominent up-and-coming fighter. For a day job, his boxing manager hired Joe for his scooter-rental agency in Park Plaza in downtown Boston. The manager also fronted him money, with which to breed money, in the process known as shylocking. His first year, Joe took the initial $2,000 and turned it into $25,000, becoming one of loan-sharking's "lesser lights," as the FBI put it. Those that didn't repay their loans faced punishment, which even Joe admitted could be excessively harsh. He warned people not to take loans they couldn't repay. Joe explained to one client (whose face he'd sliced open) that he didn't get his "jollies" from hurting people. This victim agreed he'd caused the stabbing.

Joe noted: "I was glad he said it because when I hurt a customer I always wanted to make sure it was their fault." However, having a victim out on the street displaying a scarred face and neck was like buying an advertisement. But, violence had limits, even to Joe. As he said, amused, "If anybody died from shylocking, it'd be a $90 dollar customer—it won't be the $5,000 customer, because that [murder] don't get you your money back."

Although born a Portuguese Catholic, Joe so freely associated with the Sons of Abraham he became known as the "King of the Jews." Joe boasted about his Jewish brawling buddies at Nantasket Beach, where, on weekends, he bounced in Duffy's Lounge. Being from New Bedford, he enjoyed gazing out at the open spaces of the ocean after leaving jail. After beating up some of the local rowdies, he was able to enjoy the job in peace. (He did, however, clock a police chief's son, which required a cash remedy.) Friends arranged for Joe to receive a driver's license and an unreliable 1952 Dodge. One day, when the car died, ex-con and loanshark Gaetano "Guy" Frizzi tinkered with the engine till it started. Later, the two men drank coffee and, eventually, started a partnership—with Joe providing muscle to Guy and his two brothers, Conno and Ninni.

Joe and Guy formed an odd and vastly antisocial pair. Joe claimed Guy mimicked the gangster-actor George Raft—and was foulmouthed, obnoxious, and violent. In short, he was rather like Joe. However, Guy slapped women around—which soured Joe.

Nevertheless, within two years, $5,500 was rolling in weekly "by way of interest," and Joe's bank rose to about $70,000. To handle the action, he and Guy took on four other associates, including one promising thug named Carlton Eaton.

Alone, Joe was maniac enough, but coupled with his henchmen, he was a loaded pistol without a safety. In a Revere restaurant, Guy once started a fight with a Malden bookmaker's bodyguard. Joe ended the altercation by first stabbing the tough with a broken bottle, then knocking him out with two punches. Soon after, one of Barboza's crew stabbed an off-duty Boston policeman at the Peppermint Lounge. Joe and Guy might have been arrested if the wounded officer hadn't been committing adultery the night of the fight. Later, Joe claimed Guy had started a curse. As for Guy, he soon realized that Joe was more than a partner—he was a menace, even to his friends.

3.

A RISING STAR

"This thing [the Mafia] you're in, it's going to be a life of heaven."
—J. R. Russo

It was June 11, 1939, and a crowd of reporters and photographers had formed at Boston's South Station to greet the New York City train as it pulled into the terminal. The train stopped, and given the hubbub, it seemed as if a movie star had arrived. But instead, manacled to a state police escort, out stepped a small, dapper man. No matinee idol, he was reluctant to be there, and used his hat to hide his fierce—and easily recognizable—Mediterranean features. His name was Raymond Patriarca, a Rhode Island public enemy, and currently the most notorious criminal in New England, if not the nation.

The front pages had proclaimed his name for weeks, after he'd illegally secured a pardon for his many crimes and made Bay State justice look foolish. Already, witnesses were testifying, and the political careers of powerful men, including the governor, were imperiled. Indeed, Raymond faced a serious backlash—the Massachusetts authorities were very upset and planned to punish him. Yet it was a petty crime—stealing a car in Cambridge—that had made Raymond curtail his five-month honeymoon. He had left his distraught wife Helen behind in their Miami Beach apartment.

For further humiliation, a Boston magistrate was reviewing Raymond's recent marriage license, which contained an erroneous address. Despite this, the tough and stoic Raymond had been a model prisoner on the way up north from Miami, said his escort. When the soft-spoken Raymond chatted, which was rare, it was about his winter in Florida, his family, or the weather. During the train ride, he mostly passed the time looking out the window.

A natural actor, Raymond used his expressive face, big sensual lips, and deep brown eyes to great and unforgettable effect. But today, when on the South Station platform with policemen taking him for booking, Raymond shied from the photographers hounding him, giving them his back. He asked the journalists, "Haven't you guys caused me enough trouble already? Now leave me alone, 'cause you ain't going to get nothin'."

But Raymond was wrong—he'd be providing them with juicy and unpredictable fodder for the next forty years.

To paraphrase Shakespeare, some are born crooked, some achieve crookedness, and some have crookedness thrust upon them. With Raymond it seems to have been a mix of all three. It was on March 17, 1908, Saint Patrick's Day, when Mary Jane Patriarca presented her husband, Eleuterio, with a son. As struggling Italian immigrants, the Patriarcas weren't rich—nevertheless, they gave their son a grand name: Raimondo Laredo Salvatore.

The Patriarcas lived at 161 Atwells Avenue, in the Italian ghetto on Federal Hill in Providence, Rhode Island. They inhabited a clapboard-faced four-story brick tenement in a declining neighborhood only a few blocks from Providence's elegant downtown. Nearby there also stood the Rhode Island capitol, and city hall. Eleuterio was reportedly a wine clerk, so after Prohibition he began selling liquor illegally. He prospered enough to acquire parcels of land that were soon worth $23,000 (they'd later come in handy to use as collateral when raising bail for his wayward sons).

It's a tough call just how Raymond might have turned out if the Grim Reaper hadn't intervened. But in February 1925, as Raymond put it, "I lost my father and I guess I drifted a little." His father dead, Raymond, seventeen, left school and "commenced drunk rolling and bootlegging." In May 1926, Raymond began his official record by violating Prohibition. He received a $250 fine and a month in a Greenwich, Connecticut, jail. Released, he immediately broke his probation. And so it went, with Raymond endlessly accumulating petty crimes and fines.

Raymond topped off at a mere five feet six inches of stocky nerve. But with his sharp Italian features and legendary fierce gaze, he could radiate dangerousness when needed. At some point, Raymond allied with the local Mafiosi—Frank "Butsey" Morelli and his brother Joe Morelli. (The duo and their gang were little more than bold and reckless thieves.) Raymond also moved rum from coastal Rhode Island to Worcester, working with the highly capable and discreet Frank Iacone, the local Mafia don. Under Iacone's tutelage, in 1929 Raymond apparently became a "made" (or, officially Mafia-initiated) man, responsible to the New York families. His shrewdness impressed the Empire State wise guys so much that Raymond bragged in the 1960s, "I have called every shot in New York for the last 18 years."

In the early 1930s, Raymond started enforcing for a Rhode Island Irish mobster called "Dinky." A police rumor claimed that while guarding liquor shipments, Raymond let them be hijacked for the right price.

Still a small-timer, Raymond was arrested for petty crimes such as breaking and entering and for the grand evil of rolling dice on a Sunday. But after he and his brother Joseph crossed state lines to do some pimping in New Haven (they earned $44), they were convicted for violating the federal Mann Act. Both Patriarcas headed below the Mason-Dixon Line to share lodgings in the grim and gloomy federal penitentiary in Atlanta.

Released after his year-and-a-day sentence, Raymond remained a very bold and persistent thief. He committed more stickups—including the robbery of a Webster bank's cash shipment. His gang took three bags of loot and drove off in a car equipped with a rear-mounted bulletproof iron plate. Raymond and two cohorts were later arrested for the crime, but the case evaporated. Nevertheless, by 1933, he had risen high enough—or to reverse the metaphor, sunk low enough—for inclusion in the Providence police's public enemy list. Officers could arrest him on sight if they caught him driving after sundown. "Sure I was a bad kid in Providence," Raymond later admitted. "Everyone knew I was a gambler."

Although baptized into a crime family, Raymond had to earn on his own. He wandered all over southern New England looking for scores. He racked up yet more arrests for a mixed antipasto of crimes: robbery in Southbridge, vagrancy in Springfield, larceny of an auto in Cambridge, being a suspicious person in Providence and Pawtucket, and "lewd cohabitation" in Worcester. For two years, despite steady arrests, the most the authorities could do was fine Raymond for lying about his name at a murder inquest. But he loved stealing, admitting later: "The happiest days of my life were when I was on the street clipping."

On March 19, 1937, Raymond and two associates hit the offices of Oxford Print, a Brighton payroll-printing plant. After taking the switchboard operator hostage, they tore the telephone wires. At gunpoint, the trio forced an obviously stalling treasurer to enter the vault and open the safe. After lifting the company payroll, the thieves made off in a stolen car. On February 12, 1938, in broad daylight, Raymond and a partner robbed $12,000 from Wallbank Jewelry Company in Brookline. To prevent chase, the duo forced Wallbank, a salesman, and the secretary to remove their clothes. They fled in Wallbank's own car.

Only five days later, Raymond took one risk too many when he hit the United Optical Plant—a maker of fine and expensive gold eyeglass frames in Webster. After dark, Raymond and a partner broke into the plant and ransacked it. An alert neighborhood dog's barking drew official attention, and a party of patrolmen and deputies descended on the factory. Flashlights out, investigators discovered Raymond hiding under a bench.

"Come out, and with your hands up," a patrolman commanded. At gunpoint, Raymond—briefly using the alias "Roma"—obeyed. Inside Raymond's car was a large bag that held "one of the most complete set of burglar tools ever seen in this part of New England." The police soon realized Roma was Raymond. There was also a custom pin inside the car, and a ring with the Wallbank stamp on it. State police arrived to process this special case, and one phone call connected Raymond to the Wallbank robbery.

Free on $50,000 bail, on August 13 Raymond visited Rhode Island's Narragansett Racetrack. There, the Ocean State police arrested him for transport to the Summer Street jail in Worcester. Soon after, Wallbank identified Raymond as the man who'd robbed his store, clothes, and car. Also, Raymond discovered the authorities had fingered him (erroneously) in yet another theft: that of a jewelry store in Boston. In August, while before a Worcester Superior Court judge, Raymond decided to avoid a long, risky trial and pled guilty to holding up Wallbank. The state next tried Raymond on the botched United Optical break-in, and found him guilty. A judge gave Raymond a three- to five-year sentence (to run concurrently with the Wallbank term) and sent him to Charlestown Prison.

Raymond was doing time when political fixer and disbarred law-yer Daniel H. Coakley entered the scene. Called without irony "the Knave of Boston," Coakley claimed an oculist arranged for a meeting with Raymond's brother. Joseph Patriarca claimed: "My mother was grieving and sighing and I thought I'd go around and see a few people and see what I could do."

When Coakley met Raymond, he said, "I fell in love with him." No doubt, Raymond had charm, but both his biological and adopted Mafia families had some money and influence. Soon af-ter, Coakley submitted a pardon petition to the Massachusetts Governor's Council, with forged letters from one imaginary and two actual priests. It worked: After serving only eighty-four days, Raymond gave his gray-striped prison uniform to a fellow convict awaiting parole and left jail.

At 6:00 P.M., in the darkening night of December 22, 1938, Raymond emerged from the majestic gold-domed Massachu-setts State House, his release finalized. Smiling, he announced to at least one reporter, "I'm a carpenter by trade and I'm going to work and make up for the foolishness I've done." That night, the Patriarca brothers (both Rhode Island's top public ene-mies) were in their mother's cozy picture-perfect two-story fam-ily house, complete with a chimney, bay window, and encircling fence.

On Christmas, Raymond received a few friends, and his family presented him with cigars, cards, and stockings. For a photogra-pher, he posed to trim the small Christmas tree standing on a table. When not eating turkey, squash, and plum pudding, he said to a journalist present, "My record was good enough for the gov-ernor and the executive council wants it." He'd see after his moth-er's business interests, go straight, and marry, he said. He was being honest about the wedding part, at least.

———

It was 1939, and at age thirty-one, Raymond submitted Boston marriage license number 558. He wedded twenty-nine-year-old Helen Mancini, a Worcester nurse (as his own mother had been). The Massachusetts governor, Leverett Saltonstall, himself declared Helen was "a fine girl" (her brother was a state house employee). Immediately, the newlyweds headed to Miami for a honeymoon. While there, Raymond claimed to be fishing, golfing, and watching movies. "I hope they let me alone," Raymond said of the authorities—who were watching him. The Miami police didn't— discovering he'd offered a vacant parking lot as his address, they arrested him. Raymond told reporters, "I'll go back and face the music any time anyone in authority in Massachusetts says I have to." He did just that when a Bay State police detective arrived to retrieve him to answer for some unfinished business up north.

After the train deposited Raymond at South Station, a grand jury indicted him for an old Cambridge car theft charge. He was freed on $10,000 double bail. But with his highly recognizable visage in the papers, he was soon after indicted for the Oxford armed robbery. Raymond began a tedious shuffle between jurisdictions and jails. The charges stacked up, and they included assault with intent to murder and robbery—serious crimes with heavy time attached.

Raymond finished a first sentence for auto theft. But twenty-four hours before he walked, on September 5, 1941, he faced two more Oxford indictments. Then Raymond was indicted yet again for the old United Optical break-in, as well. At one point, when strolling outside a Boston courtroom, the state police rearrested him (to answer yet more charges) as he yelled for his lawyer. The inevitable loomed before him, and on November 13, 1941, he pled guilty to the United Optical charge and the Oxford payroll holdup. He received two more concurrent sentences of three years apiece.

Reentering prison in 1941, Raymond, an aloof and persistent sort, avoided trouble and kept his eye on the release date. Exactly four years and one day after his initial sentencing, on May 11, 1944, Raymond became a free man. His kitty included $1,000 in war bonds and some $120 in his prison accounts. The state parole board had approved his plan to work in his brother-in-law's apple orchard in Johnston, Rhode Island, for $50 a month.

From nearly zero, Raymond prepared to create an empire. Powerful criminals had locked up much of the territory: they included Mafiosi such as Boston's Phil Buccola and Joe Lombardo, the Rhode Island–based Morelli brothers, and Frank Iacone, of Worcester. But ambitious Raymond's considerable reputation equaled power. All bosses needed an underboss as an executive; they also required capo regimes (heads of ten) who ran the organization; and soldiers in the ranks who did the work. The boss also had a consigliere, usually a trusted family elder, who lacked command power but could advise and intercede.

For himself, Raymond picked a nucleus of capable Mafia associates, including Henry "the Referee" Tameleo and Louis "the Fox" Taglianetti. These men could supply counsel, muscle, and business services, as required. Needing powerful out-of-state support, he also aligned with Frank Costello, the shrewd and nonviolent (unless necessary) head of Charles "Lucky" Luciano's borgata (criminal family) in New York City. Drink, treachery, and incompetence eventually left the Morelli brothers a spent force in Rhode Island's lottery and booking rackets. Sidestepping them, Raymond also began associating with the Boston family. Seeing something he liked, the suave and aristocratic Buccola took a shine to the ambitious young Raymond.

But after decades of relative stability, everything in the Boston underworld changed rapidly. In 1950, the obscure Tennessee senator Estes Kefauver, with an eye to the White House, began holding televised organized crime hearings. He even announced his road show would hit New England—and he planned to specifically examine the up-and-coming Raymond, the ancient Buccola, and

Frank Iacone. In response, Buccola and Lombardo put their gaming operations into hibernation. According to legend, this hiatus gave a small, slight, but clever man from Prince Street an opportunity. His name was Gennaro "Jerry" Angiulo. (But that is a later story.)

Feeling his age, Buccola needed a successor to run his borgata. The slick and worldly Don Buccola turned to Raymond, requesting his detachment from New York to New England. As underboss of Rhode Island, Raymond assumed control of a racing wire that relayed race results cross-country. He extended the business through southern New England. Putting his faith in Raymond, Buccola sponsored him as the new don. It was probably in 1952 when the council of elder Mafiosi convened and voted. The transition of power was not exactly clean, according to Raymond, who claimed, "There's a lot of [fucking] conspiracy; there's a lot of BS going on and now we call a meeting. . . . If I become the boss I'm forgetting everything: who's right, who's wrong."

Raymond prevailed, and Buccola oversaw his baptism into his borgata. He warned Raymond about some of the family. "They will put you in a lot of trouble; they will put you in a swindle and leave you there without ever knowing when you are implicated until the roof falls in." On April 27, 1952, in an apparent celebration of the promotion, Iacone held a party for himself and his onetime protégé at the Ranch House, a mob spot in Johnston, Rhode Island. Some eighty hoodlums, including big shots from New York, Chicago, and other places, attended. Like a cut-rate Romanov or Hapsburg of the Old World, Raymond was a member of a ruling family now.

Like many of his colleagues, Raymond had a fierce loyalty to the idea of his organization. "In this thing of ours [the translation of the Italian phrase "La Cosa Nostra"]," Raymond once told an associate, "your love for your mother and father is one thing; your love for the family is a different kind of love." He told this fellow man of honor to be very choosy about picking initiates; don't just select men for their toughness. "Look for guys with brains who don't talk a lot. Together we survive. Alone we die."

But, over time, Raymond lamented that the quality of the initiates was declining—Boston even had some "garbage" in it.

4.

THE PAX PATRIARCA

"You want to be a tough guy? All the tough guys are dead. We do away with them all."

—Larry Baione, Mafia capo

In 1954, Phil Buccola embarked on his new career as chicken farmer in his native Sicily. This left Raymond to branch out in many directions, and with a new aggressive management style. By acquisition and alignment, he became don of coastal New England, from New Haven to southern Maine. In these boundaries, Raymond kept his family small but disciplined and cooperative. In a brash American touch, he moved the family headquarters from Boston to his childhood neighborhood of Federal Hill. After all, it was easier to corrupt a small state than a large one, as legend quotes him saying.

Like Rome, Providence sat on seven hills—but Boston, although larger and richer, served as its Byzantium. Inside his domain, Raymond wasn't tribal. Like a Caesar of old, the barbarians were free in his kingdom—as long as they rendered to Raymond the things that were his. Pragmatic, Raymond judged men by the content of their wallets—not the vowel configuration of their surnames. He got along with the Jews in his Providence neighborhood, believed blacks (ultimately) deserved civil rights, and worked closely with many an Irishman.

The common law that supported this empire was Raymond's

notion of honor. For instance, Raymond claimed the worst sin was to gyp money from a trusted partner. He also said that money was nothing next to principle.

Although ruthless when needed, for him violence was a tool, not recreation. When Raymond was done with diplomacy, he deployed John "Jackie" Nazarian, one of the East Coast's most feared killers, whom he kept on a short leash. Nazarian had his own Providence club, and a gang of reckless, dangerous men. Legend boasted how he allegedly gleefully shot, strangled, or otherwise disposed of a score of victims. For instance, Nazarian killed bookie George "Tiger" Balleto in the Bella Napoli Café in front of twenty-two witnesses. When one witness appeared about to testify, Nazarian strangled him to death with baling wire. He then dumped the body in a garbage dump, the wire still encircling the throat.

So, the year 1954 started the Pax Patriarca, with a new Augustus enforcing a strict but efficient regimen. To counter his violent temper, Raymond shrewdly promoted the older and world-wise Henry Tameleo as his new underboss. The two made a formidable combination. Aloof and reserved, Raymond set an example to his employees, remaining low-key and simple. "We're supposed to have more polish than anyone else and know what we're doing," he said once to be heard—and obeyed. "We're not supposed to make a mistake."

He seldom dined out and rarely even appeared in public places—he expected his men to avoid meeting openly, as well. He shunned golf courses or country clubs, as this was "placing yourself in the limelight." Raymond dressed inexpensively but tastefully in dark suits (with white sweaters) and alligator-skin shoes with his signature white socks. In a concession to sensuality, he typically wore two rings—one with five diamonds on the right hand; on the left, a large diamond ring.

A born conservative, Raymond lived in a modest white clapboard house (worth about $35,000 in the 1960s) in a reasonably fashionable, leafy, and mostly Jewish neighborhood on Lancaster Street in Providence's East Side. The only flourish on the house was the green trim, striped awnings, and the purple *P* on the door. A three-foot-high wrought iron fence enveloped the yard on three sides; a two-car garage abutted the fourth side. Two German shepherds, Duchess and Astro, served as pets and guardians.

Like a typical Yankee owner of a small- to medium-sized business, he commuted to work with dreary regularity, driving himself the two miles to his office. When his daily business was done, he returned home to his family, rarely venturing out at night.

To outsiders, Raymond remained a sphinx. He rarely drank ("I got the sugar," as he once explained, referring to his diabetes) or gambled and frowned on associates who did. He liked to smoke— and local children vied for the privilege of buying Raymond's cigars for him; it meant a dollar tip. He spoke softly, even when uttering his frequent obscenities. But if a reporter annoyed Raymond, he'd fling his plastic cigar holder into the reporter's face. When he spoke publicly, he dispensed harmless saws, such as "They never let you forget the mistakes of your youth." Or, "I'm a man from Missouri, and I don't trust anyone. I don't trust my left hand with my right hand."

Needing a fig leaf for his enterprises, Raymond launched as a legitimate business (more or less) the National Cigarette Service. A vending company, its intent was to "install the more modern type of machine in various establishments," as he told the FBI. Leasing his machines came with a health benefits policy. The mere threat of Jackie Nazarian ensured people bought Raymond's cigarettes—in just two months, National Cigarette replaced fifty-five rival machines. Eventually, Raymond opened an office at 168 Atwells Avenue in Providence, which also housed the Coin-O-Matic distributing company. This firm handled pinball machines and other electronic amusement devices. Given his headquarters always comprised a small and shabby business suite, everyone called Raymond's outfit "the Office."

With slightly more time and opportunity as the head of his own shadow government, Raymond might have made Rhode Island as backward and incompetent as feudal Sicily. By his life's fifth decade, Raymond oversaw a sprawling and disconnected business empire. Its roots sank in dark criminal places—but it had branches exposed in legitimate sunlight. The various enterprises included bootleg liquor stills in Connecticut, dice games in Maine hamlets, nightclubs and high-stakes dice and poker games, a dump, a shirt manufactory, and a shipping firm; Raymond also provided advice and funds for start-up firms; among the ventures pitched to him were a factory with electromagnetic machines to develop drugs; a mixed-use blueberry-canning/sports arena; and a dry-cleaning shop for the U.S. Naval War College in Newport.

All day long, eighty to ninty constituents, associates, schemers, flatterers, and friends from Connecticut and Maine (and even New York City) entered his office. To the Caesar they offered tribute: money, tips, opportunities, tomato sauce, and stolen merchandise. Paternal in some ways, Raymond settled disputes, even between legitimate people. Would-be Underworld entrepreneurs proposed a myriad of felonies and capers. Schemes included buying stolen bonds, opening a gambling den catering to rich professionals, and procuring special paper to counterfeit U.S. currency. "Where there is a buck to be made, he was always interested," said Vinnie Teresa, who observed Raymond firsthand.

Over time, Raymond's heart began to fail and he developed an ulcer, while the worries and hard decisions deeply lined his aging face. He began to resemble the celluloid gangsters of his youth, and his fierce, scoured visage became ever more famous. Yet Raymond never lost his common touch, and he could also produce a charming "cat-that-ate-the-canary grin" as one writer put it. One eye canted to the side—an ideal, if almost comic, touch for a gangster. One of his wife Helen's lady friends paid a visit to the Patriarca family manse on Lancaster Street. She found the house "modest," and without expensive furniture or furnishings. Helen did her own housework, and her wardrobe was simple—no diamonds or other jewelry. The few times this family friend met Raymond, he was "very polite and courteous and acted like a perfect gentleman." Apparently, she found it difficult to connect this middle-aged man to the "big-time hoodlum" the newspapers described.

In the early 1960s, Raymond often appeared on the sidewalk in front of his office on Atwells Avenue, wearing a white sweater, watching, waving to passersby, smoking his cigar. Some might have believed Raymond "almost benign," a reporter observed. He donated regularly to the Christmas beautification fund on Federal Hill. He'd pay for a funeral or a surgery, or send someone to school on a "Patriarca scholarship." He tipped his hat to ladies who passed and said, "Salut."

Naturally, fame was a pricey commodity, and on November 14, 1957, police fingered Raymond at the Mafia conference in Apalachin, New York. Later, down in Washington, D.C., on February 11, 1958, he appeared before the U.S. Senate's McClellan investigating committee. Raymond was chagrined that Senator John Pastore, of Rhode Island, was in New York and couldn't receive him. (As a sop, a local congressman, John Fogarty, did invite Raymond for a visit.) This attention made his asthmatic wife so upset, Raymond was worried about her health. Before Congress, Raymond said he was ignorant of any strong-arming done to peddle his cigarettes. He also managed to keep a straight face when discussing the seed fund for his vending enterprise. Raymond said he used an $80,000 nest egg that his late mother had left to him in a box kept in the cellar. A skeptical and abrasive committee counsel, Robert Kennedy, asked why Raymond had worked as a burglar with that big stake underfoot.

"Why do a lot of young fellows do a lot of things, when they haven't a father?" Raymond replied.

The next year, the Senate rackets committee subpoenaed Raymond. The Colossus of Atwells Avenue, alone of the notorious mobsters assembled, declined to plead the Fifth. On February 11, 1959, Raymond, again facing Bobby Kennedy, complained, "I have been a goat around Rhode Island for 20 years." In public, he admitted no wrongdoing from 1932 to 1944, when he labored as "a counterman and manager, like" in Louie's Restaurant on Atwells Avenue. After a year there, he said, "I think I played horses until 1950."

Allegedly, after testifying, Raymond approached the committee table, faced Bobby and Jack Kennedy, and said, "You two don't have the brains of your retarded sister." Whether Raymond vented his spleen like that or not, by the time the hearings closed, Bobby, who possessed a gift for hatred, had marked Raymond as an enemy.

In 1960, reportedly Raymond took a seat on the mob's national commission—but this probably just meant more stress. Already diabetic and myopic, in March 1960 a cardiac arrest sent Raymond to the hospital, and almost to the morgue. A newly disloyal "Mad Dog" Jackie Nazarian openly bragged that when Raymond "croaked," he'd take over with his own private gang. Not surprisingly, Jackie met his violent fate soon after, while leaving a Providence dice game. Raymond now closely watched his diet and activities, and for a while, flunkies had to chauffeur him about.

He fought against his fame, still. In 1961, seeing an unflattering article in *The Providence Journal*, Raymond boldly sued the paper for libel. He also bought a large advertisement that said, "Since my release from prison in 1944 . . . my time has been continuously and assiduously employed in honest endeavors. . . . How bitterly I realize the truth of a great poet's words 'The evil that men do lives after them; the good is often interred with their bones.'"

For the second time in his life, law enforcement harassment became routine. Once in 1962, U.S. marshal John Partington, armed with a subpoena, invaded Raymond's stronghold at Coin-O-Matic. As he approached, Raymond's two bodyguards stopped him. The don, eating a slice of pizza, looked out from inside his office to see who was there. When Partington reached in his coat for his badge, Raymond dropped his pizza and jumped behind a desk; his men grabbed the marshal's arms and pinned him to a wall.

"It's okay!" said Partington. "I'm a federal man."

Raymond took Partington's subpoena, examined the document, grimaced, and then said, "Anytime you want me, kid, I am here. But don't you ever go to my house, you hear? My wife, she don't have nothing to do with my business. Capisce?" Moments later, Raymond announced on the telephone to his attorney, "A goddamn Boy Scout just left after serving me with papers."

5

THE WILD BUNCH

"I had Georgie McLaughlin in here one day to talk to him and he was so polite and quiet you'd think he was an altar boy. But let him get a gun in his hand, and whoosh."

—a Boston police detective

Minutes before midnight on August 22, 1948, Charlestown resident Bernard "Bernie" McLaughlin and a partner waited outside Wenzler's Tavern on K and West Second Streets in South Boston. After tavern owner John Wenzler locked up, Bernie and his companion closed in. "Give us your money," one of them said. Wenzler, a lawyer and state representative with a history of resisting thieves, refused. The Charlestown duo laid into Wenzler, beating his face and head and knocking him down. Bernie was five feet eight inches and 150 pounds of ferocity, and a skilled debt collector. But, through the blows, Wenzler bellowed loud enough to draw Boston patrolman E. W. Dumas, making his rounds nearby, to the scene.

"Put your hands up," commanded Dumas. The two assailants turned from Wenzler and shoved Dumas off his feet. "Stop!" the patrolman yelled, and, drawing his revolver, put a slug into Bernie's stomach. Bernie collapsed, and his colleague ran down East Second Street. Dumas handed his nightstick to Wenzler and then ran to the corner to call an ambulance. Bernie rose, staggered down Second Street, hailed a cab, and unsuccessfully tried to escape in it. Police arrested him before he got far—the driver claimed he hadn't noticed Bernie's wound. The next day, in the hospital under police guard, Bernie read about his botched attempt in the newspaper. Bernie, a true child of Charlestown, didn't give his partner up.

Eventually Bernie healed and returned to Charlestown. A year later, in South Boston District Court, Bernie faced his accusers in the Wenzler job. He claimed he'd only approached Wenzler "to ask him for one dollar. When I did he refused me and then struck me. I hit him back in self defense." Bernie was found innocent, or at least his guilt was officially unproved. He clearly had friends, somewhere, purchased though they might have been.

A community not only gets the government, but also, possibly, the criminals it deserves. After World War II, a declining Charlestown faced growing unemployment and poverty. As if in symmetry, it also had the McLaughlins: it was an unlucky place. And, like every Boston neighborhood of the time, it was a tiny village inside a small city, but possibly even more insular than the rest. Much of Charlestown sprouts from two drumlins—small hills of glacial refuse—Bunker Hill and Breed's Hill. The twin humps loom on an isolated peninsula separated from the mainland on the north by the then oil-slick–laden Mystic River. The Charles River, equally polluted at the time, cuts it off from the mainland to the south. Right from the crown of Bunker Hill, in the heart of Charlestown, a smooth granite obelisk points an accusing finger into the sky. The monument celebrates a bloody battle against the English army that the locals had lost. (That didn't stop the British from later leveling Charlestown in revenge.) The sight of the looming, vertiginous obelisk is hard for the residents to evade, like fate itself. From nearby Route 93, Charlestown almost looks like a medieval European mountain village, with its pointed monument, church spires, and fine houses, all compressed together in miniature.

In the twentieth century, Irish Charlestown was short on

opportunity, long on resentment. Here, in the "Green Square Mile," some said the babies were born with clenched fists. By 1900, the summit of the hill in Charlestown was the domain of the higher-class Irish citizenry, such as politicians and civil servants. At the bottom dwelt a rougher breed, including one "wizened" railway clerk named Johnny McLaughlin and his "gargantuan" wife, Annie. The hardworking immigrant couple produced a respectable-sized litter for that time: six girls and five boys. The children grew up in a three-story wood tenement on Main Street. They were four doors from where the elevated rail cast its shadow, and the train blasted out noise and soot. The McLaughlins always would remain crude versions of "Townies" (Charlestown natives).

Johnny McLaughlin's sons included a pair of local war heroes who died in service. The three McLaughlin sons who survived the conflict were, in order of appearance: Edward, Bernard, and George. They were part of a generation of Boston criminals who were born in harsh poverty and want. But, they had also lived through an epic global bloodbath that had made human suffering and death almost a trivial matter. The McLaughlin trio took to crime like other Boston boys took to baseball. "Those three boys were on the streets too much, even as young kids," reflected one Townie years later. "You can't blame the parents; raising a family 40 years ago was a rough job."

The brothers McLaughlin loved violence and thievery, and a dishonest buck earned by breaking a face. Boosting was a favored pastime, so Edward "Punchy" McLaughlin often wore a large loose-fitting jacket, which contained deep pockets to hold shop-lifted goods. A Boston top cop called the brothers "low animal-like cheap thieves and petty shoplifters." The policeman had a point: Eddie McLaughlin took his first collar at age eight for trying to steal oranges. This would become the first of thirty-eight entries in his police record. Light-skinned and brown-haired, at five feet ten, he was the biggest of the three brothers. He adorned his body with assorted tattoos, including an eagle, an American flag, a girl, and a ship. Eddie was a vicious street fighter—once nearly biting an opponent's ear off—and in his twenties, took to the ring. "That Punchy was a tough kid growing up," noted an aged Townie. "Always looking for a fight. No wonder he became a boxer, even if he wasn't a future world beater." Long after his boxing career had ceased, everyone but his family called him Punchy.

Both Punchy and Bernie became movers in the International Longshoremen's Association (ILA) local. Working for the corrupt ILA, Punchy roamed Florida and other places as a "labor organizer." He also started running loan-sharking and other rackets in Charlestown and beyond. "He was bad," said one associate. "Bad. Take my word for it, he was vicious. He could shoot you and smile." Punchy became the dour brains of the family, avoiding flamboyance. He was not particularly magnetic or likable, but as head of the family, he had contacts in all the large crime families in Boston and beyond.

Through ferocity and violence, (as well as Punchy's "surreptitious connections" in New York City's organized labor and crime organizations) during the 1950s, the McLaughlin gang rose to the murky top of the waterfront underworld. As leader, Punchy arranged for strong-arm jobs on behalf of the Big Apple's unions and crime organizations. Each week, a New York emissary made a round trip to Charlestown, bringing $3,500 back in tribute, said an FBI report.

Under Punchy toiled Bernie, who achieved some fame for the "vigorous" treatment—breaking debtors' legs with sash weights wrapped in newspapers. The family caboose was Georgie, who, appropriately, topped off at five feet four. A small man in a small peninsula, when young, his skinny frame carried a mere 156 pounds. With his baby face and brown hair, he was not quite a frightening sight—even with the bird tattoos that covered either side of his chest. Of him, one Townie said, "He didn't have to be big. Georgie would cut your balls off as soon as look at you."

So small was Georgie, he couldn't meet the weight requirement for the navy. He ate endless mashed potatoes to put on pounds, and eventually the navy accepted him. His service years became a disaster. After several court-martials, a psychiatrist declared Georgie possessed a "psychopathic personality with marked aggressive traits." Indeed, newspapers uncharitably described him as "a nut who would shoot his best friend if his back was turned." The navy flushed him, and he turned to low-level and violent crime. But some called him "Gentleman Georgie," as a jailhouse acquaintance recalled.

Like his brothers, Georgie officially worked as a laborer—sometimes as longshoreman or painter. Generally, he ran errands, made collections, and drank. "Georgie was drunk his whole life," said one contemporary. "You tried avoiding him. He was bad and obnoxious." Within a year of his navy dismissal, Georgie was convicted of armed assault and went to Concord Reformatory. Later, in Salem, during a botched robbery, he fought a gun battle with the police, which he lost.

Georgie was also very tight with fellow Townie Harold Hannon, a tough who once kidnapped the manager of a Howard Johnson's roadside stand to steal $3,000. Hannon and Georgie represented the crazy and unstable wing of a crazy and unstable gang. The FBI suspected them of committing "killings for hire" for mobsters throughout the United States.

And then there were the Hughes brothers, Cornelius and Stephen, whom even dangerous men feared. "The Hughes brothers made the McLaughlins look like Boy Scouts," noted one underworld figure. Individually, either brother was capable of mayhem, but together, they were uncommonly lethal. After his time in the service, Cornelius "Connie" Hughes became a laborer and thug, and in 1948 he did a jail term for armed robbery. His brother Stephen ("Little Stevie") was a longshoreman and heavily built boxer who could kill without regret. Yet, with his wavy black hair, bright blue eyes, and sensitive features, Stevie resembled a young priest or a poet. On the other hand, with a scarred upper right lip and surly cast to his face, Connie looked like the thug he was.

Another of the inner circle was Thomas Ballou, a burly, two-hundred-pound longshoreman. Bold and lethal, he once entered the car of a bookie and moneylender, put a .45 caliber pistol at his head, and demanded his money roll. This "pleasant fellow" (when sober) was also an "extremely vicious" drunk. He had a reputation for carrying a $100 bill—he'd take the money out with one hand and then, while an intended victim was dazzled, lobotomize him with the longshoreman's hook he carried hidden in his other hand. Ballou had friends in the seedier cafés of Winter Hill in Somerville, as well.

The Charlestown waterfront was a very rough and hard-drinking crust of coastline. In the worst bars, "buckets of blood," fights, beatings, and even murders might occur without raising too many eyebrows. Usually, when a longshoreman entered a bar, he put his hook inside his belt loop. If he took it out during a fight, things could get very nasty, indeed. According to legend, during a brawl at the D&H bar, one longshoreman drove his hook through his enemy's lip and out his chin. The injured man made it to the bar and downed a shot of whiskey, some of which ran out the hole in his chin.

When ships arrived for repair at the Charlestown Navy Yard, thousands of sailors disgorged themselves into the seedy rows of buildings lining the harbor's edge. The drunken mariners would pick up prostitutes and start fights. In this rowdy mess were the McLaughlin and Hughes brothers. They distinguished themselves as tough men in a tough town. To make a point, as one Townie recalled, they would enter a bar, put a gun muzzle in a debtor's face, or cut his tie off. Sometimes they stepped behind the bar and helped themselves to cash from the register or poured themselves free drinks. It wasn't like the owners were going to do anything about it.

Brawls were major entertainment in Irish Boston in those days. In the taverns, the McLaughlin gang frequently vented the excess ferocity not required for business in brawling—they beat fellow long-shoremen, sailors, whomever. Sometimes they battled over things no one could remember after the fight. By the mid-1950s the McLaughlins and Hugheses used the Mystic Tower Tavern on Chelsea Street as their office. Longshoremen could see them "with their heads together in close discussion," as an FBI report noted. It added, "most of the rest of the criminal element were afraid of these people."

For instance, Connie Hughes once started a barroom fight that ended up in Chelsea Street. After Connie's opponent went down, Ballou kicked him in the head. Naturally, the tavern owner "was displeased with the presence" of this volatile and motley crew, "but was unable to do anything to get rid of them," noted the FBI agent. After one particularly destructive brawl, the owner presented Ballou with a $600 repair bill. "When that's up to $1,000, I'll shoot you," said Ballou.

Through the 1950s, the gang remained brazen. For instance, one November morning, at the South Boston army base, Bernie issued a warning to a longshoreman who hadn't cut the gang in on the sale of a batch of stolen shoes. One Townie pinned the arms of the errant longshoreman as Bernie stabbed him, leaving him "all blood." The victim claimed an unknown "colored person" had assaulted him, before heading to Mass General Hospital. Although questioned (he said he'd heard the scuttlebutt but knew nothing), Bernie was never charged. This was typical. Nevertheless, some ILA members cringed at how the McLaughlins were turning the local into a den of thieves. After Bernie smashed a union brother in the mouth, the ILA local council ruled the McLaughlins' membership cards were forfeit. In response, Punchy threatened to break a union brother's wife's legs—before killing and burying him in the harbor. Although convicted of assault, Punchy's "considerable 'in'" at the district attorney's office meant only a whopping $100 fine.

Later, Bernie and Ballou jumped the ILA official who'd lifted the cards. They left him walking down Mystic Street, blood streaming over his face and clothes. Although the McLaughlins later won an appeal, Punchy didn't bother to reinstate his card. He didn't need it. Given his relative prosperity, Punchy joined the migration out of Charlestown. He relocated, with his wife and son, to the pleasant town of Canton, just south of Boston. There, Punchy enrolled the boy in Catholic school and brought him up strictly.

Facing the dreadful prospect of earning an honest living, the McLaughlins came up with ideas that were almost white-collar. In the summer of 1957, inspired by what he saw in New York, Punchy devised a plan to squeeze the waterfront of some of its looser nickels and dimes. The combined gang tried to persuade union officials to allow them to levy a "per capita tax" on any nonunion, or "scalawag" laborer on the waterfront.

But there were some obstacles to the gang—and not the police or the FBI. Rather, it was one brave fool named Tommy Sullivan, a former pro boxer and Southie legend, beloved by the local kids he trained. Although, in the manner of the time, he took a few numbers, he was notoriously honest and decent. In 1957, Sullivan and Punchy (who was with the local ILA president) chanced to meet in a South Boston bar. Punchy had tried to cross Sullivan's picket line a few months prior, and the two began arguing. This soon became a brawl, and Sullivan and a companion gave Punchy and the union president a "severe beating." In response, Punchy hit Sullivan with a five-inch railroad spike, in the head. Really mad, Sullivan chased Punchy under a car. In view of the amazed crowd, Sullivan moved the auto to the curb to get at Punchy, who begged for mercy. Or so goes the legend.

Thereafter, Punchy and the entire gang avoided Southie because they were "afraid the South Boston guys will take care of them," as the FBI noted. Once, when working on the Charlestown waterfront, Sullivan deliberately shoved Bernie and Connie out of his way. This was unwise. On December 23, 1957, while Sullivan walked from his house to his job at the South Boston army base, a Chevrolet sedan, stuffed with men, pulled up close to the curb nearby and idled. Someone stepped out and approached Sullivan, who crossed the street diagonally, heading toward the vehicle. Sullivan may have known the oncoming man. Perhaps Sullivan even saw the .38 caliber pistol come up, because he raised his hand, as if to protect himself. The .38 flashed quickly three times: bullets penetrated Sullivan in the right eye, jaw, and forehead. He was so close to the muzzle, powder burned his face and the back of his uplifted hand. The ex-boxer collapsed forward, feet on the curb. The shooter put three more slugs into his shoulder and spinal cord, and then reentered the Chevy.

The car sped off. The glow of Christmas-tree lights from nearby houses illuminated Sullivan's body and the sidewalk it lay on. Soon after, at the Sullivans' house, the Christmas lights dimmed and the shades were drawn. A witness said the face of the getaway car's driver matched Punchy McLaughlin's portrait—but it's likely Harold Hannon or someone else was the shooter. ("Punchy has always been one who made the snowballs and had others fire them," as Raymond Patriarca once observed.) Despite the public uproar and the police's questioning of Bernie and Punchy, no one was charged. The FBI, which had been monitoring the McLaughlins, guessed at what had happened but couldn't make a case.

At the start of 1958, Punchy avoided Massachusetts for several months, going cross-country as an ILA organizer. Returning to Boston, despite the money rolling in from the lending and other enterprises, he kept at thieving. However, Punchy bungled the robbery of two televisions in Lynn and was arrested. Police found other stolen wares in his car. Convicted, Punchy was fined $500 but received no jail time.

Naturally, there were loose ends. In August 1959, in the West End, Stevie Hughes shot and stabbed a longshoreman who was a potential witness in the Sullivan killing. The outcome: the victim never testified; there was a bullet hole in a furniture store; and Stevie got a stretch for attempted murder. Little Stevie had graduated to the big time—but in jail he made friends with fellow boxer Joe Barboza. He liked Joe's style in the ring—presumably, the all-attack, no-defense method suited Stevie Hughes just fine.

In 1950, a squat, fat Boston master thief and comedian named Tony Pino assembled an unlikely eleven-man gang of drunks, oddballs, outcasts, and career thugs. Together, being far more than the sum of their parts, the gang performed the near-genius robbery of the Brink's facility in Boston, taking $3 million—the largest theft in American history at that time. The FBI and other authorities harshly squeezed Brink's conspirator Joseph "Specs" O'Keefe. Fearing Specs would fold, the robbers retained the services of homicidal maniac Elmer Francis "Trigger" Burke.

Georgie McLaughlin, currently a fugitive from justice on an assault and battery charge, roomed in Somerville with Burke. On June 16, 1954, Burke, with an assistant (presumably Georgie), met Specs near a public housing project in Dorchester. The chat ended when Burke opened fire with a machine gun on Specs—who escaped, although slightly wounded. In all, Burke got off thirty shots, riddling parked cars, peppering the project's walls, and shocking three hundred locals. With his partner, Burke fled in an expensive green sedan.

The next day, the police arrested Burke in the Back Bay, where he was behaving like a regular tourist, except for the machine gun concealed under his coat. The police sought his accomplice, although they only had his alias—"Edward Donovan." A detective dusted a beer bottle from Burke's Somerville apartment—and the prints matched Georgie's. When authorities realized Georgie and Edward Donovan were one and the same, they ordered the twenty-seven-year-old McLaughlin arrested on sight—leaving Donovan free, so to speak.

Georgie drove to Old Orchard Beach in Maine in a green sedan. On July 8, 1954, carrying $700, he entered a Sears, Roebuck & Co. in Portland. When he shoplifted a woman's seventeen-dollar bathing suit, a clerk took note, and police picked Georgie up as he left. After his arrest, Georgie said he represented a union (soon proved nonexistent) from Jamaica, New York. Police also found a license plate in his trunk—it matched that of Burke's getaway car. Soon after, Massachusetts police arrived to drive Georgie back to his home state for trial. Never charged for the machine-gunning, he was found guilty on a lesser charge.

On August 5, 1954, the unlucky Specs received two years on a parole violation. Jailed in Springfield, Specs met with Edward Albert "Wimpy" Bennett. No mere thug, middle-aged Wimpy and his brothers ran one of Boston's largest bookmaking and street-finance enterprises. Wimpy's moniker derived from his sleepy-eyed resemblance to the hamburger-munching cartoon character Wimpy, from the *Popeye* comic strip. The real Wimpy also frequently feasted on hamburgers from Tremont Street's White Castle restaurant.

Wimpy was as violent as he needed to be. Yet he could show a light touch and often used others to do the necessary brutal tasks. Because of this, the Brink's gang sent the venerable Wimpy to Specs with an offer of future cash. After Specs shot the deal down, Wimpy threatened Specs with death for testifying against the Brink's gang. He also warned they'd find a way to certify Specs as insane and commit him to an asylum. This frightened Specs, who turned state's evidence instead and complicated many lives.

The ripples from the Brink's robbery touched other McLaughlin gang members. The loyal Thomas Ballou ran errands for the last two Brink's robbers still on the lam. Now broke, the two fugitives skipped paying rent on their Roxbury apartment. Their landlord turned them in for a reward. One of Ballou's friends, Thomas Callahan, an ex-convict and waterfront tough guy, beat the landlord in revenge. Later, someone shot the landlord to death.

On August 7, 1958, Ballou entered a Charlestown café with a twenty-two-year-old woman. When an ironworker refused to give up his seat at the bar, Ballou, armed with a box cutter, slashed his throat from ear to ear and stabbed him in the stomach. Ballou and Callahan went on the lam together. The next evening, a rookie state policeman engaged the duo in a high-speed car chase on the Massachusetts turnpike. This ceased when they met a roadblock in Southbridge. The police charged the wayward Townies with possession of two pistols and hit Callahan with a driving to endanger charge (he also lacked a license). Ballou got eight to ten years—while his victim got to survive, albeit barely.

6.

THE BEAR AND THE RIFLEMAN

"Vincent was such a good boy."
—Mary Flemmi, describing her son, Vincent James Flemmi

On December 16, 1954, three "cowardly young punks" stood before a judge at the Suffolk County Superior Court in Boston. One of them was the stocky Vincent James "the Bear" Flemmi of Lenox Street in the South End. With three North End companions, the Bear had beaten two officers of the U.S.S. *Tarawa*—so savagely, the victims carried permanent scars. A lower court had found the Bear and his associates guilty of assault, and they'd received six months each. The quartet had appealed the decision, and now the judge agreed the sentences required adjustment—but not for the shorter.

Declaring this the "most despicable assault ever committed in this city," the judge gave Flemmi two and a half years in the Dedham House of Corrections, two more years suspended, and five years' probation. The Associated Press publicized this legal buffoonery.

Subsequently, the Bear remained in the headlines off and on for the next thirty years. Indeed, the Bear's voluminous arrest record almost indicates he believed being captured was a civic duty.

"He was one of the worst people to walk the face of the earth," recalled one contemporary and partner. "He killed everybody," as his own brother, Stephen "Stevie" Flemmi, observed. Soon after his birth in 1932, something went very, very wrong in the Bear's head. Genetics doesn't seem to have been the cause, as his parents were honest and decent Italian immigrants. His father was a hard worker and frugal man who toiled as a bricklayer and pushcart driver; his mother was a kindly and generous homemaker.

But South End residents said the Bear, when a cub, was shy, prone to softly giggling at his own odd jokes, and violent. His official crime résumé started with a charge of malicious injury (filed in March 1949 in Boston Juvenile Court). Between then and the *Tarawa* beating, police arrested him more than twenty times. Jail became his second home for infractions that included larceny, wanton destruction of property, operating without a license, leaving the scene of an accident, breaking and entering, assault and battery, drunkenness, and armed robbery. The Bear's baby face disguised a destructive and psychopathic personality. Briefly, he entered the boxing ring, but he was prone to taking off the gloves to murder his sparring partner. The Bear's unique qualities, and those of his younger brother, Stevie, caught the eyes of the local underworld.

In November 1956, the Bear made parole for the *Tarawa* assault. He quickly joined an amateur criminal gang that worked out of a handful of South End cafés. On Wednesday, December 19, 1956, with a companion, the Bear entered the Boston & Albany Railroad employees' credit union in venerable South Station. The duo produced pistols and forced a black porter into a chair, tied him in place, and stole his seventy dollars. Then the Bear shoved the sixty-eight-year-old credit manager into a room, pushed him down, and jumped on him. After choking him and stealing his wallet, Flemmi forced the old man to open the safe, and extracted the $4,090 it contained.

Unsurprisingly, the Bear and his partner were indicted and

arrested for the South Station job. After making bail, Flemmi went on the lam, starting a lifelong personal (and family) tradition. By July 22, 1956, the FBI had located and arrested him. On July 23, wearing a broad-brimmed fedora, he entered Roxbury court to answer a previous $97 larceny-by-check charge. This was a small technicality before his big trial began. Seeing a chance to evade the hard time looming for the South Station job, the Bear bolted. He knocked down a court officer on the second floor, made the stairs, and hit the street running. In pursuit was a bespectacled court clerk (a former Boston College football star), who caught Jimmy with a flying tackle "in the best B.C. tradition on Kent Street." Despite the powerful young Bear's kicks and punches, the clerk held on until police arrived.

There was a failed attempt to bribe the porter not to testify (the Bear refunded the stolen seventy dollars, sans interest). But on October 11, 1957, he received a sentence of seven to twelve years. But he proved too nasty even for the newly opened MCI Walpole: Soon after his entry, Flemmi was one of twenty-three of the suspected ringleaders, troublemakers, and agitators moved to solitary in Concord. The next year, he was back in Walpole—where he put a guard in the dispensary with a vicious blow.

In February 1961, Raymond Garbiel, one of Walpole's model prisoners, was in the prison gymnasium awaiting a basketball game. Amidst the athletic ruckus, as the rear of his T-shirt turned red, Garbiel staggered toward a guard and gasped, "I'm hurt." An hour later, Garbiel died of a stab wound. Soon after, witnesses fingered the Bear, who, in a Bay State legal first, was tried in the prison—and, because of witness intimidation, acquitted.

While the Bear was doing his considerable time in the 1950s and 1960s, his brother Stephen "Stevie" Flemmi represented the family criminal interests out on the street. The brothers contrasted: The

Bear, at five feet eight and 185 pounds, was burly, powerful, and loud. He was manifestly demented and said odd things that unsettled even fellow criminals. Demonstrative, he'd kick down doors and take on a crowd of enemies to make a point (eyewitnesses said he did both). On the other hand, Stevie was a slim five feet six, prone to calculate and wait. Nevertheless, he was tough, quick, and ruthless and could handle himself well against larger men.

Almost from his exit from the womb in 1934, Stevie took to the life felonious. Police picked him up at age fifteen for "carnal abuse," and he did time at a juvenile facility for assault. In 1952, as an incorrigible youth facing jail, he dropped out of high school and enlisted in the U.S. Army in New Jersey, using an alias to dodge the age requirement. He landed in Korea as a paratrooper in the 187th Airborne Regimental Combat Team. On his first eight-man patrol, he opened fire first, killing five Chinese regulars. The patrol started shooting and nearly wiped out the Chinese platoon. After that, his comrades called him the "Rifleman."

Stevie had a knack for killing. During two tours, he nailed many communists, of both the Chinese and North Korean varieties. Sometimes he could look out from his position and see the faces of those he was shooting at. Once, during a nasty fight against the Chinese in Kumwha Valley, Stevie and a partner bravely rescued a wounded soldier.

"He's a very mild person," said the soldier with whom Stevie performed the rescue, years later, after Flemmi became famous. "He doesn't really get excited, but when he says something, he means it. I've never seen anyone so sincere." He concluded, "Steve is just a terrific humanitarian."

In 1955, a corporal, he received an honorable discharge. Now married, kids coming, he needed to earn money, so he started various businesses, legal and otherwise. He repaired church roofs, opened the Jay's Spa market, a bookstore, and a tavern. He also bought up Roxbury real estate on the cheap. Still a crook, he robbed and stole—but eventually drifted to white-collar ventures. His second year stateside, he chanced to meet Roxbury kingpin Wimpy Bennett, who was from nearby Dudley Street and a major street financier, of sorts.

When Wimpy asked if his shylock customers could leave their payoffs for him at Jay's Spa, Stevie complied. Wimpy and his brother Walter were men to imitate—successful and almost exclusively white-collar crooks. Although Irish, they worked closely with the local branch of the Mafia. In fact, Raymond had assisted Wimpy in building up his businesses—for which Wimpy offered gossip and reports on the local underworld, but no cash tributes. And there was money to spare: Walter's vast profits required him to recycle them legitimately (more or less): he owned two bars, real estate, and even a TV repair shop.

The Bennett brothers complemented each other in their businesses. Baby-faced, heavyset, and balding, the unsmiling Wimpy was a master schemer. He looked out on the world with ice-blue eyes, visible through half-closed lids. His brother Walter was steady and reliable: a cool man who could talk about a murder as if it were a horse race. During the 1950s, Walter relocated the family headquarters from the South End into Roxbury. The new location, called Walter's, was in a decaying (and mostly black) neighborhood on Dudley Street near Upham's Corner. If there were fifty men inside Walter's, there would be about forty guns, too. In the gloom and cigarette smoke that pervaded the lounge, gangsters planned scores, borrowed venture capital for capers, and bought and sold stolen goods. (Walter charged 20 percent on loans to ex-convicts.)

Seeing potential in Stevie Flemmi, Wimpy gave him the seed money for a shylocking business. So it was that Stevie began his white-collar criminal apprenticeship with the Irish Bennetts and not the Mafia. The Bennetts groomed Stevie to collect and take bets;

they launched a numbers ring as well. Stevie didn't much like Wimpy Bennett's cartoonish nickname—over time, fittingly, he renamed him "the Fox." Under Bennett tutelage, Stevie took to the business like a vulture does to a carcass. The Rifleman loaned so much money and caught so much attention so flagrantly, the police arrested him in 1961. Paying a $500 fine made the problem evaporate.

Unlike most gangsters, Stevie was a "handsome bastard," with his somber eyes and black hair. Although frequently sullen, he could be pleasant and quite charming, and drew women easily. As the Bennett heir apparent, Stevie was often in Walter's, with a beautiful date on his arm. One avoided violating either the Rifleman's women or money, observed his partner, Francis "Cadillac Frank" Salemme. Cash and females were Stevie's life. "That's what it was to him, his money and his women, not necessarily in that order," Frankie said. "The word to describe Steve Flemmi was a spontaneous reactor. If you messed with either one and two or two and one, forget it." The Rifleman was also touchy. "Anything against him, it's personal," claimed Frankie. He wouldn't overlook anything for the good of the gang.

And he wasn't just a sociopath: He was an egomaniac. "He thought he was invincible," as one girlfriend noted. That Stevie had been an army sniper and could shoot from a long distance unsettled people. But he was hard to read, and his mood might change quickly, as those in the underworld knew. South Boston gangster Kevin Weeks noted that as "I got to know him I understood that Stevie enjoyed a good murder. . . . I'd see him explode" at people who owed him money or didn't do what he asked.

Stevie's bad temper was dangerous to him more than once. As a budding gangster during the 1950s, Stevie befriended South End Mafia soldier Ilario Zanino—always called "Larry Baione." Stevie worked some numbers with Larry and the "In-Town" Angiulos. Once, Stevie accepted a bet that paid $3,000; however, his runner was arrested before he could place the bet In-Town. The Mafia wouldn't honor any wager not officially registered. Stevie ate the loss, which always rankled him. Eventually, he got into a beef with Larry—a volatile and highly lethal man himself. Bullets and fists flew, but Stevie survived long enough to collect his money, and the heat subsided. But Flemmi never looked at In-Town the same way again. Indeed, Stevie "had a natural dislike for the LCN [La Cosa Nostra], that's for sure," Frankie noted. The Rifleman could also take revenge at the long range.

7

THE MAN AT THE TOP OF WINTER HILL

"Winter Hill, from Marshall Street to Adams, is a most pleasant community."

—*from the* Somerville Journal

In August 1961, four men entered Porter's Diner on Mystic Avenue in Somerville. They included brawny teamster James J. "Buddy" McLean and a surly dark-haired guy named Andrew "Bobo" Petricone. Also in the company was the six-feet-two Metropolitan District Commission policeman Russell Nicholson, and a middle-aged pizza parlor owner. For some reason, a fight between them and four young men broke out, leaving the diner a wreck. Someone struck the sixty-five-year-old owner, Porter, with a mop and dishes, smashed his eyeglasses, and put him in the hospital for three days.

Soon after, the police charged Buddy and his colleagues with malicious destruction of property. Buddy's codefendants were a mixed lot. Bobo was a bespectacled "hulking bartender" with a large gut and wide fat face who spoke a thick Somerville dialect. Then there was Nicholson, a brave police officer with an exemplary record. But he was also close to Buddy, and some other hangers-on from Winter Hill. Such interactions weren't particularly noteworthy in the Hill—a very tough working-class neighborhood.

A bit of history may help. In 1900 or so, Somerville was a

pleasant, genteel metropolis, crisscrossed by railroads whose freight kept it prosperous until the twentieth century arrived. As the rail traffic dropped, so did the city's fortunes. One of the barely surviving hardscrabble Somerville communities was Winter Hill, a four-hundred-foot drumlin in the heart of the city. The wide and busy thoroughfare of Broadway divided the Hill like a blue-black vein and connected it to Charlestown.

Buddy McLean, the man at the top of the Hill, inevitably stood out in tiny Somerville. Born on the wrong side of the blanket to a waterfront clerk, a local woman had brought him up with her family, as if he were her own. Buddy, as his name indicated, had a way of making friends. "You just liked him," claimed Frankie Salemme, who saw Buddy around at area sporting events. While still a child, Buddy made a best friend for life: Howard "Howie" Winter. The son of a disgraced policeman, Howie was originally from West Roxbury, and his family had just discovered dire poverty.

Like everyone else, Buddy and Howie needed cash, and they shined shoes, sold newspapers—anything to support and preserve their families. Before leaving their teens, in 1942 Howie and Buddy dropped out of school to work full-time at the Fay Strapping Company. Then war broke out—with an underage Howie joining the U.S. Marines. But, unlike so many other young men from the area, he returned alive and whole. After World War II, there was a future again. As close as David and Jonathan, Buddy and Howie united in business, vowing they'd never forget their suffering and would help out the little people. They had no fears about the future, Howie claimed.

Ambitious, Howie and Buddy opened the trucking firm Travelers Transportation. They started by driving rigs to New York to deliver fabric bolts for the garment district. This required two trucks with two men in the cab—one resting for the next shift. Buddy found this boring and juiced it up with antics—he'd jump on the rig ahead and creep across the load till he could slide his feet on the hood. Needless to say, working with Buddy wasn't for the faint of heart. Howie even claimed Buddy, a born stuntman, could tip a car over on two wheels and drive it balanced that way.

A ladies' man, Buddy was handsome, with honey-colored hair and a "smooth, fair countenance that sometimes made people think of a grown up choir boy." In 1957, Buddy married a local girl, Jean Kelley, and started manufacturing babies, four in all. By 1961, he was spending most of his time working at his company, hauling fish and lobster from Boston to New York. He also headed a five-man team of "lumpers," who performed the backbreaking task of unloading fish from a truck as fast as possible. As a sideline, Buddy also trained German shepherds. So well were the canines disciplined, he'd leave his children at the cinema and go quench a thirst, two vigilant dogs at the theater entrance. If the McLean offspring tried leaving before Buddy returned, a shepherd (literally in this case) prevented them.

Buddy also earned respect from those who didn't readily give it. Broad of shoulder and stout of limb, he was quick to challenge and didn't back down. He was solid and unusually strong, didn't smoke, and worked out frequently at the Cambridge YMCA or ran laps at the Tufts track with his dogs. He loved to brawl. "Buddy was one of the roughest baddest suckers around with fists or a pistol, in your life," said one associate. Working-class, meat-eating, red-blooded, brawl-loving Somerville followed his exploits up and down Broadway. Everyone knew the tales of the latest fights—and Buddy became the father of many legends. For a time, at least, if opponents didn't come to him, he'd go to Charlestown's Alibi Lounge and issue an open challenge for a fight. Some takers left by ambulance.

Somerville was a haven for official corruption, gambling, and blue-collar thefts, such as hijacking and bank robbery. The city joyously and stubbornly resisted all attempts to reform it. Not surprisingly, Buddy also leaned toward crime (he took fifteen collars in 1960 alone), a field where his natural charm and authority made him a leader of crooks. During the 1950s, he began to piece together a loose group that ran numbers, moved stolen goods, loan-sharked, hijacked trucks, and pilfered from the waterfront. The gang ran operations in a handful of seedy taverns dotting Broadway: the Winter Hill Athletic Club, the Capitol Grill, and the 3-1-8 Lounge. Yet Buddy also remained a hardworking soft-spoken family man who attended Mass.

"You would have liked Buddy," said an underworld associate. "He was a rough-and-tumble guy and gruff, but he could be very gentle. Until it came to business, and he could really handle himself."

The coastal town of Salisbury is at the edge of the line dividing Massachusetts and New Hampshire, where the wide mouth of the "mighty" Merrimack estuary meets the frigid Atlantic.

Here, on Labor Day weekend, 1961, some very bad things happened. At one point, anyone strolling along the beach in Salisbury might have noticed a drunken party of city toughs, about forty strong. Boston wise guys often headed north, where the police wouldn't recognize them. One of the revelers on this day was thirty-six-year-old Georgie McLaughlin, whose receding hair and pudgy build made him resemble the comedian Lou Costello. Among the other roughnecks celebrating at the party were Buddy McLean and pals from Somerville and nearby. They included a roofer named George "Red" Lloyd, thirty-two, and his partner, thirty-nine-year-old Billy Hickey, a grocery store employee from Medford. They were sharing a cottage with Georgie and another local tough; Hickey's wife, Ann, was there as well.

On Saturday, Georgie got on Buddy's bad side by insulting a woman, said one witness. Buddy loomed over him, and, feeling threatened, Georgie threw the first punch. Georgie was tough and, though small, threw all his terrier ferocity into his assaults. But Buddy was a match for all three McLaughlin brothers at once. Repeatedly, Buddy hit Georgie, knocking him down and back. Each time, Georgie would get back up and open his mouth again and attack. After slugging McLaughlin twenty-five times or so, Buddy walked away.

"It was just another fight," said the witness. A beaten Georgie made his way to one of the many bars near the beach, where he started to mouth off, calling Buddy some choice names in a bar full of Buddy's friends. He also mouthed off to a woman and received another beating. Eventually, Georgie returned to the cottage with Lloyd and Hickey and their women. Downstairs, Georgie— as an FBI agent drily noted—used "very vulgar language" with Ann Hickey. McLaughlin then made a pass at her—even calling her a whore and spitting beer. Adding to the burlesque atmosphere, upstairs in the cottage Somerville patrolman Billy Breen was proceeding to fornicate with his girlfriend. Before he could succeed, one of the hosts flung open the bedroom door.

"Jesus," Breen said.

"Billy, you're going to have to get the fuck out of here," the host said. "I got Georgie downstairs and he's going crazy. . . . He grabbed the wrong broad, now they're coming after him. And all hell's going to break loose. So do yourself a favor, get lost. I'll come back and get you when it's over." Breen and his girlfriend got dressed and headed back to Somerville.

Back downstairs in the cottage, Georgie brawled with the aggrieved husband. Looking for an equalizer, Georgie broke a whiskey bottle and stabbed Hickey in the face with the shank. That was it—it was time for Georgie's third and final thumping of the day. Lloyd and Hickey beat McLaughlin—after he went down, they kicked him almost to death. It was then they dumped him in an alleyway in the maze of cottages. They hoped someone would find him—and figure a car had hit him.

Regrettably for them, someone brought Georgie to a North Shore hospital. He lay in critical condition for two weeks: He'd lost all but two teeth, the tip of his ear was bitten off, and his scalp was split. The police visited Georgie in the hospital to question him. "I'll take care of it my own way," Georgie said, through what remained of his teeth.

Almost immediately, elder brother Bernie McLaughlin started hunting for Lloyd and Hickey—who'd wisely skipped town. (The Somerville police and the FBI both started looking for them as well.) About a week after the beating, Bernie appeared at Buddy's door and, before entering, loudly demanded the two men dead. Buddy disagreed—Georgie had brought this on himself, and Bernie should let it pass. Bernie left without going inside. Soon after Buddy's rebuff, a car carrying the unwelcome forms of Bernie and Punchy pulled up near Howie Winter. The brothers McLaughlin invited Howie inside to discuss Georgie's beating. They asked Howie, sweating heavily, his thoughts—the number-two man on the Hill sided with Buddy. Bernie leaned over and let him out, but Howie, as he recalled later, knew that wasn't the end of it. Not helping the McLaughlins kill Lloyd and Hickey was a major insult—maybe just as bad as Georgie's thrashing itself.

8.

THE BASTARD SHOULD GET A MEDAL

A month passed. On October 30, 1961, Buddy McLean was at home with his wife and children. Buddy's house was a simple two-story affair at the crown of Winter Hill. It occupied the very end of a small drive with no setback, called Snow Terrace. The next day, he was due in Middlesex Superior Court to face the Porter Diner charges (which predated the mess in Salisbury). Buddy was also scheduled in court later that week, for his alleged stabbing (possibly by accident, with a fork) of a nineteen-year-old driver—whose car he'd backed into on the Broadway-McGrath Highway.

Buddy's brother in-law had borrowed the McLean family car and dropped it off at 12:30 A.M. in front of the house. It remained there at the curb for Buddy's wife to use, as she did every day. Buddy was watching television when his shepherds began barking. His wife, Jean, looked out the window and called for her husband. Sending Jean into the back room, Buddy fetched his Luger from the closet and headed out the front door. Seeing a few men grouped by his car, Buddy fired off three or four 9 mm bullets. The group scattered and ran down the street to a waiting car. Buddy returned inside and quiet resumed in the hilltop neighborhood.

No one immediately called the police, but a Snow Terrace neighbor looking out his window noticed the McLean convertible's hood was up. At 6:30 A.M., as the neighbor left for work, the hood was still raised, and something hung from under the auto's passenger side. On inspection, it proved to be a cluster of dynamite wrapped in paper.

Now the neighbor alerted the police to the night's events. The dispatcher radioed the call to none other than Billy Breen. When, after his Labor Day vacation, he'd reported for duty in Somerville, he'd heard about Georgie's beating. Now, with his blue lights out and no siren, Breen drove up the tangle of streets that led to the top of Winter Hill. It was still dark and quiet, and he recalled the neighborhood "seemed to be holding its breath." Breen saw the dynamite hanging below the car, walked to the door, and rang the McLean bell.

"Waddiya want?" boomed a voice from an upstairs window.

"Patrolman Breen. I got reports of a shooting. . . . if you're Buddy McLean, I got something to show ya."

"Yeah? Okay. I'll be right down."

Buddy appeared in his shorts, and then dropped into a push-up position to see the bomb. When Breen took out his notebook, Buddy, trembling, said, "Put that away, I'll handle this myself."

Investigators located three empty 9 mm shells in front of the McLean house—Buddy denied their ownership. He'd already secreted his pistol in a woman's purse. Police also deduced that if the culprit had connected all the contraption's wires, the bomb would have exploded at ignition and killed anyone inside the car. Someone might have supposed Buddy was taking the car to court—and somebody really had erred. Buddy's wife had planned to drive the full McLean litter that day.

On Halloween morning, before noon collections, Bernie McLaughlin drank at the Morning Glory bar on Chelsea Street in Charlestown's City Square. Perhaps knowing police wanted to question him, Bernie had packed his car with his belongings, as if he were leaving town. The square, all but hidden under an on-ramp to the Mystic River Bridge, usually looked like a sunless slum. Today, longshoremen by the dozen were milling about—lunch, often consisting of liquids, was about to begin. Just around noon, a singer named Linda Lee walked by Bernie, standing in his collection spot under the highway ramp.

"Hi, beautiful, how are you today?" Bernie asked. Lee kept moving to the opposite side of Chelsea Street. At about 12:35, a black sedan pulled up near Richard's Bottled Liquors at City Square; stepping out was a six-foot-tall brown-haired man in a brown suit and trench coat, wearing tortoiseshell sunglasses. Another man joined him; Lee had seen these two companions earlier that day around the square. Now they were moving toward Bernie, who, just then, was accepting a client's money. The man in the brown suit pushed an old bystander in his path aside, stopped about six feet from Bernie, and raised his hand, which held a .38 caliber pistol.

The weapon's muzzle flashed five times: two bullets entered Bernie's head and brain; two more penetrated his back, left side, and arm. A fifth went wild. Bystanders stood transfixed or petrified as a bleeding Bernie collapsed headfirst into the sidewalk. From there, he rolled into the gutter, where a parked car concealed his body. The shooter handed his weapon to his companion and the two both fled in separate directions. Lee watched the gunman run under the Mystic River Bridge and duck under the tailgate of a trailer truck. From there, he crossed to the other side of the street and leaped into a waiting car, its trunk raised. This car drove directly up a ramp and onto the bridge—the trunk still open, so no one could see the license plate. The culprit with the gun ran toward City Square and escaped in another car. The event was over in two well-scripted minutes.

Three policemen found Bernie, who'd been hidden. "What happened, Bernie?" asked a kneeling sergeant. "Who shot you?"

Bernie's body in death, as in life, refused to cooperate. In minutes, the police blocked the Mystic River Bridge and searched all entering cars, but it was too late. Some longshoremen stopped to gaze at the small corpse. "They looked like they couldn't have cared less," said one policeman. "Most of them didn't even bother to cross the street to see the body."

One man wearing a peaked cap said, "Whatever bastard did that should get a medal. Bernie's dead—really dead!"

For his part, Buddy told Howie and some select members of the crew what happened. They all concluded the McLaughlins wouldn't stop till Winter Hill existed only as a point in a map.

Bernie's corpse went to the Boston Northern Mortuary—proof that death makes even the most law-breaking rebel quite docile and law abiding. Although Buddy had pumped four bullets into Bernie rather deliberately, the obituaries reported the death as by "accident." After a Mass, Bernie joined his parents and brothers in the Holy Cross Cemetery in Malden in the McLaughlin family plot, which was proving it had been a wise real estate investment.

That afternoon, Bobo Petricone and Russell Nicholson entered the Capitol Lunch on Broadway. Outside, Somerville detectives waited with their eyes on Bobo's car. The car's plates were also expired—a good reason to leave the trunk up during a murder getaway. When Bobo and Nicholson emerged, the detectives arrested them both on suspicion. They were taken to Charlestown's Division 15 headquarters, where police booked Petricone but released Nicholson.

Learning he was a suspect (along with Hickey and Lloyd), Buddy voluntarily entered the Somerville station at 7:45 P.M. for booking. There he remained until Boston detectives transferred him to the Charlestown precinct station, where a captain interrogated him. Like his friend Bobo, Buddy kept his cool, giving just his name, age, and address, and saying, no, he didn't know why he was there. Unfortunately for the Hill, Linda Lee fingered Buddy and Petricone as the shooters. A chemist performed a paraffin dermal nitrate test on Buddy, and found residue "consistent with a recently discharged firearm." Buddy revealed he'd fired his pistol from his front steps the night before. A captain arrived with an official police stenographer, meaning the quest for the suspects was over.

Boston newspapermen descended into Somerville and Charlestown and printed stories about McLean the "tough guy" and "berserk fighter." One writer said Buddy's baby face hid a "vicious nature and great strength, which he uses to commit savage acts and spread terror." On November 2, under a heavy police guard, Buddy and Bobo were arraigned. The proceedings were on the second floor of the Charlestown courthouse, a fine building overlooking City Square— less than a hundred yards from Bernie's murder site. The suspects entered court handcuffed together, looking respectable in their suits. The photographers snapped their likenesses; the duo held up their hands to cover their clean-shaven faces, making them appear as if they were in deep thought.

The judge ordered Buddy and Bobo held without bail until a November 16 hearing. Facing the electric chair, on December 7, Buddy left the Dedham jail to appear in Boston in Suffolk Superior Court. But, the grand jury dismissed the evidence against him and Bobo, issuing a "no bill." But Lady Justice wasn't quite done with Buddy—he had to answer for his October 10 frolic in Porter's Diner. Just hours after beating Bernie's murder charge, he was in Middlesex Superior Court. There, he was arraigned for his previous stabbing charge and released on $5,000 bail. Life on the street for Buddy would be dangerous—the McLaughlins wanted him real dead and, no doubt, in hell.

From about 1962 on, the underworld feud made life ugly on either side of the Somerville-Charlestown line. There were many cross-border connections, established through friendship, marriage, or family. Everyone had a relative or friend in someone's crosshairs. Legitimate businesses suffered—the thought that violence might break out in an establishment could choke off the flow of customers. Some houses emptied completely of men, who, to protect themselves and their families, began a migratory life. They rented different apartments and frequently changed cars and passed messages to their wives—who could only hope the communications were still current. When people vanished, turned up dead, or were found represented by only a few constituent parts, everyone naturally just blamed the feud.

Illegitimate businesses suffered on both sides of the lines as well. Luckily for Howie and Buddy, independent operator Sal Sperlinga took some of the gang's action and let a trickle of money flow into the Hill's coffers. Tommy Ballou left the Hughes brothers and McLaughlins to stay with Buddy. (He spent much of the gang war in jail; even after he was eligible for parole, he stayed inside.) The one advantage to squaring off with the McLaughlins was that the job didn't require tremendous brain capacity. Reportedly, Harold Hannon had been driving a car around Winter Hill. If he sighted Buddy, he'd signal Georgie, hiding in the trunk with a machine gun, to emerge and open fire.

Yet, Howie never missed church at East Somerville's St. Benedict's Church, faithfully believing no Irishman would kill even an enemy on his way to Mass. No wonder the local bookies kept raising the odds on Buddy's and Howie's survival. To ensure loyalty on the west side of the line, Buddy instituted "preventative maintenance." Over a couple of days, a designated clocker would tail any potential Hill defector and fill a notebook page with his observations. Then Buddy would visit the subject of surveillance and demonstrate the notebook. Buddy would tear the sheet out with the information on it and hand it to the subject as a warning.

On Monday, April 30, Buddy got two years for his part in the

Porter's Diner dustup. The court cleared Russ Nicholson as a suspect in Bernie's murder—but he'd already resigned his Metropolitan District Commission job over charges of keeping "company of persons of ill repute." Now, Nicholson claimed he'd reapply for his old MDC job. But reportedly he became a gambler and full-time crook, instead. His former colleague, Joe McCain, testified against the Hill before a grand jury. Subsequently, someone began calling McCain's wife, threatening to kill Joe Jr. and burn the house down. Acting on a tip, McCain then visited the Capitol Café, saw Bobo Petricone, and called him outside. McCain grabbed Bobo by the throat, shoved him against the picture window, and accused him of the telephonic threats. "It stops today, right now, or I'm gonna come back here and shotgun every last one of you motherfuckers." The calls ceased.

Now doing time, Buddy—like the McLaughlin gang—began recruiting men to assist him back on the street. One of his inductees was Tony "Blue" D'Agostino, who later supplied "boilers" (hot vehicles with guns and masks in them) all over the city. In Walpole, Jimmy Flemmi did time with Buddy, as well as Joe "Joe Mac" McDonald, a major Winter Hill enforcer. Born in 1917, McDonald had served on the ill-fated U.S.S. *Indianapolis*. After it had delivered the atomic bomb earmarked for Nagasaki, a Japanese submarine sank her. During a waking nightmare, schools of tiger sharks feasted on the bobbing and swimming survivors.

Joe Mac had somehow awoken from the nightmare on the ocean alive—a brother serving onboard with him hadn't. Joe Mac never discussed the *Indianapolis*—but he did go on periodic drinking binges. Reputedly, he favored the handgun as a killing weapon—it allowed him to shoot his victims at close range, to ensure he'd be their last sight. Coupled with his partner, the expert driver Jimmy Sims—an orphan and a sometime steeplejack—Joe Mac was a formidable weapon.

So eager was McDonald to fight in the gang war, he walked out of his minimum-security forestry camp, where he'd been doing time for robbing a dairy. Rumor spread of his dark deeds on the street. Later, he was arrested after a brawl and gunfight with police in Boston, boasted up-and-coming maniac Johnny Martorano (Joe Mac's devotee). After overturning McDonald's original conviction, the authorities released him. He'd never been, technically, a fugitive of justice, since there was never a true cause to arrest him in the first place.

If, as someone once said, Waterloo's outcome had been decided on the playing grounds of Eaton, the New England gang wars of the 1960s were determined in the mess halls, cells, and ballparks of the Walpole and Norfolk prisons.

While Buddy was in jail, the gang war continued to simmer on the street. Just before dark, on July 9, 1962, someone found the decomposed corpse of George "Ox" Joynt, of Somerville, in a clay pit in Medford. Joynt had been a friend of Georgie's—and someone had put a bullet in his head, allegedly after forcing him to dig his own grave.

One key member of Wimpy's Roxbury group was old-time gangster Earle Smith. He'd been particularly close with the McLaughlin brothers. Wimpy also bankrolled the McLaughlins—so he and Stevie both initially threw in their lot with Charlestown. But Stevie admitted he'd never warmed up to the dangerous Georgie, who was a "vicious" drunk—and so often vicious.

Nevertheless, on September 4, 1962, Wimpy the Fox drove Stevie and Georgie to Somerville. They found Howie Winter's car, and Georgie affixed a time bomb to it. In the meantime, Howie loaned the car to a woman who suspected nothing—until she pulled the car up to the curb by the Mystic Avenue projects. Some twenty-four hours after it had been set, the bomb belatedly exploded. The nearby building shuddered, interrupting a card game inside and sending the players to the floor. The car hood landed in an adjacent playground; the front seat was a mess of plastic and steel. A cloud rose over the wreck, and eventually, as the approaching sirens became louder, the neighbors emerged to eye the damage. Howie appeared and removed his belongings, smoking a cigarette and smiling awkwardly while the photographers snapped his picture. Winter had never known what didn't hit him, and there was even greater mirth on the McLaughlins' tab.

Still at a distance from the miniature, if savage, Charlestown-Somerville war, Joe Barboza was trying to improve his estate. At this point, still out on the street, Joe wanted to enter the Office by his own means. Passing through the state's most elite criminal colleges, Joe had realized they contained an especially elite varsity. Its Porcellian Club (to borrow from Harvard) was exclusively Sicilian-Italian. Together, the members formed a shadowy but powerful upper class not just in prison, but on the street. These Italians formed a consortium of criminal enterprises whose scope and influence dwarfed the heft of puny gangs such as Winter Hill. "Younger inmates in Walpole and Concord would do anything to get in with these people, figuring that they would become big men," as Joe later observed.

Like one of his barbaric Visigoth ancestors, Joe had looked upon the prosperity and power of a Roman dominion. He'd seen the strength of its legions and its wealth, and coveted it with barely disguised resentment. Although he didn't understand the empire, he was inching toward it now. Gutsy Joe hoped somehow he could avoid paying "rent" on his shylocking business to the Office. He was willing to work for this privilege, too.

An opportunity arrived in September 1962. His criminal sponsor, Leo Schwartz, called Joe to the dry-cleaning store on

Massachusetts Avenue that fronted for his booking operation. Leo took his protégé into the cellar and explained a "Greek" was running for the head of the bakers' union at a North Station factory. The Office wanted to discourage this man, and required he be "bundled." Schwartz had proposed Joe.

Although the contract was worth $1,000, Joe offered to take it gratis, to show "some class" and buy some Mafia goodwill. It was easy: Schwartz gave him the man's description and Dorchester address; his car's make, color, and license plate number. Joe even knew where the Greek typically parked at work. The Animal waited two weeks, until it "was beautifully stormy," as he put it, and the street was bystander free. Joe and two henchmen approached the Greek's house and then converged on their victim.

Leading the assault, Joe hit the baker on the side of the head with 20-pound sash weights. The Greek staggered against the side of the car before running into the middle of the street. The two enforcers followed. Joe beat the victim on his knees and wrists, while his partner hit him on the shoulder, and he collapsed. "We left him in a heap, a bloody heap in the middle of the street, and took off in the hot [getaway] car."

As Joe bragged, they'd "popped his roots in," dislocating his shoulder blade and leaving him with a gash on the knee requiring sixteen stitches. The next day, Joe told Schwartz, "You'll read all about it in the papers." Schwartz pulled out a roll of money, but Joe stopped him. "I don't want it," he said. "The expenses are one dollar for two sash weights. I'll see you later."

Joe left, feeling that he was slowly rising to the "real money." The goodwill from this job came to about $70,000, Joe later estimated. He was still fighting and shylocking, and now had a front job at an auto agency owned by a friend.

Also working there was a slender, good-looking young blonde: Claire Cohen. With her large brown eyes, in light makeup, she could appear as fresh as a model from "a Talbot's advertisement."

She had pleasant manners and a sense of humor. Joe had been seeing her regularly, and declared he was in love. Up until now, as he
later depicted it, his sex life outside jail had comprised a series of
adulteries and crude affairs to punctuate his violence. Claire, at
least, might give him one special woman to cheat on. Before September 1962 closed, Joe's good luck soured when he violated his
1958 parole in a botched break-in. Before he returned to his second home, Walpole prison, Claire promised to marry him. There
was one condition: He must convert to Judaism on his release. Joe
agreed, and returned for a two-year stretch, knowing someone on
the outside waited. That someone could prove very useful, too.

9

THIS BUNCH OF BOOKIES

"In Italian, La Cosa Nostra is also known as 'our headache.'"
—Jerry Angiulo

The Somerville-Charlestown fracas had wide implications for the regional underworld. From his North End perch, Jerry Angiulo briefly contemplated hitting Bobo and Buddy. He even discussed tracing their daily habits and activities to arrange the hit. Presumably, this was for matters of policy, as Jerry had his fingers in Somerville. As a rule, Jerry protected his cash like a she-bear does her cubs.

Under Raymond, the abrasive and obnoxious Jerry was one of the most powerful men in the Boston underworld. For a crook, Jerry was born with a leg up, being a child of the sunless and poverty-ridden North End ghetto. There, only the strong survived the poverty, racial and religious slights, and crushing despair. Most residents were Southern Italian peasants, who often spoke little English. These "dagos" and "guineas" fought hard for the crumbs—jobs and contracts and educational and political slots—left by the Irish who'd preceded them.

Jerry's parents, Caesar and Giovannina (Jenny), had emigrated from the same Southern Italian town. They married in a North End apartment in 1915 and opened a grocery store on 96 Prince

Street. As it also served franks, it was called the Dog House Restaurant. Their apartment, also on Prince Street, soon filled with five sons and a daughter. Jerry took after his mother, who was a shrewd, sharp-tongued woman and cardsharp. Like his siblings, Jerry worked at the family store—but, clever and willful, he stood out.

He talked back to teachers and publicly ridiculed other students. He managed to graduate from high school; his yearbook quote was from Shakespeare: "One touch of nature makes the whole world kin." He grew up prickly about his Italian heritage and resented the Irish domination of the city's civil service, businesses, and political machines. He was, in essence, born to hate the Kennedys.

A natural bookie, Jerry racked up an arrest in 1941 for registering bets. After World War II erupted, Jerry tried to enlist in the navy. But flat feet kept him out—until he switched middle names on his enlistment papers. In four years, Jerry rose to boatswain and drove landing craft in the Pacific. In 1946, at age twenty-eight, carrying battle awards, he was honorably discharged with $12,000 in hand. Like his brothers, he worked menial jobs, driving a truck and vending from a pushcart. But Jerry's arrests also continued: registering bets and booking outside the track, and malicious injury to telephone company property. In 1947 alone he faced six collars—one by a state trooper from the boondocks, who managed to arrest him for booking at Prince Street.

Sometime around 1950, Jerry took his operation into the Boston big time. Jerry allowed free "agents" to take play up to ten cents apiece—exceed that sum, and then they must lay off or bet with the Angiulos. A master of odds and street math, Jerry knew when to go heavy on bets and when to lay off others to avoid large payouts and long-shot number lotteries.

Raymond cultivated Jerry and oversaw his baptism as a Mafioso, which brought him new respect. Now if a local hoodlum borrowed money from Jerry, he made sure he repaid it. For this, in the 1960s, Jerry kicked up to Raymond about $50,000 a year, although estimates varied over time. Mostly a businessman, Jerry at least half believed the myth that the Mafia was a noble society that had fought the misrule of Sicilian "land barons."

In any case, the organization was good enough for Jerry to graft his brothers into it, in varying degrees. They included Donato ("Danny"), and Nicolo ("Nicky"), the only blue-collar crook among the brothers Angiulo. The Dog House on Prince Street remained a working deli, with an office. At their height, the Angiulos maintained a nearly round-the-clock operation of betting on horse and dog races and numbers running. And Jerry was there with money to lend to gamblers—preferably those on a losing streak. This "bunch of bookies," as one old-school Mafioso called the Angiulos, was more successful than any other branch in the Office.

In the early 1960s, there were an estimated quarter million Angiulo dollars out on the street, garnering 1 percent interest. With this cash, the local street bankers floated the final loans out from pizza joints, bars, candy stores, and other establishments, at higher rates than Jerry charged. Eventually, the Jerry fund became something akin to the U.S. Federal Reserve Bank. Of course, if a network bank went bust, the manager wished he only faced jail.

Jerry had fierce eyes, a hawk nose, and a sort of haughty thin-lipped sneer that might have fit a Renaissance prince. Jerry's slender five-feet, six-inch frame carried a mere 145 pounds. While he could display the courage of small wiry men, his appearance just wasn't frightening. But to succeed, Jerry had to manage dim-witted, if more physically imposing, underlings. He complained that some of his older long-term employees "could not even add" when they started working for him. Angiulo wanted "kids right out of high school" as bookies—not dropouts.

To flunkies, particularly slow ones unable to keep up with his quick mind, Jerry was explosive—then his mouth ran to the obscene and nasty. Nevertheless, Angiulo employees became "greatly in-debted" to the brothers from borrowing (presumably to cover gam-ing losses), so tended to stay with the firm. Jerry became "very disturbed" when the family of a hospitalized employee asked if the Angiulos "had provisions for unemployment benefits."

White-collar Jerry wasn't a warmhearted man, and grasped the power of pain. He kept muscle at the call, and in 1963, had a par-ticularly violent bodyguard. He noted his bodyguard "would kill nine people, but if he cuts his finger, he gets sick. Some people like him like to kill, but don't like the idea of dying themselves." His job also let Jerry express the pent-up rage of a small man in a fringe minority community in a miniature and fragmented city. Once in power, he rarely had to listen, and often bullied. Once, an Angi-ulo debt collector received a pistol whipping instead of an install-ment from a client. A furious Jerry sent two men to retrieve the debtor at gunpoint. In Jay's Lounge, the club owner begged for his life. "I'll give you one more chance," Jerry said.

His hardness extended to colleagues. In February 1964, Jerry learned that an old Boston Mafiosi had shuffled off the mortal coil. "He better not be dead," Jerry said. "He owed me $14,000." When he called Beth Israel Hospital to verify the announcement, he was rebuffed, not being a relative. Jerry then ordered an underling to call the hospital, and pretend to be the deceased's brother—but this ploy also failed. In any case, the venerable Mafioso was in fact dead.

Small and slight, Jerry was also crafty, and could use psychol-ogy as a weapon. "Seeing him was like going to see a priest," noted one Irish associate. Jerry warned one careless shylock partner: "You better have an explanation for your stupidity in handling Raymond's money I can pass on to Raymond." Raymond wasn't going to be happy, Jerry promised.

The various Angiulo methods worked on a Midas scale. Money entered the street, multiplied, and returned to the Angiulos in such increased volume that, by necessity, it needed outlets in ever-expanding and varied enterprises, legal and otherwise. Jerry's embarrassment of riches even forced him to haul stacks of paper cash personally to Miami to launder. To handle these far-flung activities, in 1955, with his brothers (as always, located at 95 Prince Street), Jerry founded the Huntington Realty Trust. From one side, gambling and loan-sharking dollars entered the trust—and exited for use in a cleansed, untraceable format. This cash bought heaps of protection, including from law enforcement—and Jerry boasted the could afford to buy 300 of the 360 detectives in Boston.

The Angiulos frequently partnered with legitimate small businesses—and over time, plied the owners with so many loans that they were, essentially, bought out. They also acquired properties and enterprises from Maine to Florida. The Angiulo ventures included a jingle business for radio commercials, an advertising and publicity firm, a vending machine operation, a bowling alley, an automobile-bumper-repair company, and the Indian Meadow Country Club in central Massachusetts.

So upwardly mobile he was skyrocketing, Jerry married a lovely model (of the blond sort) and produced two children (always well dressed). Leaving Boston, he relocated north, to the pleasant town of Medford, to have a place to sleep through the morning. After a poverty-stricken childhood, he enjoyed the good life. He dressed impeccably, ate fine Italian fare at the high-end restaurant Giro's, and visited the racetrack. Sometimes, to relax at night, he'd bowl. Naturally, as a onetime navy man, Jerry bought a yacht and, generously sharing his own name, called it the *Saint Gennaro*.

To his family—sometimes—and to those who pleased him, he could be pleasant, soft-spoken, and polite. He fawned on Raymond, to whom he once pledged himself and a flunky, saying: "We belong to you." One of his cousins described Jerry thus, "A gentleman's gentleman, and no matter what they say, he was a good guy."

10

THE DUKE OF MEDFORD

"When [Bobby] Kennedy takes a dislike to you, the FBI will be all over you."

—Raymond Patriarca

In 1960, John Kennedy, with assistance from connected men in special places in Chicago, narrowly squeezed by Richard Nixon to become president—as Nixon's and the mob's story goes. Later, kingmaker Joseph P. Kennedy forced John to pick his brother Robert as attorney general. Then Bobby did the unpredictable: He actually viewed organized crime as a serious threat, and treated it accordingly. In him, the Mafia had an enemy whose malice was bottomless (as Jimmy Hoffa discovered, to his regret). With his brother as president, Bobby could empty his spleen on anyone, including "that pig on the [Federal] Hill."

In any case, the dons, generally good Democrats and fellow Catholics, were shocked, angry, and frightened, and declared, fairly or not, the Kennedys were ingrates. "Everybody that went to intercede for somebody with the Kennedys not only wound up in trouble himself, but the guy that he was interceding for also wound up in trouble," Raymond observed. He also complained: "He's got more law and pretty soon you won't be able to do nothing."

Bobby ordered Hoover to make good on his intention to go after the Mafia; Hoover followed his instructions, and the Boston

FBI office followed Hoover. Charlestown native and FBI agent Dennis Condon began to dog Jerry Angiulo and other choice regional mob leaders. Condon and other agents, such as H. Paul Rico, also started recruiting informers and contacting local police departments and businesses for information about New England's organized crime network. In May 1962, Condon even spied on Raymond when doctors at New England Baptist Hospital removed a calcified lump from Helen Patriarca's lung. While she recovered, Raymond visited her faithfully—conducting business from the hospital parking lot from inside a car. He even met with a governor's councillor to spring Larry Baione from jail.

From another (and slightly more unsavory) angle, the FBI attacked by recruiting informants, such as Vincent "Fat Vinnie" Teresa. Born in 1928, Vinnie claimed nothing less than the royal blood of the Bourbons pumped in his stressed veins. He boasted his grandfather was a Mafia don and a duke in Sicily—however, Vinnie's father violated family tradition by living honestly.

The genes had only skipped a generation, as Vinnie quickly became all those things the story of Pinocchio warned us that boys become without a guide. Try as he might, his father simply couldn't beat the devil out of his son. Vinnie admitted to being "a thief and hustler" since age twelve. "I'd have ripped Christ off the cross in those days." For fun, Vinnie and his friends played tackle football on cement, mixed it up in street fights, or rolled dice in the school basement. While still in seventh grade, he committed his first burglary—eleven more break-ins resulted in a pile of five thousand stolen dollars. He blew the stake gambling. In fact, Vinnie was such a gaming addict, his mother couldn't even trust him with the family's twenty dollars of weekly meat money. When Vinnie reached the ninth grade, his school principal asked him to drop out.

During World War II, Vinnie managed to resist the tide of patriotism until 1945. But with the entire neighborhood in uniform, including the scoundrels, a bored Vinnie felt compelled to join the army. Vinnie, still a crook, was dishonorably discharged. Without regret, he became a civilian; married a long-suffering woman named Blanche; and moved into his father's house to breed sinners.

As his legitimate sideline, he worked as a truck driver and deli operator, among various other pseudo-professions. To make real money, he stole, cheated, extorted, conned, usuriously loaned money, committed arson, and forged drivers' licenses. Just as Vinnie always preferred the wide and crooked path, he also became a wide and crooked man. Of all his deadly sins, gluttony was a specialty. He punished himself and his health with excess food, drink, and smoke. Over a few years in the 1950s, his five-feet, eight-inch frame grew in weight from 155 to 300 pounds. He chain-smoked until his voice was a rough bark—and all this caused him a heart attack in his thirties.

Clever and scheming, he was still no Dr. Moriarty-like mastermind. Vinnie maintained that every day in the underworld was like going to school. "Graduation is staying alive," he observed. Multiple times, Vinnie nearly flunked. Needing a sponsor, he turned to Henry Tameleo and stuck with him for years, as a pilot fish does to a shark. Always, he kicked up tribute to Henry and built trust—to the degree Henry trusted anyone. Seeing his uses, Henry employed Vinnie as a driver, gofer, and debt collector.

As a trusted flunky, Vinnie had access to Raymond and Henry. Seeing how the Office's top men operated, Vinnie knew how to lie on a grand scale. Despite his inflated palaver, reality was less accommodating to Vinnie than his imagination. Most hoodlums found him laughable—one of the nastier young turks even spat on him. His colleagues called him "Fat Vinnie," a moniker he hated, despite its aptness.

Nor, when push came to stab, was the hanger-on Vinnie a blood member of the family. For instance, once he scammed Henry's friends with eighteen hundred dollars' worth of bad checks. Soon after, under the underboss's orders, Joe said that he caught Vinnie and gave him a modest beating. (Thereafter, Vinnie called him the "Nigger," even though their skin tones weren't too far apart.) Much worse, Vinnie and a partner stole $40,000 from the house of one of Raymond's Worcester cousins. He nearly left Raymond's office in a box after that one—but walked after pleading ignorance to the mark's lineage.

In 1963, Vinnie, to his peril, crossed Jerry after buying $1 million in "queer" twenties for ten cents apiece. Soon after, Jerry dispatched someone to bring him into his club Jay's Lounge. For his audience with Vinnie, Jerry appeared in gray silk pants, patent leather slippers, black velvet smoking jacket, and ascot. With his filter-elongated cigarette, Jerry resembled George Raft.

Sitting down, Jerry said, "Oh, so you're the kid. You brought some queer twenties into the city. You may not walk out of this joint alive tonight."

The underboss explained how Vinnie's counterfeits had flooded crap games and racetracks, creating beefs with the law and just about everybody else. After calling Raymond, Jerry dismissed Vinnie, but screamed, "Get outta here. Don't come back and keep outta my sight." That Raymond, from his lofty perch, spared Vinnie proved the New England Mafia had a sense of humor.

But Vinnie's greed was only matched by his cheapness: in fact, he relied on slugs to make pay-phone calls. He dropped so many of these dummies into one unit, the telephone company disconnected it. During his long criminal career, Vinnie pulled scams everywhere he could find a fool with money: Miami, San Francisco, Las Vegas, Baltimore, and even overseas in London and in the Bahamas and Haiti.

But, unfortunately, he remained a self-admitted "degenerate

gambler," and no matter how much he stole, he blew it all. "I used to be at the track so much that my legs used to ache from the cement—every day, every meet," he said. "I'd bet as much as two and three grand a race, every race, when the money was rolling in." Usually he lost—"on a real bad day it would be as much as twenty grand."

Luckily for Vinnie, Hoover wanted a "Top Echelon" informant with access to the top levels of the organization. It was the highest status a source could achieve—akin to an award the Sanhedrin might have given Judas Iscariot. Vinnie honored no cause except his own, needed the loot, and wanted the job. By 1960, Vinnie was on the FBI payroll, through a cash-on-delivery transaction system, and had earned a total of $190. He got a promotion in 1963, when Jerry fronted mafioso soldier Nicky Giso $114,000 of his and Henry Tameleo's money. Instead of lending this cash, Giso gambled it away, and the family considered eliminating him. Instead, the wise men demoted him to mere worker and recompensed him a "small week's pay" for his efforts. The rest was credited to his considerable bill. Giso's bad fortune was Vinnie's good luck. After Vinnie shared that tidbit, the FBI promoted him to its Top Echelon Informant program.

II.

UNEASY LIES THE HEAD

"Pretty soon the U.S. government will be running the country."
—Raymond Patriarca

Besides clownish and dishonest pawns like Vinnie Teresa, Bobby Kennedy had other means to attack the Office. They included various forms of electronic surveillance. That brave new world humbled and terrified even Raymond: Electronic surveillance was like a witness he couldn't threaten and kill. As a matter of habit, Raymond believed all his phones were tapped. He walked blocks away from his office to make calls from phones he presumed were clear. The Office feared an FBI walkie-talkie could pick up conversations twenty miles away, and had cameras that snapped photos from five miles. Raymond even warned Jerry "to be careful about people wearing hearing aids."

Given it was a criminal headquarters, by necessity, the Coin-O-Matic building also housed more or less legitimate businesses. Because of this, it held a lot of hard currency, which a truly enterprising thief might try to filch. So, security was considerable. Despite Raymond's caginess, the FBI planted a bug in Coin-O-Matic, with a listening plant at nearby St. Margaret's Home for Working Girls. The listening room cost $45 a week in rent, but the results were priceless. (The communications were interrupted once, for two days, by an auto that crashed into a telephone pole carrying the wire.) Gangster lingo and innuendo encrypted many conversations to unintelligibility. But, among the various nuggets the agents did shake out was that on December 18, 1962, an emissary of Rocky Marciano had visited Coin-O-Matic. Someone had recently stolen Marciano's fur coat, and he wanted to ask for Raymond's help directly. As far as we know, Raymond was unable to recover the garment.

By November 1962, the FBI had also targeted Jerry (code name June). FBI agents traced calls and interactions between Jerry and contacts in Scranton, Philadelphia, Niagara Falls, Myrtle Beach, Yakima, Fort Lauderdale, Old Lyme, and other far flung places. They interviewed credit agencies, banks, police chiefs, neighbors, informers, and officials of every stripe.

Nailing Jerry was tough, too. The North End remained a fortress for the Angiulos and their cohorts—twice, over several years, when federal agents or state and city police raided the Angiulo operations, riots broke out. And nobody got an audience with Jerry at Jay's Lounge unless permission was granted. This was the era of James Bond, and Jerry was healthily (for his profession) paranoid—he particularly feared cigarette packages that carried bugs. (His lieutenant Peter Limone said the feds had stuff that, rubbed in, could transmit inculpatory signals from one's clothes.)

The Boston FBI focused on Jay's Lounge, which bore Jerry's name, and from which he ran his money-lending operation. It was ensconced in the rough-and-tumble Combat Zone, Boston's answer to Times Square. Inside a few city blocks that edged Chinatown were embedded a series of garish nightclubs, strip joints, and pornographic (semidisguised) bookstores.

The FBI secretly traced the door lock of Jay's Lounge to make a key for a smooth break-in. After examining some building blueprints, they settled on placing a microphone in the closet of

Jerry's new basement apartment. A drill bit had to penetrate from the historic Shubert Theatre through nearly fifty inches of concrete and cedar. To do the job, the New York office flew in a special drill, apparently water cooled and armed with a special diamond tip. But the drill tip froze and required a new motor and custom-built extension replacements. Nevertheless, the agents persevered, and inserted their electronic ear successfully. The Angiulo radio show went live in a nearby "monitoring plant" at 10 P.M., January 16, 1963. This was none too soon, as the New York office needed the drill back in time to bug the Cuban United Nations delegation.

"The law would give $1 million to have a microphone in my place," Jerry observed. The government paid far less—$5,368.75 to be exact, including $3.75 for a leased line. The canny Jerry also installed a special machine that picked up radio waves. He believed the feds could never tap his place—the walls, even the ones in the closet, were cement. Yet Jerry told an expert bug sweeper he still feared there was a device that could detect a distant conversation through glass. The expert said that was impossible, "unless these guys have become space men."

And there was always Vinnie. Jerry's abrasive demeanor made it easy for Teresa to betray him to the FBI. But Vinnie didn't limit his snitching to Jerry—he gave up anyone he could. So it was that in 1963 Vinnie informed the FBI about $57,000 in stolen jade and ivory awaiting a fence. As Vinnie told it, Jerry and Henry Tameleo became involved. According to FBI records, on March 2, 1963, the FBI found the jade in a burned-out car in a Roxbury parking lot, covered with Vinnie's and Henry's fingerprints. An agent approved Vinnie's $300 expense claim and stated grandly that this sort of work would "enable this office to make an inroad into the empire of [Raymond Patriarca]."

The incident caused an uproar at the Office. Soon after, Jerry and Henry visited Providence to discuss how the jade caper had become known to the FBI. Jerry accused Henry of having picked up a tail. Not so, said Henry—he'd avoided arrest for thirty years, and claimed his skills made it impossible for anyone to surveil him. He checked and double-checked for that very subterfuge. Rather, Henry deduced, the FBI had tapped the phone line. "Forget the whole thing, it's gone, there's nothing we can do about it now," said Raymond to end the conversation.

When Henry left the office, Raymond vented to Jerry: "He's [Henry's] handling too much. He's more active than six bosses and is all over the place. This will lead to trouble."

"He doesn't have the experience you and I have in the field," Jerry said.

On another occasion, the don's observant night driver also told Jerry that Raymond "was very worried because of all the federal heat and [he] should go away for a vacation."

"Everything is bothering him," Jerry noted, believing Raymond had suffered a nervous breakdown. "If they indict everyone who is rumored to be indicted, they'll need a new jail. . . . I wouldn't let this upset me like it's upsetting Raymond." He considered hiding for a few weeks in Florida, by renting a house across from his mother's place in Fort Lauderdale.

April 1963 was a particularly cruel month for Raymond. On the sixteenth, at Boston's New England Baptist Hospital, a surgeon operating on Helen Patriarca discovered cancer. Raymond told Jerry, who, behind his back, accused him of being a "crybaby." Jerry told Limone, "I wonder who he'll tell his troubles to, as he won't be able to tell his wife any longer. That [police pressure] will break them down. My brothers are being watched constantly, but they're not going to break down." Nevertheless, the next day, Jerry secured three special nurses to attend the don's wife twenty-four hours a day. (Later, Jerry said he wished Helen "would die and get it over with.")

Raymond's woes made the FBI salivate. An agency director instructed the Boston office: "In view of Patriarca's emotional state due to this illness [Helen's cancer], you should be alert to be in a position to exploit the situation."

Retrenching, Raymond ordered his flunkies to kick everyone out of his front office and keep them away. At times, Raymond's suspicion became paranoia, which was very dangerous for suspected informants—whom he might eliminate, just to be on the safe side. Learning someone had broken into his mistress's summer cabin, he narrowed the suspects down to the state police or ignorant kids. A car parked near one of his meeting places prompted him to get his official friends to run the plate. After Raymond told a friendly local dentist he was off to Boston to see Helen, the FBI surveilled the don. Wrongly, Raymond surmised the innocent neighbor was a snitch—but we have no record that Federal Hill mysteriously lost a dentist.

Again, Uncle Sam hammered away at Jerry, using the IRS as instrument. The government demanded Jerry and his colleagues provide their tax returns. After Jerry spent many hours with an adding machine calculating his finances since 1956, he realized he was vulnerable for at least two years' income.

Making his life more difficult, Jerry's wife had filed a separate support petition and contempt citation against him. Alleging cruel and abusive treatment, she'd obtained a restraining order in Middlesex Probate Court. Jerry blamed the FBI agent Dennis Condon for using this domestic legal mess to get him "nailed" and make him reveal his secrets. Angiulo was convinced he was going to jail. "If Dinny Condon comes in I'll split his [fucking] head open," he declared. "No one ever went to the can with Jerry Angiulo." That was tough talk, given Jerry had emphysema and needed to reduce his cigarette intake.

But, as Condon wrote, "Angiulo is known to be dramatic and often boasts to impress his associates." The FBI planned to watch him more closely, just in case.

The feisty underboss confronted Condon in the street. "I saw you parked down the street and thought I'd come by and say hello," said Jerry. "Anyone investigating me or my brothers won't find anyone who'd knock us." Another afternoon, Jerry, his brothers, and Peter Limone stood outside their stronghold at 96 Prince Street. They watched Condon watching at a distance; Jerry approached him. "How did you enjoy your vacation?" He hinted he knew about Condon's influencing the court against him. "I hope to God you never have the personal problem I have." Jerry also warned: "I don't mind if everything is on the up and up and there aren't any low blows."

12.

INTO THE PUBLIC EYE

"That's the FBI training. Stay with it until you prove it."
—Jerry Angiulo

The heat on the Office became more intense. In August 1963, Peter Limone noted an article in *The Saturday Evening Post*, then a major publication, depicting the operations of the Office. "They never had a breakthrough like this before," Limone told Jerry when he brought him a copy.

A perturbed Jerry concluded that in three to five years, the horse and numbers business would carry federal felony penalties, putting him out of business. "If worst comes to worst, we can go to Canada and operate there," Jerry said. Noting the organization hadn't had a good break in the last two years, he called his Washington, D.C., contact for more information. Gloomily, he whined: "If things get any worse for me, I'll probably do better if I go to the old country."

During his routine visit to the Office in Providence, Jerry took the troublesome magazine with him. "The Kennedys are putting them [the media] on this to cover for all their blunders around the country," Raymond told Jerry.

The gravy pot positively boiled over on October 8, when the infamous, if not necessarily accurate, informer Joseph Valachi stated the obvious fact that Raymond was "king of the New England underworld." Following Valachi's performance, Raymond's oldest and most powerful enemy testified: Colonel Walter Stone, the superintendent of the Rhode Island state police. The colonel claimed: "He [Raymond] is the most powerful man I've ever dealt with. He is a shrewd, scheming individual as well-versed in the ways of crime today as he was yesteryear. He is as ruthless in the sixties as he was in the thirties," said Stone.

In private—just Raymond, an associate, and the FBI's bug—the don claimed a Kennedy-brainwashed Stone only "made a fool of 'himself' with his testimony." He noted: "Some of the young punks coming up might figure I was at one time a stoolie and kill me. . . . He made a goat out of me—with the neighbors—the family—I have nieces and nephews—no one could go to work the next day. If I don't answer back I can never walk the street again. He said I was a dishonest man with friends. I have always been an honorable man with friends."

Nevertheless, the "heat" was so intense that he told his men to avoid his headquarters. If anyone asked if he was mafioso, he planned to say, "The only Mafia I ever heard of is the Irish Mafia that the Kennedys are in charge of." Publicly, Raymond said Stone's approach "smacks more of the legal practices under the Nazi regime in Germany and the present Communist regime in Russia." Of Valachi, he said, "I never saw or talked to the creature. . . . There's a lot of crazy people in the world. What do you think we are, animals or something?"

This was bad for business. By now, Raymond had already lost eighteen accounts at Ace Dumping, a grand jury was impaneled to investigate it, and the venture was destined for bankruptcy. "This is a move by Robert Kennedy to get me before he leaves [the Attorney General's] office," Raymond claimed. "I want to see Kennedy lose in [the senate race in] New York." Then there was a joker in Congress's deck, in the form of the stocky five-feet, nine-inch ex-boxer Paul Colicci. Nearing forty, he was a familiar—and unattractive—face on Federal Hill, "capable of anything" in terms of crime, with a record twenty years long.

While doing a stretch at Charlestown State Prison, Colicci had written a letter to Raymond that said, "Hello Boss: Do you notice how I respect you and call you boss. But do you have to leave me in jail? . . . By, big boss." Stone read these letters before the Senate, making Raymond "very perturbed," as the FBI noted.

In October 1963, during his Senate testimony, the Boston police commissioner, Edmund McNamara, made Jerry Angiulo a household name via television. Ominously, McNamara was an ex–FBI man—competent and honest, and not some malleable, crooked hack under the Office's thumb. Worried, Jerry shot back, "I'll give McNamara more trouble than he bargained for."

Jerry observed the Angiulos were now the "hottest thing in Boston." The attention was so fierce, Jerry considered a trip to Hawaii. Instead, he sent his girlfriend to the Sandwich Islands, armed with $3,800 in spending money—he later complained about all the cash she went through.

In the midst of the turmoil in 1963, Revere's Jewish rackets boss, Louis Fox, died, rather prosaically, of a heart attack. This was a godsend to Jerry, who'd long coveted access to the Fox's prized and protected (through New York) markets. Already, Jerry had bought a liquor store to create a base of operations to befriend city officials and expand his illegal enterprises. Minus the Fox, the city and the numbers business of the "Revere Jews" was wide open.

And Jerry needed money. One of his biggest investments (with Raymond and other mafiosi) was the Indian Meadow Country Club—a "financial monster" as Jerry phrased it. This cash-bleeding white-collar enterprise was becoming a public disaster. Sniffing mischief and fraud in the meadows, the IRS had demanded the club's books for an audit. On November 7, 1963, Jerry visited the club office to strategize with his fellow investor, a relation of the Worcester don, Frank Iacone. Jerry shook hands with the venerable Iacone, and the two entered the office. Soon, the discussion became an argument, and Jerry's famous temper exploded. Jerry touched Iacone's head and called him an "obscene name" four times. So angry became Iacone, he feared he'd kill Jerry. However, he refrained because, as he put it, "Angiulo was Raymond's boy."

(No mere henchman, Frank Iacone had been one of Raymond's own mentors in the honorable society.) On November 8, Iacone complained to Raymond directly. "You should have killed him then," said Patriarca. "If he ever calls you that name again you have the right to kill Angiulo on the spot and no questions will be asked," Raymond promised.

But on November 9, at 3:30 A.M., Jerry parked his $7,000 Cadillac on Huntington Avenue in Roxbury. He then made his way to the Boston apartment he shared with his mistress, and went to sleep. Soon after, a green convertible with several men inside drove by Jerry's Cadillac. Someone sloppily fired five bullets—two smashed the rear passenger window; another flattened the left front tire.

The shooting awoke Jerry, who wondered if this was a warning or just a badly timed hit. Those who disliked Jerry were legion— the McLaughlins had briefly stopped talking to him after Bernie's murder, suspecting his involvement. But as Jerry told Peter Limone later that day, few people knew his 902 Huntington Avenue address. He suspected the FBI—or someone seeking revenge. Jerry said he believed someone was displeased he'd "gotten too big too fast." He vowed, "I'll find out the reason for the shooting and who did it, no matter how long it takes."

For public consumption, Jerry said: "I haven't got an enemy in the world." But now Jerry's bodyguard carried a weapon in his pants round the clock. Rumor claimed even Jerry started packing a pistol in his briefcase. There was still the ongoing fear of the Boston

Strangler. After someone burglarized his girlfriend's apartment, Jerry taught her to defend herself with a knife and gun.

Possibly in response to the shooting, on November 14, Raymond presided over a sit-down with Iacone and Jerry. Angiulo claimed he didn't remember being obscene—or he didn't "mean it in the literal meaning of the word." He apologized "from the bottom of his heart" and vowed to "put this word out of his vocabulary." Debate erupted, until Raymond shouted for it to cease.

"That ends it," Raymond declared. In a later reprimand, Raymond told Jerry, "If you're able to improve your handling of people, you'll go a long ways in the organization."

The Office was facing a financial slump. Raymond and Jerry would sink an astronomical $400,000 into Indian Meadow before they managed to sell it (they'd nearly torched it). Jerry decided the FBI had forced the club into the ground. Moreover, the agency knew for a fact that Raymond had, by using Byzantine accounting and ownership methods, acquired a majority stake in Berkshire Downs. This was an ill-fated horse-racing track in Hancock, which bled out up to $18,000 daily. Raymond estimated that the golf course and Berkshire Downs had put him back financially for ten years. His Las Vegas investment in Caesar's Palace was paying a poor return. And the casino skim was so blatant, Raymond said he feared the FBI could detect it. He'd even recently skipped his usual donation to the Federal Hill Christmas beautification fund.

But, after all this Kennedy-inspired mischief, the Office received pleasant news on November 23, 1963, when three bullets transformed the plaza named for Dallas businessman George Bannerman Dealey from a commemorative site to a crime scene. The event prompted Jerry to make choice comments, such as: "They shot the wrong Kennedy." He openly uttered "obscene remarks" about the thirty-day national mourning period. "I hope the attorney general and his brother both get hit in the head because they are no [fucking] good," Jerry vented. That December, Jerry said he planned to be around "for a long time to come" and "to hell with Bobby Kennedy." But when publicity spread that Oswald's murderer, Jack Ruby, had been a nightclub owner. As proprietor of his own club, Jay's Lounge, a fretting Jerry asked: "Why the hell couldn't he [Ruby] have been a lawyer or something else?"

13.

THE BODIES START FALLING

"All it takes to be a tough guy is to lose the fear of dying."

—Joe Barboza

In the early 1960s, male gangsters murdered other male gangsters with regularity. But the Boston Strangler was simultaneously helping balloon the death toll. He (or they) kept asphyxiating women of various ages, creeds, and colors. Police were baffled. So, after Punchy's arrest for stealing a pink negligee from a Roslindale department store, police gave him an extra grilling. Going underground for safety, Georgie McLaughlin burrowed into the first floor of the three-story Orchard Park Housing Project at 55 Yeoman Street in Dorchester. His consort apparently was Maureen Dellamano, a thirty-three-year-old divorcée who rented an apartment with her mother.

On March 15, 1964, on the third story of the building, the Buckley family held a christening. From the first floor, Georgie emerged in a brown suit and joined the party. Other revelers included William Sheridan, a twenty-one-year-old "freckle faced" bank clerk. Sheridan, who remained uncommonly sober, argued with the host's aunt and left the apartment at about 11:00 P.M. The elder Buckley followed him downstairs, hoping to talk.

"I want to go back and apologize," Sheridan said.

"Forget it and do it later," Buckley advised.

Back upstairs, Georgie gave Buckley ten dollars to replenish the beer supply. But since the festivities were concluded, Buckley refused. Around 12:15 A.M. the party began to disintegrate and the Buckleys attempted to empty the apartment—at first politely, then more forcefully, using fists and shoves. "Clear the hallway," Georgie commanded, but no one obeyed.

Gentleman Georgie interrupted his chat with a reveler named Lynch to grab at a beer bottle in his hand. After Lynch refused to yield the bottle, the two men argued. Georgie reached into his pocket, as if he were looking for something, before heading downstairs and entering the first-floor apartment. He soon emerged into the hallway, carrying a long-barreled revolver, and sought out Lynch. But Lynch had left, passing by Sheridan, who was returning to the apartment upstairs, with an apology. As Sheridan entered the hallway, he saw squat Georgie blocking his path a few feet away.

About twenty feet away in the courtyard was a tall, lanky ex-marine and Dorchester native named Herbert Josselyn. Through the illumination of the nearby hallway light, Josselyn observed Georgie facing the taller Sheridan. Georgie's lips moved and Sheridan shrugged. Then Georgie raised the pistol, pointed it into Sheridan's face, and pulled the trigger, creating an explosion. Sheridan collapsed as a bullet passed between his eyes, and someone yelled, "Yahoo!" thinking a cherry bomb had gone off.

Everyone in the courtyard stampeded, leaving Sheridan alone, half in and half out of the doorway. He lay on his left side in the front hall, blood spurting from the cataract between his eyes and forming an expanding puddle on the front-entrance landing. Upstairs, Buckley was clearing the living room of dirty glasses when he heard the ruckus in the hallway below. Opening the door, a hysterical Maureen Dellamano rushed in from the second-floor landing. "Georgie just shot somebody," she yelled. "Get him out of here—please, please, please!"

Soon after, someone drove Georgie away into the night in Harold Hannon's car. Later that day, armed with riot guns, squads of patrolmen searched the project but only turned up a bloodied bullet in the hallway. After Georgie blended into the landscape, the FBI exalted him to being a public enemy.

During the week of May 8, 1964, the Commonwealth of Massachusetts released thirty-two-year-old Joseph Barboza. Immediately, he took his blond-haired, brown-eyed fiancée, Claire Cohen, to Maine's quaint seaside city of Portland. There, a justice of the peace presided over the nuptials (a rabbi later remarried them). As part of his bargain with Claire—fittingly enough, given his Old Testament demeanor—Joe was now officially a Child of Abraham. To prove his loyalty, Joe presented himself to Beth Israel Hospital and submitted to the ancient and unpleasant rite of circumcision. Given the size of his penis (by his own account), he had some flesh to spare, at least.

Joe also changed his last name to "Baron," possibly because he wanted to provide a cover for his wife and future children. There was "too much history" connected to the Barboza name, as Joe explained. (This betrayal of name and faith reportedly upset Old Man Barboza.) But Joe's move from Catholicism to Judaism didn't gentle his condition. Once, Joe asked, "How important is it what we're doing here? We're so fuckin' small in the universe. We don't even exist." This worldview was ideal to let a murderer sleep well at night.

Joe returned to East Boston with a stitched and sensitive penis. Unwilling to use a "filthy bathroom," Joe requested admission to the toilet at the Benbrook Drugstore in Eastie. The owner refused—and a gravely offended Joe offered him the choice words: "Well, I'm not threatening you; I'm promising you."

The Eastie crew went to work that night. The next day, when Joe returned to the drugstore, plywood had replaced all the windows.

"Can I use your bathroom?" asked the Animal.

"Sure, go ahead, Joe," said the chastised owner.

Needing to revive his enterprises, the onetime leader of the Cream Pie Bandits assembled a new crew of violent and unstable men. Primarily misfits, they all had their own reasons for joining Joe's East Boston gang. The Frizzis—Guy, Conno, and Nini—we have met. Early after Joe hit the street, Guy introduced him to Joseph Amico, a "good kid" (at least in the inverted criminal sense) in his twenties. Joe habitually assigned associates nicknames, and he called the two-hundred-pound, six-feet-two Amico "Chico." In Chico, over time, Joe found an obedient friend, pet, and younger brother— who, as a former short-order cook, was also lethal with a blade.

Another minion was the rotund Nicky Femia, whom Joe affectionately called a "fat bastard." Dark complexioned, although in his twenties, he looked about forty. Femia reminded Joe of a quack named Zorba, who always figured things to perfection but managed to never get anything right—so he called him "Dr. Zorba."

Among the ten or so other young henchmen was Patrick Fabiano, of East Boston—basically more an ill-fated clown than thug. More formidable was Carlton Eaton of Medford, who had replaced Joe as a bouncer down in Nantasket. Eaton was an ideal swap for the Animal, having drifted through his brief life as laborer, salesman, and convict. Joe also recruited him to shylock and fronted him money. Along with the Bear and the Frizzi brothers, these men formed the rotten core of Barboza, Inc. For headquarters, Joe appropriated Chiambi's Grill in East Boston, which became "Barboza's Corner." The owner was too terrified to tell Joe to leave. When Nicky Femia rented an upstairs room, the proprietor never bothered to collect a cent from him.

———

When not in Eastie, Joe frequented North Station, near Boston Garden. He was also on various payrolls as salesman and clerk, and in another position in a "public relations capacity." With a growing reputation as a hair-trigger thug, rumors soon circulated that Joe committed uglier deeds—including murder most foolish. Joe claimed his "first hit" was a "stooge" ex-convict, performed with a partner. "It's not like you see on TV. We're all set to do him in," Joe said. "We knock him down and he's out of it. Then I take my gun and start shooting till it's fucking empty. I see his eyes pop out, there's blood everywhere. It's unbelievable. Not everybody can kill. It's not easy. You can break kneecaps. You can punch people out. But to take a life, you know? . . ."

That was his start. Joe was a car with one speed—he smashed, maimed, or killed at will, and didn't bother to hide the bodies. High on uppers, Joe became a paranoid megalomaniac, said critics. Indeed, he admitted killing had a "very tranquilizing effect" on him. After a murder, he felt humble, at peace with the world, and slept in a babylike peace for weeks. He wasn't that imaginative in homicide, nor was he a gun wizard. "I don't know anything about pistols," he once noted. "I fire guns. I can squeeze a trigger." Of his few tricks, he boasted cunning disguises. One of his favorite TV shows became *Mission: Impossible,* and he emulated its appearance-shifting heroes. As an actor-killer, Joe bragged his most outrageous role was that of an old lady—including long dress, pancake makeup, gray wig, and a hat with a veil covering the face and mammoth jaw. To complete the ensemble, Joe carried a .45 in a handbag.

The brothers Ventola, Arthur and Junior, formed a petty-criminal-entrepreneur duo. On the main strip in Revere, they opened the Ebb Tide, a club and restaurant which became a focal point for Joe and his flunkies. Inside, besides a bar and dance floor, there were hidden offices, ideal for secret meetings. The establishment, under paid Office protection, became a safe place for dangerous people.

Arthur also operated his own ramshackle roadside vegetable stand, named, not so imaginatively, Arthur's Farm. No actual farm, it sold vegetables and groceries—but in the back of the store, Arthur also offered hot clothes and toys for crooks and honest citizens alike to rummage. Even pro ball players driving home from Harvard Stadium stopped in.

After the Ebb Tide's grand opening, Guy Frizzi's youngest brother Ninni complained "about a watered drink." In response, Junior Ventola beat Ninni—and this quickly drove Joe and five of his crew to Arthur's farm to dispense justice. On arrival, armed with a bat, Joe ran right for Arthur, a big man in his mid-fifties, and "wiped" at his face. Arthur took that blow on his hands, but then Joe "thumped him across his back a couple of times" and even connected with the back of his head.

From the ground, Arthur blubbered: "It was Junior, my brother, that hit Ninni."

"You're a big tough man, you give up your brother," Joe said. "Would you give up your mother?" Joe claimed this beating wasn't a mistake, as Arthur "had it coming," in any case. In Joe's Darwinian-Nietzschean jungle, Ventola was a mere "buzzard," who had to rely on the strength of the Office for protection. (Joe would view Jerry Angiulo in the same light.)

Joe returned to the Ebb Tide, beat manager Richie Castucci, and promised to return the next night and kill no less than everyone. Soon after, an Office-connected man from Chelsea named Ronnie Cassesso called Joe to chat. A career thug, Ronnie was fat and rotund, with a massive double chin and thick lips that rarely formed a smile. Although not made, he worked for the Chelsea-based capo regime of Joe Burns. Under Henry Tameleo's orders, Ronnie asked Joe to forget the "Ventola beef."

Naturally, as an aspiring strongman, Joe knew of Tameleo—and that he frequented the Ebb Tide. Joe also knew it was unwise to cross this distinguished-looking old man.

"I am only here in the way of strength," Joe told Ronnie. Although still feeling Junior's legs required breaking, he let the matter slide.

Joe accepted Henry's invitation to meet at the Ebb Tide. While chatting, Henry said: "Joe, this is what happens when you get involved with weak assholes. . . . They run off at the mouth because of your [borrowed] strength." He promised there would be no more insults. Joe swooned at this treatment.

After nearly blowing Junior's brains out, Joe fashioned a working truce with him—always calling him "The Shit." Once, for a hefty price, Joc and his crew even beat up the lover of Junior's ex-girlfriend, in a movie theater.

Henry Tameleo, like many who use violence as a business tool, didn't want recreational mayhem near his own properties—in this case, the Ebb Tide. As Henry also was frequently a guest in the Ebb Tide, it became the "hottest spot in town" with the hottest telephone number. By October 1964, Joe's duties included keeping order there and dishing out beatings to rowdies. He discovered Henry was the "glue" that held the Office together, preventing it from disintegrating into a mere street gang. "The guy is more or less public relations for Raymond Patriarca, smooth talker, the man that has a father image, very sharp-minded man, a tremendous personality," Joe reflected later.

The Animal, who'd lacked a father and who hated authority, had finally, in early middle age, found a powerful man he didn't despise. Over time, Joe developed an infatuation with the powerful Henry. He once told Tameleo: "Everybody in this city knows I look up to you more than any man living. I told Raymond to his face I like you more than him because I've spent days with you and only hours with him."

"Raymond respected you more for saying it than he does those other ass-kissers," Henry replied. But even Joe could see Henry wasn't like anyone else in the New England underworld. His last collar dated way back to 1931, when Providence police picked him up as a suspicious person. ". . . I got arrested . . . as a professional gambler," Henry admitted of that incident, many years later. "I've learned a whole lot from then up until now." In any case, the Providence charge hadn't stuck.

Born in 1901, Henry, at age thirteen, legend boasted, was cleaning spittoons in Detroit. Henry's theft of an automobile at seventeen in Rhode Island officially started his underworld career. Caught and convicted, he earned a stay at the state's adult correctional institution—and that sentence, if anything, confirmed him in his vocation. By twenty-seven, Henry was a great "mechanic," or card player, a master of gin, with or without cheating.

During the next two decades, Massachusetts convicted Henry of a string of petty gaming and motor vehicle offenses. During this time, claimed Vinnie Teresa, Henry expanded his already-extensive curriculum vitae. Besides placing wagers, Henry murdered and ordered killings, robbed, handled stolen goods, loan-sharked, and set up fraudulent diamond rackets. But he avoided the worst wrath.

In the early 1950s, Raymond's decision to make Henry his underboss may have been his shrewdest ever. Given his seniority, Henry could have been the boss himself—but he liked the good life too much. He didn't want to be aloof and reserved, like Raymond. "Henry and Ray got along famously," said Tameleo's close friend. "Not even Raymond would duck Henry for any reason. Not even Uncle Ray would interfere when Henry called something. If that's not power, I don't know what the hell is." As Mafia statesman and diplomat, he also made the peace, and kept many people alive, as he saw it necessary. This is why some called him the "Referee."

He could use politicians as playthings; when necessary, he'd reach a governor, police chief, city councilman, or congressman. He could have remained in Rhode Island, but, as he put it, "Some fellow was in trouble in Revere." Henry needed to intercede, and over the northern border he came into the Bay State. It was "the worst move I ever made in my life." As the 1960s rolled around, Henry was possibly the most respected, well-recognized, and feared man in New England organized crime.

He looked the part of a statesman: at five feet ten and 180 pounds, he was, by his own boast, "all arms and chest, no belly at no time." He carried a hard-lined face with a frown for a mouth; his somber eyes were brown-black. Except for a fringe of white hair on the sides and back of his head, he was bald. Rounding off the image, he wore glasses and dressed conservatively, favoring white socks and suspenders. Possessing a diplomat's manner, Henry was soft-spoken and deceptively gentle and pleasant, and he carried himself with uncommon dignity. In the right office, someone might have taken him as a financier (a legitimate one) or a priest. Some called him "Henry the Banker."

To the right people, Henry demonstrated strict scruples. "I did the right thing with anybody," he once reflected. "If I make a promise, my word is my bond." Raymond appointed him to oversee the weekly kitty (a multipurpose fund to cover legal bills or offer short-term disability) that all Office workers paid into. In admiration—and few men are heroes to their chauffeurs—Vinnie called him "Uncle" Henry. He warned Vinnie, "Never trust anyone, no matter who it is."

His effect was powerful. "I knew Henry when I was kid," recalled one particularly dangerous associate. "I loved Henry. He was the most wonderful human being in my life. A gentleman. He was a good, good man. He was gentle. But you didn't cross him. If you did, you ended up in the grave. He'd ice you in a heartbeat. Henry could snap his fingers and have someone put in a box." (As opposed to burying bodies in a reputed land-based "Mafia graveyard," Henry preferred burial at sea, where the sharks could devour the evidence, said one acquaintance.)

On paper, Henry was wealthy, with real estate and other investments. Although a family man, Henry enjoyed a playboy's life— tasty food, attractive and rentable women, expensive liquor, and cabaret entertainments. Henry would drop $30,000 in a weekend and think nothing of it. He was the sort of diner that waiters fight to serve—the size of his tip often matched the cost of the meal itself. Henry came up to Boston and Revere once a week, frequently engaging the services of women, with whom he'd spend the night at a hotel. Henry could handle more booze than anyone Teresa had seen, able to drink from 11 A.M. to 3 A.M. the next day and function on three hours' sleep. Vinnie claimed he would drop Henry off in a Boston hotel and would, in a few hours, receive a call to hurry up and retrieve him.

His great vice was wagering: horses, cards, and dice. The Banker blew as much as $1 million on gaming, Raymond estimated. In 1961, Henry admitted losses that forced him to mortgage his family house. He didn't always care about the stakes. In fact, he once bragged to Jerry and Raymond about a $140 pot he'd pocketed after playing until six that morning. He required five dollars in change so he could place his cross-country bets, using a pay phone. Naturally, he took great interest in a device that illegally made the pay phone spit the coins back out.

Henry also gambled on certain street toughs he thought might be useful. He drew dull-witted men who craved the prestige of dealing with the Mafia—in short, suckers like Joe. He noticed Joe wanted as much of the rackets as he could rip off, and he cultivated the younger man expertly. Once, when "down below" (as Joe called a Providence trek from Boston) with Henry at the Roman Gardens restaurant, Joe ate calamari and listened closely. Henry discussed the recently and unnaturally deceased Jackie Nazarian. Henry walked Joe to the lounge section, pointed to a corner, and said: "He [Jackie Nazarian] was sitting right there drinking." Obscene and drunk, Jackie boasted of taking over the Office. "I calmed him down and took him home," Henry recalled. "He was of no use to us anymore. Uncontrollable."

One of Joe's first jobs for the Office was to chastise an independent bookmaker at the track. After someone fingered the bookie (named "Bozo") Joe grabbed a banister post and beat him, with the warning to stop working that venue. Joe also recruited jockeys to "pull" for the Office. In this operation. Joe loaned the jockey money and then threatened the athlete—only to have Henry intervene at the last moment and clear the debt. After that, the jockey would do as Henry commanded in a race. Given his role as enforcer, Joe also had to go "down the street" to meet with the Angiulos.

Joe offered at least one beating on behalf of Raymond and Henry's aptly named Piranha, Inc. "finance and insurance" company. (A Piranha loan could come with a 20 percent-plus interest rate.) However, not even Joe's reputation exceeded that of Pete and Gladys, the two actual piranhas that swam in the company's fish tank. After employees stuck one deadbeat's hand into the tank for the fish to chew, everyone paid up, said Vinnie Teresa.

Joe also enjoyed side jobs for impatient legitimate creditors unwilling to endure the law's delay. Given his predilection for violence, some observers believed that Joe, excepting his Portuguese nationality—not to mention Jewish faith—might have taken the sacred communion of La Cosa Nostra. That is dubious, and was like saying J. Edgar Hoover could have become pope, except he was a

Protestant and not Italian. Certainly Joe envied and resented the Office's monopoly on the rackets, particularly the lending one. But, it's dubious he ever seriously thought of merging with the Italian faction.

Nevertheless, when Joe learned Raymond wanted to meet him, he naturally obeyed the summons. For the interview with Patriarca, he, Ronnie Cassesso, and Jimmy the Bear drove to Federal Hill and parked in the Roman Gardens' car lot. Raymond liked Ronnie, having appreciated his silence at their first meeting. ("Someone who is very quiet is either a fool or very smart," Raymond had observed later.)

Joe and his friends ate a quick breakfast, and at 11 A.M. walked to the Coin-O-Matic address—one of the city's two rival capitol buildings. Almost in eyesight was the magnificent domed edifice of marble, where the governor and the assembly pretended to run the upper world.

On entering Coin-O-Matic, Joe discovered the Office, hidden behind a partition on the left side. It was twelve feet wide and twenty feet long, and far from classy—more poor than rich—but would-be gangsters climbed ladders covered in blood to be there. Henry knew of the appointment with his protégé, and arrived with coffee. Joe laid eyes on Raymond, in a dark blue suit and white socks. On his finger was a white gold ring sporting four diamonds, each a karat or more, in a line.

Henry said, "This is Joe Barboza."

"My pleasure, Mr. Patriarca," said Joe.

"Call me Raymond." Joe looked into Raymond's "piercing eyes" and noted the don's features, under the combed-back black hair, were those of a hawk. However, the mouth resembled a lizard's, and was purplish from diabetes.

After an hour, the trio left. During the ride back to Boston, the Bear noted, "You didn't have much to say in there. What were you thinking?"

"I was thinking how I could bite his finger off and get that diamond ring," Joe said. The Bear and Ronnie laughed.

Joe asked, "What the fuck is funny?"

The meeting, however brief, was the beginning of another career-advancing professional relationship, or so Joe hoped. Over time, he and the Bear regularly visited the Office to receive assignments and clear jobs, including assassinations. The don enlightened his dull instrument about the width of his grasp. Raymond mentioned New Bedford, and said, "I got a bookmaker down there, Sullivan, that wants to quit." Joe had never heard of him, even though he ran the "biggest pot" in town. "I want you to rough him up but not really hurt him. Just give him a slap in the mouth and toss him around. I don't want to break any bones or anything." Two weeks later, Raymond canceled the contract, without explanation.

The Animal was a free agent. "Raymond Patricia kind of isolated me," as Joe put it, "which met my approval very highly because I didn't like Jerry Angiulo and his ways and I didn't like a lot of people involved in the family." If his own borgata caused a problem, Raymond could assemble thirty-seven professional assassins within a half hour and place them anywhere in New England.

"They [the mafiosi] did something ten years ago and they figure they don't have to do anything but play center field for the rest of their lives," Raymond confided to the Animal. For Joe, a mere hired hand, the alliance was a strategic move—as a freelance contractor, he avoided paying a tribute on his shylocking business that could have cost as much as $5,500 a week.

Just then, Peter Limone was shutting down all the independent operators around Joe. Those who remained had to pay 50 percent of their take. "I gave them a little more than that in the way of strength," Joe concluded. "I was an enforcer that kept the enforcers in line."

Jerry resented this, Joe believed, and bad-mouthed him, as did the other made men. One night, Joe tried to enter the mob-upped Coliseum with his crew. He'd recently performed a hit, and the police were tailing him like "seagulls." Manager (and Mafia capo) Sammy Granito stopped the East Boston crew cold, and said, "What the fuck you think you're doing coming in here bringing heat on my place? What are you, stupid? Get the fuck out of here before you get us all in trouble." Joe shrugged like a confused dog and left.

Another Mafioso who got on Joe's bad side was Louis Greco. He was a 230-pound mountain with great, powerful hands and a knockout punch. Greco warned Nicky Femia not to front money to teenagers in his East Boston neighborhood. Femia kept loan-sharking anyway, and Greco cornered him. "I knocked him down," as Greco said. "One punch. Femia ran into this store at the corner of Bennington and Brooks Street. Barboza was there. I was chasing Nicky around the store, trying to catch him, but I can't run." Joe never forgot the humiliation.

Other independents weren't interested in partnering with Joe. They included Frankie and Stevie Flemmi, who both disliked him. Frankie even told Joe he didn't want him around his shops. (With a gang war going, you didn't want "everybody mobbed up down there," as Frankie observed. "The more you keep away from your area, the better off you are. The normal truck thieves, that's one thing . . .") However, besides doing muscle work with the Bear, Joe partnered with two Office-affiliated Italians—Ronnie Cassesso and his partner, Joseph "Romeo" Martin. Although he wrote poems (which was the wherefore he was called Romeo), Martin was a very tough U.S. Army deserter in his late thirties, and a professional gambler, housebreaker, and strongman on both coasts.

Everybody on either side of the law liked him. On the East Coast, Romeo and Ronnie worked under Ralph "Ralphie Chong" Lamattina, who reported to capo Joe Burns. Romeo also snitched, and even bragged, falsely, he'd done time with Raymond and become his pal. In early 1964, Joe Burns approached Raymond for the first time in three years and asked to baptize Romeo. Raymond felt Burns hadn't proposed the name properly. Burns hadn't shopped Romeo around the organization yet to see if anyone had an objection. Shrewdly, Raymond observed Burns was building up his ground with a lot of young fellows—looking for his future advantage. Romeo wasn't made.

At 4:15 P.M. on Thursday, May 14, 1964, a patrolman was making his rounds driving near 3 McDonough Way in South Boston. He took note of an 1963 Pontiac sedan, minus plates parked at the Old Harbor Village projects. The police pried open a window, and through the windshield's registration sticker, traced the car's origin. The prior November, someone had stolen the vehicle, with the owner's golf clubs in its trunk. The police left the car in a garage on West Broadway, where its owner, fifty-seven-year-old Marvin Cohen, could retrieve it.

At around 8:00 P.M., Cohen arrived at the garage with his wife. "I then went to the trunk to see if my golf clubs were still there," Cohen recalled. "It was dark when I lifted the lid . . . and found a body lying on its stomach." He pushed his wife away and told the garage attendant to call the police. A sergeant arrived and examined a body that, he soon learned, was minus the head. Using the fingerprints, the police discovered it had been a thirty-two-year-old ex-convict named Francis Regis Benjamin. He'd been a frame carpenter, roofer, laborer, and petty crook. After serving five years for armed robbery, Benjamin had left MCI Walpole two weeks before and moved in with his wife on Norwell Street in Dorchester. He appeared to favor the McLean group—officially, the Bennett Roxbury group then sided with Punchy and Georgie. Worse, he'd threatened one of Wimpy's clients, a local restaurant owner. Wimpy, wanting to bind the customer even closer to him, prodded the Flemmi brothers to swat Benjamin. Late one night, the unlucky Benjamin was in Walter's Lounge sitting with Wimpy and the Bear; Stevie was also present. Suddenly, one of the Flemmi brothers shot him in the head with a policeman's revolver. This officer then complained that the bullet was traceable to his weapon—so Jimmy the Bear lopped the head off with a meat saw, claimed one story. (Possibly, the Bear entertained leaving the head someplace where it would maximize shock value—such as a front doorstep—but thought better of it.) The conspirators dragged the body from the booth where the shooting had occurred to the kitchen and, from there, to the storage room. The corpse spread blood everywhere it went.

The Bennett brothers declared Walter's closed and summoned Stevie's partner, Frankie Salemme, an electrician by trade. Frankie arrived and noted the lounge door had a sign hanging there stating, "Closed for electrical problems." At the Bennetts' request, Frankie proceeded to "mess up the electrical box" so it looked like a fire had disabled it. Frankie, with the group, wrapped the body, then blocked off the adjacent alley while it was taken to a car. Frankie drove a second vehicle, the crash car, to block any police cruisers. "For a disposal operation to be successful you needed five men," as he later observed. Although a career criminal, Frankie claimed he'd been a virgin when it came to snuffing people, until now. Later Stevie torched select areas of the lounge to eradicate the bloodstains.

Benjamin's trunk and head would have to wait till judgment day to end their divorce. No one ever made public who actually took the head or where its resting place is—sunken, burned, or buried somewhere. But the gruesome news traveled fast in the underworld, and the prime culprit was the Bear. When Joe saw Jimmy, he said, "I heard you killed Benjamin and cut his head off."

"I heard you did it," was the reply.

Months after the grisly discovery, the Bear claimed the hit on Benjamin had paid off well; some even began calling him "the

Butcher." Perhaps it had been profitable—but such a murder was more than just a business necessity: the Bear liked killing people. The simmering war was a great opportunity—he wanted notches on his gun, as if these were the days of the O.K. Corral, and the more notches, the bigger the man he'd be, Frankie Salemme observed. "Plus, he wanted to be Mr. Macho around in the gang."

"I am going to be the number one hit man in the area," the Bear told an informer. "All I want to do is kill people. It's better than hitting banks," as FBI agent Condon reported. Flemmi offered to help the informer kill anyone. He contrasted his own professionalism with that of his rivals. Some hit men even took money for contracts without fulfilling them. One pair of would-be murderers had even spent all their fronted contract money drinking, without executing the commission. The Bear offered full services, as he also disposed of the cadavers. His onetime South End neighbors believed he used the furnaces in the public housing projects as crematoriums. (A local noted how, once, the newspapers trumpeted the Bear's killing of the wrong man. "I've got to stop doing that," Flemmi promised, and giggled softly.)

Despite the savagery with Benjamin, Hoover wanted the Bear as part of his Top Echelon effort.

On Tuesday, May 12, 1964, a Wilmington parks department employee was about to cut a stand of grass near the town pumping station. Something unusual caught his eye, just ten feet from the road—it was a long body under a jacket, clad in a T-shirt, black trousers, and black shoes. Nearby, on the road, was a pair of sunglasses with one broken wing, and a wallet containing a diamond ring and $78. Two patrolmen arrived and fanned out to search. Soon, police identified the body as having been Russell Nicholson. The prior night, someone had pumped a .32 caliber bullet into his left temple. The killer might have even used Nicholson's own weapon on him before dumping him into the ditch from a car.

Georgie had terrified Nicholson—and just weeks before, he'd even admitted to Joe McCain he was a "dead man." As a sideline, the onetime Metropolitan District Commission detective worked with a Charlestown hoodlum, one "Fat Harry," shaking down legitimate businessmen, the FBI claimed. At 9 A.M. on Monday, May 11, Nicholson had left his home with Harry—and now he was dead. Both Georgie and Harry were suspects. The state police found bloodstains in Harry's car, which also sported a new front seat. The interior had also been wiped down with a liquid that left the floor tacky. Harry, however, refused to answer any questions about his onetime partner's demise. In February, as Harry faced trial for extortion, the prosecutor possibly considered charging him in Nicholson's murder, too. To avoid that, Harry pled out to extortion and was sentenced to a three-to-five-year term. It was probably safer in jail, anyway.

14

FOUR SALESMEN AND A SPANIARD

"Raymond would jump into a cage full of lions before he would hurt anyone."
—Providence gangster, commenting on Raymond Patriarca

For several days during the week of Thursday, July 23, 1964, a white 1963 Chevrolet sedan sat parked unobtrusively against a fence behind the parking lot of the Sheraton Motor Inn in North Quincy, off Hancock Street. A pool of dark liquid forming under it caught the attention of a guest's dog, and then the manager, who called the police. Around 10 A.M., a squad car arrived with several policemen. They noted a "strong odor" emitting from the Chevrolet's interior; inside, they discovered several air conditioners without motors. The trunk remained unexplored—so a Quincy sergeant pried it up and discovered there a liquefying, putrid mess.

This decomposition soup contained two bodies, one short, and one tall; one was spread-eagled, the other slumped over; both wore shorts. The heat had reduced one corpse to almost a skeleton; a sweatshirt covered the other body, whose skin was dark-complexioned. Each victim had been dispatched with a single bullet to the back of the head. A Providence dentist solved the mystery when he identified the corpses as the late thug Paul Colicci and Vincent Bisesi (a nonentity and salesman). Although facing bookmaking and gun-carrying charges in Rhode Island,

Colicci had been wandering the South Shore selling what he claimed were air conditioners. (After finding the units lacked motors, some customers had complained to the police.) Colicci's father, with whom he lived, had reported him missing on July 13. Given that Colicci had annoyed Raymond with his "Hello Boss" letter, lingering in New England was most rash.

Raymond had already put Colicci's name in a hat. Then, publicly, Colicci argued with Samuel Granito at 2:30 A.M. at the Coliseum. Not long after, Granito's men J. R. Russo and Vincent DeScisio (whom Joe dubbed the "Gold Dust Twins") shot the victims in a Braintree restaurant. "The two kids would have done a good job and would have done well even if I hadn't been there," as Granito reported to Raymond. "They were unable to bury them, so they went toward the Cape and got rid of the car." Raymond promised to give "each one of the kids" $150, as a "gift from him."

Although Georgie was in hiding (and in drag, as needed), he and Punchy prowled around to kill any unfriendly witnesses to the Sheridan murder. In the meantime, the McLaughlin allies turned a buck wherever they could. Harold Hannon performed dangerous jobs with his partner Wilfred Delaney—a murderous laborer, roofer, and sandhog from South Boston. He and Hannon "never did anything straight," said one Irish compatriot. From a car they also sold air conditioners—ones that were exceptionally quiet, given they were either inoperable or plain watercoolers. Stickups remained an occasional paycheck, including the home of an Everett Mafia-connected bookie, from whom they took as much as $100,000 and twenty-five expensive suits. This was most unwise.

From what police gathered, on Wednesday, August 19, Hannon was driving through Franklin Park, presumably with Delaney. (Hannon was motoring in the same car that had whisked Georgie from the Sheridan murder scene.) At some point, Hannon was forced off the road—the car, when found, bore dents on the front and rear fenders. Kidnappers bound and gagged Hannon and took him and Delaney away, leaving Hannon's car behind.

On August 20, 1964, while examining a Logan Airport runway, two federal aviation inspectors noticed a body in the water below, caught in some pilings. Soon after, a Boston police barge crew fished out a naked male corpse. The eyes were taped over and blindfolded with a rag; a stocking was stuffed in the mouth and covered in tape. Thermal underwear was knotted around the neck, and tape and rope trussed the hands and feet behind. A piano-wire noose circled the neck and ran past the groin and wrapped around the legs. The wire formed a Chinese torture knot: The more the victim struggled, the more he would choke himself.

Investigators learned they had fished out Hannon's fifty-four-year-old waterlogged body. He'd been viciously beaten, strangled to death, and then dropped into the harbor, or one of its tributaries. Soon after, the police discovered Wilfred Delaney's nude body floating by Pier 9 in Charlestown. He'd been struck on the jaw, and while unconscious (and possibly drugged), was dumped alive into the water, where he drowned.

"That's the end of one tough guy," Jerry said of Hannon. There were any number of possible reasons why the two petty thieves were murdered. One Winter Hill legend claimed Buddy lured the duo into a trap, using a comely woman. Then Buddy (or the fierce Joe McDonald) unlocked Hannon's secrets through torture. Allegedly, and less credibly, someone even used a blowtorch on Hannon's privates. On the other hand, the FBI suspected Wimpy Bennett and the Flemmi brothers had kidnapped the two to find where they'd hidden the bookmaker's stash. And yet again, the doubleheader also could have been Mafia retaliation for knocking over the bookmaker.

In any case, Hannon had kept the bookie's stolen suits in his house. His murderers reportedly took them back. When it came time for Hannon's wake, there wasn't a suit in his wardrobe—so, reportedly, the aggrieved bookie sent one to the funeral home.

But, there was a rumor that Hannon's killers had left a loose end—a third man who'd assisted in the big robbery, one Edward "Teddy" Deegan.

As the FBI watched, bodies of underground players began showing up in the oddest places—and with ever-increasing frequency. One corpse belonged to the small, freckle-faced Leo "Iggy" Lowry, a Walter's Lounge barfly who ran with a gang of South End thieves. For some reason, the McLaughlins decided Lowry had set up Hannon and Delaney and handed Jimmy the Bear a murder contract. The Bear also had a personal score with Lowry—Iggy had been feuding with his brother, Stevie the Rifleman.

On September 3, 1964, Lowry entered Walter's Lounge, where Billy Bennett allegedly doctored his drink. Soon after, the Bear dragged Lowry out, administered a beating, shot him in the head, and cut his throat, nearly decapitating him. The Bear put the body in the car and drove around Roxbury until he found Stevie. The Flemmis, in two cars, drove south toward Plymouth, where the Bear ran low on gas. He pulled over in the rural town of Pembroke, dumped the body in the town's lovers' lane, and fled into the night. The corpse, almost in two pieces, lay there a day or so, until someone chasing a cat stumbled on it. Lowry's pants pockets carried two house keys, two automobile keys, and the unlikely sum of $7.77.

The Bear ran out of gas on the return trip; he couldn't recall if he'd dropped a pack of cigarettes by the corpse. Stevie noted that "these mental lapses of his brother concerned him, but did not appear to bother the Bear."

On Friday, September 4, at 11 P.M., Ronald Paul Dermody stopped the English compact car he was driving. Dermody was at the intersection of Belmont and School Streets in Watertown. Although tough and brave, Dermody was in deep trouble and frightened.

Once, some years before, Dermody had been a bank robber. In that endeavor, he'd partnered with a Richard Barchard, and one James Bulger, whom some called "Whitey," because of his blond hair. The trio was bold, reckless, and incompetent. Eventually, FBI agent Paul Rico arrested them, and they were tried, convicted, and sentenced to hard time. Paroled after eight years, Dermody returned to Somerville. Given his access to the Hill, a Townie asked Dermody to set up Buddy. Rather than take on this risky assignment, Dermody informed Buddy of the plot. Punchy "recontacted" Dermody and renewed the assignment, with the proviso that if Buddy survived, Dermody wouldn't. On September 3, Dermody, liquored up, entered Somerville's Colonial Café and opened fire on a cluster of Hill associates with a .22. Fleeing, he shot Buddy McLean lookalike Charley Robinson in the leg and dropped his weapon.

Robinson may have been honest when he told police he didn't know why Dermody had shot him. On the other hand, Buddy was dead certain—and a now-desperate Dermody contacted Rico and scheduled a fix-it meeting in Watertown. Possibly, he may have threatened Rico in some way. As planned, Dermody arrived and parked to await Rico. Soon after, someone approached his car, pointed a pistol through a partially opened passenger window, and fired four shots. Three entered Dermody, the fatal slug passing through his neck—so close to the gun's muzzle, powder burns were left on the skin before exiting through the left side of his head.

The shooter dropped the gun into the car and, leaving Dermody behind, entered a blue sedan, slamming his door shut. A driver started the engine and drove to School Street and kept going until reaching Belmont. Then, according to Frankie Salemme, Buddy

McLean emerged and entered Rico's house. There Buddy stayed "safely tucked away for a few days" until the heat subsided. The police found the thirty-year-old bank robber's body slumped over the front seat, a trickle of blood running down the face. Dermody carried the driver's license of one James "Spike" O'Toole of Norfolk Street, Dorchester—a violent felon and McLaughlin pal.

As Jesus said his place was with sinners, so it was with H. Paul Rico, who sought informants to break the power of the Office. Being Irish and Spanish—a rare ethnic flavor in Boston—people called Rico the "Spaniard." He had a perfect all-American Catholic résumé. Rico had graduated from Boston College, did a stint in the service, and joined the FBI. Brash and ruthless, he had a Machiavellian way (to put it politely) of law enforcement. Criminals who knew him claimed Rico was himself a crook—suave, devious, and very dangerous. He excelled at turning one gangster against another.

These traits had let him nail Jimmy Bulger and Dermody. A natural opportunist, Rico saw that, like a piece of marble with a wedge in it, the cracks of the Winter Hill–Townie feud were spreading outward beyond Charlestown and Somerville. Rico could give J. Edgar what he wanted—and neither would be too picky about the means. Looking over the criminal landscape, Rico picked Francis Salemme as one of his targets. A lean five feet eleven, Frankie could be soft-spoken and polite. But he "was a guy who could cut your throat and eat a sandwich as he watched you die," said a Dorchester contemporary. "And he was far from stable." Given his typical ride in youth, Salemme had earned the moniker "Cadillac Frank." Although he claimed to be a licensed electrician, Frankie chose the crooked path. He admitted, "I've been involved in crime all my life. . . . I had a reputation for not backing down." He boasted, "If I told someone to do something, they would do it." A boyhood friend from Roxbury was Stevie Flemmi. Together, the two were a formidable—if uneven—pair.

"Where you saw one, you saw the other, all the time," said North End gangster Anthony Fiato. "They were a left and a right, both knockout punches. They would kill at the blink of an eye, and they hung out with killers."

Also, as Frankie admitted, "I was good at making plans." He plotted schemes, even murders, so well that Wimpy dubbed him the "General." Stevie, not so patient or subtle, would join in Frankie's plots as an executor. With Stevie, and partner George Kaufmann, Frankie operated two garages that provided cover for his side businesses, including loan-sharking and gambling. A big part of the auto work involved insurance fraud, declaring cars wrecks after minor damage or switching out the engines and reselling them.

Frankie liked Buddy and passed him some heads-ups—although at this time, he didn't want to commit to a war. On the other hand, just two meetings with Punchy convinced Frankie he "wasn't my cup of tea." As for the Hughes brothers, they were "dangerous guys, just enough to keep your distance." Eventually, Buddy told Frankie that Rico wanted to meet with him. Frankie suspected Buddy was feeding the Spaniard choice tidbits about rivals. "Paul's an all right guy, this is what he did for me, you'll find he's all right, Frank, you can trust Paul," Buddy told Frankie.

But when Frankie eventually mentioned a meet to Raymond, the don said, "Go, by all means, be a good listener, but remember, [Rico] he's a [prick]. Be careful of him. Just be careful." Yet, over time, Rico formed a relationship, of sorts, with Frankie. Rico visited Frankie's garage several times weekly. Once, when Rico was at the track, someone struck his parked FBI vehicle. He brought the damaged car to Frankie's shop, expecting to benefit from that portion of Salemme's auto business that was actually legal. Frankie accommodated him; Rico drove the car from the garage with the paint still drying. He never mentioned any compensation.

Rico and Condon were agents of different mind-sets, reflecting Boston itself. Being a member of the Knights of Columbus and an FBI agent from Charlestown, Condon knew the McLaughlins fairly well, as Frankie observed. On the other hand, while Rico liked and used Buddy as an informer, he considered Georgie "dangerous" and "psychopathic." Also, according to some less charitable gangsters, while listening to a wiretap, Rico had overheard one of the McLaughlin gang accusing Hoover of being a homosexual. Maybe. In any case, Rico had as little use for the McLaughlins as most everyone else in Boston. The agent even fed the Winter Hill gang the Dorchester address of two McLaughlin gang members (possibly Hannon and Delaney). This helped the Somerville crew with its hunt through the terra incognita of Dorchester, Stevie Flemmi claimed.

The physical and legal pressure on Raymond increased through the early 1960s. One summer day, while walking around in New York City, Raymond felt a pain in his leg and nearly collapsed. Yet worse, in 1963, the authorities had summoned him to testify before a grand jury in Providence.

On October 24, 1964, the camera-shy don drove a borrowed Volkswagen to the courthouse and parked it in the public lot. He walked unrecognized by the waiting newspapermen and photographers and slipped in through a back door. He testified of his innocence, his wife's illness, and his son's withdrawal from the University of Rhode Island. Later, Raymond boasted how he "took the ball away" by telling the jury he was there only to clear his name for Helen. He complained that he suffered from diabetes and a heart condition "that could result in my death in two days, two months, or two years." Before finishing, Raymond noted several women on the jury had tears in their eyes.

But once outside the court, Raymond reverted to type. He

unleashed a glare of contempt on a newspaper photographer who snapped a shot that became a famous signature portrait. The grand jury agreed with Raymond: despite occasional gambling, there was no organized crime in Rhode Island.

Eventually, to share his burden, Raymond promoted Jerry Angiulo as his direct underboss in Boston. The local dons gave their blessing to the exaltation, and now Jerry was the "Boss Man," or chief lieutenant. "Everyone knows to kill someone you have to get my OK," Raymond explained once. "In the case of an emergency, however, Jerry is allowed to give it." Only Raymond's personal instrument (or the other way around), Henry Tameleo, could contradict Jerry.

Despite his promotion, with the FBI and IRS snooping around, he was vexed. "I have enough troubles to last me 3,000 years," Jerry said in summer 1964. After his name became famous, letters came in from as far away as Oklahoma, from people he didn't even know. He didn't much like commuting to Providence, either. "The one thing lacking in this organization is Raymond Patriarca," Jerry once complained to Peter Limone. "Patriarca should be on the scene in Boston, but everyone they got to go forty miles to get in touch with him." During the visits to Providence, Jerry rendered unto Raymond his dividends, Boston gossip, and flattery.

But Jerry's displays of ego riled even Raymond, who at one point commanded him to stop acting "like Jimmy Cagney."

Aware of the fault line in the Office management, one FBI agent anonymously called Henry. He said Jerry had accused Raymond of being a "crybaby" over Helen's cancer—which was true—and of going soft. Jerry planned to take over the Office, too. For reasons of his own, Henry told Raymond about the call, and how upset he was hearing this slanderous message.

Puzzled, Raymond said Jerry was "very fond" of Helen. The two agreed not to tell Jerry, hoping the caller would contact them again so they could detect his identity.

Nothing came of this FBI ploy. But Jerry realized the ferocious Larry Baione would soon hit the street. That would cause problems "since they were enemies before he went to prison." Vinnie concluded, "Eventually there will be a showdown."

Unlike Jerry, Larry performed his own violence, and with a fierce gusto. His signature tool was the baseball bat, although we don't know which hand he favored. Once, Larry warned a deadbeat teamster who worked the garment district by saying, "If you don't come up with the money in ten days, I will cut off your head and throw it through your kitchen door." To comply, the borrower arranged the theft of his own truck—he told Larry to sell the cloth inside and keep the $2,300 he owed.

Larry would keep Jerry sharp.

CITY ON FIRE

"Well, I've always been considered a cuckoo anyways . . ."
—Joe Barboza

"Read the papers tomorrow and you will see what happens to a punk," Joe announced on Saturday, September 26, 1964. Later that day, in Malden, Joe and Nick Femia entered Carlton Eaton's 1957 Cadillac. Joe took his place behind the wheel, while Eaton sat catercorner in the front passenger's seat. Nicky sat in the back.

Now Eaton was relaxed, high from a joint he'd just shared, as the Animal later boasted. But Eaton was in grave danger. Joe had fronted Eaton money, which he gambled away, leaving Joe's bank short $600. When Joe discovered Eaton's borrowers were phony, he told the Office. Then Eaton had borrowed scuba equipment from Chico Amico—and sold it. Now stoned, Eaton closed his eyes, and reached up with his left hand to touch Joe's shoulder. "Oh, Joe," he said. Just then, the Animal raised a .38 special to the level of Eaton's head and pulled the trigger twice. One bullet entered the lower part of Eaton's left ear and exited the other side. The other passed through the left temple and emerged from the middle of the right cheek. The body went rigid as it convulsed in death spasms, and blood "poured like thick syrup from the hole in his head," as Joe later told a friend.

"Look at this motherfucker, Nicky," Joe said. "I am having a conversation with him and he goes to sleep on me." Before fleeing, Joe pushed Eaton back into the corner of the front seat and shot him in the head again. Joe claimed a "lot of matter" splattered while plugging Eaton. Later, he brushed his hair and found a "hard substance," which he put in his mouth. He spat it out when he realized it was a splinter from Eaton's skull.

The list of suspects for the Eaton job was slim, and the papers all but named Joe as the killer. The Animal headed to a New Hampshire hideout, but with nobody to maim or kill, predictably, he became bored. While visiting the Malden police station for an Eaton grilling, one officer asked if Joe could beat Buddy McLean in a fight.

"Who is Buddy McLean?" Joe asked. Laughter.

To distance himself from the heat, Joe checked into the Sands in Las Vegas, as a guest of one of Boston's elder Jewish gangsters. With a female escort, Joe lounged around the hotel pool, rode Arabian horses in the desert, caught the famous Vegas nightclub shows, and left the craps tables $100 ahead. Joe was happy: He'd just killed someone, he was earning big money, and he'd be a father in seven months. "I was sure the baby would never want for anything like I had," he observed.

The Eaton affair cooling, Joe returned to the East and its tensions, having to remain alert for suckers, cops, and hit men. That didn't prevent him from holding a bachelors' party at Hotel St. George on Beacon Street. Attending was "every well-known hoodlum in Boston," who paid $20 a ticket, said Vinnie.

On October 17, just before noon, a ten-year-old boy retrieving a ball passed a car on Russell Street in Everett. He noted blood streaks on the auto's right door, stopped, and opened it. Inside was a man's body on its knees, the face resting on the front passenger seat. Soon after, the local firemen and policemen arrived, and an autopsy revealed two bullets in the back of the neck and four stab wounds.

The body, investigators learned, had belonged to twenty-four-year-old Anthony Sacramone. Although only a painter and without a record, police decreed he was gangland victim number ten. His criminality was limited to selling pills and palling around with Chelsea underworld tough Edward Deegan, with whom he frequented the Ebb Tide. Rumors flew about how Deegan had murdered his partner. Apparently, the Hannon and Delaney killings had unnerved him. As Sacramone had kept talking about the mob bookie theft, Deegan decided to quiet him and to signal the Office he was a serious man. Deegan, along with a minor mobster named Anthony "Stath" Stathopolous, even met with Jimmy the Bear in Deegan's car. They discussed an "arrangement to silence" Sacramone—but the Bear's participation ceased after he shot himself (more on that shortly) and couldn't complete the job. Later, after Sacramone turned up deceased, the Bear worried he'd left his fingerprints in Deegan's car.

Through the bloodshed, Raymond had declared publicly the Office would take no sides: It was an Irish matter, after all. The Office policy in Boston had been, "Let them all kill each other and we'll pick up the pieces"—a statement variously attributed. Raymond "had no animosity towards [McLean]" and promised [to] assist neither side in McLean's "'war' against the [McLaughlin] brothers," an informant relayed to the FBI. Yet the informant also was sure Raymond quietly favored Charlestown. Under the cover of the feud, Winter Hill was absorbing booking enterprises formerly "exclusively within the domain of [Angiulo]," as the FBI noted. Fretting, Jerry took the matter up during a confabulation with Raymond. The don was already acquainted with the McLaughlins but didn't know Buddy much at all. In any case, Raymond told Jerry, "Just sit back. Don't do anything about it. When the feud ends, I'll recover the territories." In the meantime, "If [McLean] comes on strong he [Raymond] indicated steps would be taken to curtail his prog-ress," the informer claimed.

Despite Office neutrality, when Jerry returned to Boston from his meeting with Raymond, a McLaughlin man asked him to set Buddy up in a parole violation. Jerry contacted someone in the Massachusetts State Police to arrange for Buddy's arrest. Rico might have blocked this move.

After Sacramone's murder, the Bear and Deegan began sniping at each other. The Bear pressed Deegan to repay a loan to his brother Stevie. Deegan refused, so now Flemmi wanted to kill him, and even tried to enlist an accessory—who informed the FBI. The Bear claimed Deegan was bad-mouthing the informer to the "Italian element" at the Coliseum restaurant to get him killed.

But Deegan had competition when it came to trying to bring down the Bear. Assassins would attempt to kill the Bear; he'd visit the hospital; and when he left, people would die. However, in Sep-tember 1964, the FBI noted the Bear "had shot himself by accident and it had nothing to do with the gang war." At the hospital, the Bear claimed that two men had fired at him six times. The story in the South End was that the Bear visited a black heroin dealer, an-nounced they were partners, and pulled out a pistol to prove the point. However, the pistol had accidentally gone off and had hit him in the foot.

In any case, by mid-October, the Bear was well enough to visit Peter Limone's West End Social Club on Cambridge Avenue. Limone's place was (along with the Coliseum) a magnet for all late-night aspiring criminal wannabes and zeros. The Bear asked Limone about Teddy Deegan—telling him Deegan owed him $300, by way of a loan. Limone said Deegan didn't visit his place. Limone had already even complained to Raymond how the Bear was uncontrollable. Now, given the heat on the Bear, Limone asked him to leave. The Bear denied the heat—but when Limone insisted, he left peaceably. Limone immediately called Deegan and told him about the Flemmi loan. Deegan denied it and both agreed the Bear probably wanted Teddy gone.

For most, a prowling Bear was a terror—but not so for the uncommonly tough Deegan. At age thirty-five, small and slight, Deegan was a longshoreman and convict with twenty-five arrests, starting from age eleven. He was a very hard man. "He beat people up and the wrong people," said one contemporary. Soon after, the Bear openly admitted he wanted to kill Deegan, the FBI learned. And did nothing.

16

IRISH LUCK

"There's one thing in this game. Either you kill me or I'm going to kill you."

—Joe Barboza

At around 11 A.M. on November 23, 1964, Punchy McLaughlin sat behind the wheel of his 1962 Oldsmobile. He'd parked in Brookline's Regent Circle, which served as the Beth Israel Hospital parking lot. With Georgie on the run, Punchy was the weary, troubled-looking, and public face of the McLaughlins. The Brookline police had asked Punchy to stay out of their fine city, although Punchy claimed he bought candy there. Today, he violated the constabulary's injunction to meet Wimpy's henchman, Earle Smith, on business—but, as a cover, in the back were two pounds of confectionaries. On the seat in Punchy's car was the book *Mafia*, with a smoking-gun illustration on the cover. As Punchy waited, a 1962 Pontiac with Rhode Island plates pulled up nearby. Two men dressed as rabbis exited it—but if someone had looked closely enough, they might have recognized Frankie Salemme and Stevie Flemmi.

One "rabbi" walked to the driver's side and aimed a 12-gauge sawed-off shotgun into Punchy's face and pulled the trigger twice. The shots nearly obliterated Punchy's jaw; the other "rabbi" fired into his chest. The two assassins left him for dead to escape down the driveway, staying just ahead of hospital security. This wasn't a good spot at all, and "you couldn't finish what you started," as Frankie lamented later, noting he hadn't really "sanctioned" this hit.

Gushing blood, Punchy pulled himself from the car and staggered toward a nearby hotel. "I'm shot. I'm shot," he cried. Two men helped Punchy inside and let him slump to the floor. "Help this man," said one Good Samaritan, "he's been shot," before fleeing.

The Brookline police found Punchy in a pool of blood outside a barbershop and rushed him to Beth Israel, next door. "Meet somebody, meet somebody," Punchy mumbled. A priest administered the last rites as the staff wheeled Punchy into the surgery. Yet, after an eight-hour operation, the doctors gave him a fighting chance. The Boston police and FBI fortified the hospital. By November 26, although Punchy was minus much of his jaw, under police guard, he improved.

When Revere capo Sammy Granito told Raymond that Punchy would probably live, Raymond said, "They should have used Double 00 instead of bird shot. One of the hardest ways to kill someone is from outside a car."

Eventually doctors wired Punchy's jaw together, but steel remained embedded in his chin, and he could consume only liquids. Punchy was discharged from the hospital under a police guard and immediately hid. He talked of heading to California, but instead remained in the middle of the shooting. The following April, in Brockton, he clumsily shoplifted two cans of rug-cleaning fluid and a transistor radio. After his arrest, a judge fined Punchy $100 and released him—even if he were safer in jail than outside it. Right after Punchy's shooting, two Charlestown crew members (one of them was Spike O'Toole) awaiting release from the Dedham jail, received identical telegrams, stating, "You will receive the same benefits as Harold [Hannon]."

———

On December 4, 1964, authorities took aim yet again at the Office in Boston, when a grand jury convened to present evidence to the Massachusetts Crime Commission. Among the tough-looking old-school Mafiosi, invitees included underwhelming Jerry with five Angiulo brothers. After arriving in court, Jerry noticed the newspaper photographers keeping a wary distance. He said, "What do you think we are, monsters or something?"

Seeing the television cameras, he removed his glasses, dusted off his blue suit, removed a cigarette from his mouth, and adjusted his tie. "My tie straight?" he asked. "Wait until I say something to make me smile . . . cheese, cheese." Obviously concerned, he asked if the sound-recording device was on. It wasn't, so he kept saying "cheese." Then he said, "Wait a minute. If you are going to take my picture, take my good side." A photographer snapped a picture of the four Angiulo brothers together—with their square haircuts, slight builds, and middle-aged features, they might have been attending a convention of clerks and accountants.

Soon after, though, Jerry was indicted for a blue-collar offense—an assault on an IRS agent the prior May.

Before 1964 closed, the Bear's handiwork appeared publicly at least twice. On November 24, a hunter was pursuing his game through Towers Brook in the staid old South Shore town of Hingham—that is, until he stumbled on an ice-encased skeleton. It lay faceup, the arms crossed behind it, the legs drawn up and also in an X position. There was a pair of green socks on the feet, contrasting with the floral summer shirt; a pair of dark brown, size 8D-wide shoes lay on the bank nearby. After the mystery corpse had thawed in the police station car garage, the authorities matched the teeth to the prison dental records of small-time ex-convict Edward Huber, of the South End. The case wasn't solved.

On December 27, 1964, the Bear met up with his pal, the

forty-one-year-old ex-convict George Ashe. Recently, Ashe had acted out of line at the West End club, arguing with a bartender, kicking the cigarette machine, and stealing the money that tumbled out. Perhaps worst, Ashe was also "saying unkind things about [the Bear's] group." He'd just become an approved FBI informant, to boot.

The two men entered a borrowed Corvair; during the subsequent and one-way fight, the Bear stabbed Ashe fifty times in the back. After shooting him in the head, the Bear exited the vehicle and escaped, unmolested—while two patrolmen watched. Unwilling to fill out the paperwork, the patrolmen pushed the vehicle, with the body, into the next district. Hidden by an overcoat, Ashe's body remained in the Corvair, parked on Harrison Avenue near St. Philips Church in the South End. The next day, someone found Flemmi's handiwork, and soon after, Ashe's brother, a Boston policeman, identified it. Later, the two patrolmen who'd seen the Bear kill Ashe visited Stevie at his Roxbury corner to receive a $2,500 silence fee.

After the Bear bragged about the murder, Stevie "chastised" his older brother. He "reminded Jimmy how lucky he was that he ran into two police officers who were his friends," said an FBI report.

Sometime around January 11, 1965, someone shot petty gangster John Murray in the head, in an automobile. Those nearby said it sounded like a car backfiring. The culprit dumped Murray in the frozen sands of Tenean Beach for discovery that morning. The why was a mystery. A small-time hood, Murray had just left jail and claimed he'd kill for anyone (including the Bear) as the only way to make real money. Police never solved the crime, but the consensus was this was the Bear's paw-work.

Just about then, Frankie Salemme told Raymond, "All the people are getting scared of Jimmy." He urged Raymond to talk to him and stop this killing in Boston. Raymond agreed. Of late, the heat was so intense, he was unable to arrange a legitimate janitor's job for a friend.

"If the killings don't stop, I'll declare martial law." But he admitted he thought "very highly of James Flemmi."

So did Rico, whose specific task was romancing the Bear as a potential candidate for the Top Echelon program. Another informer told the FBI how the Bear was "an extremely dangerous individual" and "extremely conscientious" about "stool pigeons." For instance, just months before, the Bear had entered a barroom and immediately started a fight. During the fracas, Flemmi took a chemical from his pocket and threw it in his opponent's eyes, blinding him before he knocked him out. A week later, the victim's eyes remained sightless.

Early one night at the Ebb Tide, Joe was hobnobbing with Henry Tameleo, Ronnie, and Romeo Martin, along with henchman Nicky Femia. Then, in through the Ebb Tide's back door, entered three hoods. One tall man, wearing a suit, waved to Joe, who recognized him as Stevie Hughes. He looked impressive—broad in shoulder, slim in waist (he'd lost fifty pounds since Joe had last seen him), with jet-black hair crowning his head. Hughes was out of Walpole and raising four sons and a daughter, with his wife, in their Bunker Hill Street house in Charlestown.

As Joe recounted the story, after everyone shook hands, Stevie Hughes sat down at the table and introduced his brother, Connie, and their associate, Maxie Shackleford. Stevie didn't know that Joe was a "sympathizer" of the Hill. "The war had broken a lot of friendships but it wouldn't break mine," Joe had decided. Wary, Joe signaled Chico to call Dearborn Square to retrieve guns from a cellar. More gangsters arrived, including Wimpy, the Flemmi brothers, and Frankie Salemme. A nervous Richie Castucci paced and wrung his hands and threw the crew glances. As the Office was (officially) neutral, Henry drifted off without anyone noticing. Convening a sort of professional conference, the different factions shoved together two tables.

Stevie Hughes said, "I want to make peace with Buddy McLean. If Buddy gives his word, I'll accept it."

"I'll talk to Buddy and do my best," said the Bear. "If this war keeps up, who knows how many people sitting here tonight will die."

"All I want to do now is make money," Stevie Hughes claimed.

After some small talk, the Hughes party left without incident, Joe claimed. The Bear's report of the proffered peace deal only angered Buddy, who said, "I don't want peace with him because he is a lying, sneaking weasel. The only peace we'll ever get between us is when one of us is dead."

Obviously, concord just wasn't on Buddy's mind—if anything, with the stress and fear of assassination, he was becoming more violent and ruthless. As a lumper, Buddy owned the keys to waterfront fish stores. A rumor persisted that one morning, the operator of a retail fish shop found someone's ticking watch in his lobster tank. The rest of the timepiece's owner had, presumably, become feed—assuming this wasn't just a dark Irish joke. Vinnie Teresa claimed he sold Buddy pistols and silencers and hand grenades (at $150 apiece). Personally, Buddy avoided automatics, as they tended to jam. One particularly dangerous man called "the Undertaker" even met with Buddy to sell him a "typewriter" (machine gun). The deal fell through. Each side would kill each other firing one bullet at a time.

Back in August 1962, there had been a big shift in the Boston underworld's bedrock. A crew of bold thieves expertly stole $1.5 million from a mail truck in Plymouth. It was "a good score down on the Cape—good money," as Raymond described it. One of the first suspects was a slippery man named Red Kelley. A career criminal, Kelley supplemented his thieving by working as a real estate agent and a vendor of "religious statuary." F. Lee Bailey dubbed him the "smiling Irishman," and for a time kept him out of jail. Another suspect was the middle-aged, potbellied, and highly successful white-collar crook Henry Reddington.

Over time, perhaps six men died because of their entanglement—intimate or peripheral—in the Plymouth mail robbery. It was dangerous to have that kind of money—or even to know who had it. When paroled on November 16, 1964, extortion artist Robert Rasmussen allegedly tried to shake down Red Kelley. This apparently resulted in a contract. At least two killers (possibly Joe and the Bear) lured Rasmussen into an apartment, where he thought a nonviolent bookie kept his stash. The last thing Rasmussen might have noticed was that the carpet was covered with plastic.

An "ex–baseball player" (possibly Joe Barboza, who told the story) swung his bat into Rasmussen's head. Then again. And again. Rasmussen collapsed to the floor, his blood collecting in the plastic, which the killers wrapped him in before carrying him to a car, as Joe said. The murderers drove to Silver Lake in Wilmington, and, as a final touch, someone fired a bullet into Rasmussen's head. At 1:10 A.M. on January 15, a patrolman thought he saw a bundle of clothes just a few feet off Grove Avenue, then realized it was a body.

For some people, the war was an opportunity. Some believed Wimpy was using it to eliminate rivals and thus called him "the Great Deceiver." During a meeting with Jerry, Wimpy complained about the slayings. "I'm disgusted with the situation and don't know what to do. Hoodlums are coming in from New York and I don't know who is going to be killed next, or when, or what side to take in the argument."

"You have to choose a side and stick with it," Jerry said. But, as Jerry doubtless knew, Wimpy was always on his own side. Wimpy had no great love for Georgie: He'd even asked Raymond if the don could make peace if Georgie were killed. The Office viewed Wimpy as a protected colleague. For some reason, someone had once approached Jerry looking for permission to kill Wimpy by poisoning his coffee. "Angiulo thought the guy was crazy and ordered him not to kill anyone or he would be killed himself," as the FBI had noted.

The police, responding to the mounting body count, circulated a confidential list of felons. It provided a hood's name, photo, address, and auto information. The document was divided into two groups—Georgie McLaughlin's friends and his enemies. Officially, Henry Reddington was a friend of Georgie's. A mischief-making Wimpy told Spike O'Toole one of Reddington's guests (he hid New York Irish hoodlums on the run) had hooked his paramour, Dottie Barchard, on heroin. Spike had fathered two daughters with her, born almost exactly a year apart. Wimpy then borrowed $25,000 from Reddington, knowing Spike would, in effect, cancel the debt.

On January 23, 1965, Reddington was about to leave his Ab-Way office in Weymouth for a late-night "business" appointment with a real estate agent and Dottie Barchard. But Spike entered his office, drew a pistol, and fired four bullets into Reddington's head, body, and face. Dottie dialed Reddington's number to no avail; after midnight, arriving at his house, she walked into the office and found Reddington, facedown. No surprise. "The police circular is beginning to take on the appearance of a list of those marked for death," said one reporter.

Raymond called Wimpy and Stevie Flemmi to ask who the culprit was. They pled ignorance, leaving both Boston and New York abuzz. Dottie rewarded Spike by having him arrested on a morality charge.

Before Spike was bailed out, a Somerville policeman asked him, "You're a buddy of George McLaughlin, aren't you?"

"Yeah, that's right."

"Where is he now?"

"Probably murdered somewhere."

On January 10, Revere resident Jack "Ass" Francione shoveled his car out of its driveway after a snowstorm and went inside his apartment. Obviously, Francione was no big shot, yet for some reason—or many—Boston hoodlum and Nazi Party sympathizer Frank Smith cleared a hit on him, on his own authority. Joe Barboza and Jimmy the Bear, carrying the authorization, passed through the rear door into Francione's apartment. Expected or otherwise, Francione turned to speak to his guests when Joe shot him. They left him facedown on the floor, "looking as though he was praying to Mecca," as Joe said.

Two days later, Raymond declared this "out of order." Indeed, it was. The reaction grew, with the Commonwealth throwing a thirty-trooper special task force at the underworld. By February 1, there was very little nightlife available to Boston's unfortunate hoodlums. Men were being picked up for petty crimes such as larceny or nonpayment of child support. These criminals were akin to junk fish caught when fishermen were baiting for better game.

The man who'd authorized the Francione murder, Frank Smith, was a political activist: He supported the American Nazi Party, whose eccentric, if not outright psychotic, head was George Lincoln Rockwell. Associating with megalomaniac Rockwell may have affected Smith, who was freely giving orders to "hit this guy and that guy." Several months later, Raymond commanded Jerry to tell Smith the killings must cease—unless he received Raymond's imprimatur. As for the Bear, Jerry admitted, "He doesn't use sufficient common sense when it comes to killing people." But he'd already spoken to the Bear and explained Raymond's "high regard" for him. Then he'd explained the necessary protocol to Jimmy. "You shouldn't kill people because you had an argument. . . ." He added that if there was an argument, Jimmy should leave and get word to Raymond, who would either okay or deny the hit.

In February 1965, Raymond's world was rocking—Helen's cancer soon was so advanced the doctors wondered what kept her alive. The feds kept the squeeze on, too. Raymond's onetime right-hand man, Louis the Fox, faced a seven-month sentence for evading income taxes. He wanted to fight the rap, and was becoming unsteady. As further insult to the Office, a bold thirty-one-year-old drug addict named Raymond "Baby" Curcio burglarized Joseph Patriarca's house. An outraged Raymond sloppily recruited assassin Nicky Palmigiano, and paid him by stuffing fifty-dollar bills in his pocket.

On the very cold evening of February 20, a pajama-clad Curcio sat behind the wheel of his car, parked on Hyacinth Street in Providence's North End. Palmigiano shot Curcio six times in the head and neck. Curcio's blood froze, so the coroner allowed the police to tow the vehicle to headquarters to thaw the body. The supervising detectives stopped for coffee at the Eveready Diner on Admiral Street. While there, they sent the waitress out to see if the passenger in the vehicle wanted anything—shocked, she rushed back in, face whitened and lips shivering. As Colonel Stone said, the streets of Providence were a "jungle."

The law wasn't alone in its pursuit of Georgie. In the privacy of the Office, Raymond lamented the violence shaking his kingdom. "It's too bad the McLeans and the McLaughlins can't settle their feud over a handshake," he said. Of Buddy, Raymond lacked any opinion, as they'd only met once before. However, he did want to summon him to Providence to discuss the gang war.

During one chat in the Office with the Bear, Joe, and Wimpy,

Raymond declared, "This war has got to get over with, one way or another, even if I have to declare martial law. It's costing too much money. We can't operate properly." Raymond said, "That little ass-hole [Georgie] has done nothing for two years but hide and cost his friends money. I'm going to sit him in that chair in front of you guys and tell him to forget this beef and stop the war. If he says no, then you can kill him right in that chair."

"If you can get them to stop trying to kill us, we'll stop on our side," said Wimpy. "But how can you trust the word of that sick little bastard, Georgie McLaughlin?"

"I'm going to call him up here and speak to him. I've called him to come in four or five times but he won't come." Raymond said Georgie mistrusted him.

A wary Joe thought, "Sure he don't trust you, Raymond. You had [Nazarian] killed after he worked for you for years. Georgie worked for you and now you want him killed. Nobody means nothing to you, you cold-blooded bastard."

On January 1, while in a cocktail lounge, a police officer asked Spike O'Toole about Georgie. "I don't know the bum," said Spike. But that month, Spike and an attractive twenty-year-old woman rented the second- and third-floor apartments of a Dorchester triple-decker tenement. With them was a short, squat man they called John T. O'Connor, who in his other guise was public enemy number one, Georgie McLaughlin.

Somehow, Dennis Condon discovered Georgie's lair before the Hill did. The FBI made ready to pounce. Rico even asked Frankie for a "throwaway"—a clean pistol with obliterated serial numbers, making it untraceable. Frankie claimed he picked a .38 from one of his two arsenals (one in each garage) and slipped it to Rico. The Spaniard said the team would plant the gun on a dresser next to Georgie—and then claim they had gunned him down in self-defense. The slick and ruthless agent boasted, "If I get the op-portunity to bang Georgie McLaughlin, I'm going to do it."

At just after 2 P.M. on February 24, Leonard Frisoli, his FBI badge showing, led twenty agents and Boston policemen to the McLaughlin address on Duke Street. Frisoli pressed the useless buzzer, then knocked on the door of the left-side apartment loudly and announced, "FBI and Boston police."

After two minutes, Frisoli heard children, and feet coming down the stairs. The door opened, and just inside was a toddler, behind whom, halfway down the stairs, was an attractive woman, Frances Bithoney. Frisoli and several agents entered the house and started moving upstairs.

"We're looking for George McLaughlin," said Frisoli.

"You're not going to search," Bithoney said. Eight law enforce-ment officers passed by her and poured into the vestibule. En-gulfed in this tide, Bithoney rose to the second-floor landing, where an officer finally sat her down in a reception room. She wept, while the child, in the custody of one of the lawmen, screamed. Knowing the apartment's layout, the officers and agents ascended another flight of stairs, weapons drawn. Up in the third-floor attic bed-room, Georgie and Spike lay in bed, oblivious to the ruckus down-stairs.

The team reached the bedroom door, knocked on it, and screamed, "Federal agents!"

Once in the room, the agents found Georgie, who said, "Please don't shoot." They forced the two gangsters to the floor, cuffed them, and removed Georgie's shirt and trousers. The FBI arrested Spike for harboring a fugitive and charged Bithoney and Maureen Dellamano as accessories after the fact to murder.

Outside, a frustrated Georgie kicked at any photographers who came within range of his short legs. "My name is George McLaugh-lin and that's all I have to say to you," he told the court. A judge sent Georgie to Charles Street Jail, an ancient, dilapidated, and

insect-infested Italianate palace-prison. So unpleasant was the facility, some men confessed to major crimes just to get out and into
the state prison system—itself no great shakes. Georgie's new home
was a cell in a secluded section of the prison's massive rotunda.

Soon after the arrest, Rico appeared at Frankie's garage and
glumly admitted that four out of five men on the FBI team had
agreed Georgie wouldn't survive the raid. But because of one
holdout, Rico couldn't risk killing McLaughlin. Rico kept the
throwaway.

Undaunted, Joe, who considered Georgie a "worm," kept plotting. First, Joe scoped a "beautiful 75-yard shot" down into the jail
exercise area. He nixed that and decided a window shot was better.
To guarantee the gang nailed its small target, Joe wanted three rifles
aimed at Georgie, with each shooter dressed like a house painter.
That plan died when Joe learned Georgie wouldn't leave his cell.
Next, Joe devised a fifty-yard shot from a window on the third floor
of the Mass General Hospital into Georgie's private yard. Joe even
asked Ronnie to procure a diesel truck filter for a silencer—it was a
hospital, after all. The plan was, again, absurd. Deciding Georgie
faced the chair, anyway, Joe gave up on it. Punchy would be easier,
and he "needed personal attention."

For John Eddy, chief of Providence detectives, Raymond was a
noontime near-daily sight outside Coin-O-Matic. Eddy was even
comfortable enough with Raymond to summon him to his office
on March 4, 1965. When Raymond arrived, Eddy discussed William "Willie" Marfeo, who ran a Sunday dice game at the Veteran's
Social Club at 375 Atwells Avenue. Eddy told Raymond he wanted
Marfeo's now-notorious game closed. "I've already told Willie to
shut down but he is a fresh bastard. I can't control him," Raymond
confessed. He also feared Marfeo might say something he "would
have to do something about."

State police moved next. To gain entry to Willie's game required passing a guard who opened the front door to the establishment electronically. To circumvent this, Rhode Island state trooper Vincent Vespia devised a plan. Armed with an ax, a machine gun, and a very bad attitude about the Mafia, the Federal Hill native entered a cherry picker basket. Vespia, in the basket, ascended to the second floor and crashed through the window. Willie still had cash and dice in his hands. Six men tried to hide in the two bathrooms; the police retrieved the dice from one of the toilets.

This was too much heat. Now Henry Tameleo personally instructed Willie to quit.

"Go fuck yourself," said Marfeo (as Joe heard it). Henry gestured with his hand to Marfeo's face and said, "You understand you are to close down." Marfeo pushed Henry's hand and head away—Henry later claimed if he'd been carrying a gun, he would have shot Willie on the spot.

A frustrated Raymond said "that he would love to kill Marfeo himself." When by chance Willie saw Raymond in public, Willie appeared as if he "was going to die right there on the spot." Old-timer Louis the Fox received special permission to do the hit. His favorite tool was the shotgun—but in February 1964, just as he was about to strike, a massive snowstorm intervened. Before the Fox could move again, the police picked him up, embarrassingly, for carrying a concealed pencil-weapon. This gadget, favored by ladies, ejected only tear gas. Now the Fox was out. Willie still was alive and well. This had to be fixed.

17.

AN ALLEY IN CHELSEA

"So the Mafia is great for this, for getting the friend to kill another friend."

—Joe Barboza

The Bear planned to end, permanently, his waltz with Teddy Deegan. Joe signed on to this project: He knew Teddy from North Station and the racetrack and considered him a McLaughlin ally. Deegan also recently had been "out of order" at the Ebb Tide, pulling a gun, Joe claimed. On March 4, Frank Smith gave them permission to visit Providence to discuss the murder and other matters. Raymond was infuriated at Smith for granting an audience without "prior authorization." This demented pair, Jimmy and Joe, was white-hot. Naturally, Raymond didn't want them contacting him at his "place of business," and so told a worker at the Office to take them to a nearby garage.

During the meeting, the Bear claimed Deegan had done for "the kid [Sacramone]" only to "impress some people." Deegan was an "arrogant, nasty sneak and should be killed." Raymond asked if they'd discussed Deegan with Jerry—yes, they claimed. Raymond told them to get more information, and Jerry would make the final decision.

They took this as a yes. The Bear and Joe put Deegan's murder on a fast track. On March 10, the Bear claimed the conspirators had already made a "dry run." Moreover, "a close associate of Deegan's has agreed to set him up." This Judas was balding Roy French, a horse trainer and Ebb Tide bouncer. Now in his midthirties, the stocky French was uncommonly fast and tough. Joe claimed French had once hid Georgie from Buddy's vengeance—and for that McLean had anathematized French as a McLaughlin man.

In a meeting at the Ebb Tide, French promised to set up Deegan—in turn, Joe would intercede for French with Buddy. The conspirators formed a plan. They would pretend to take the Lincoln National Bank, located on the second floor of a downtown Chelsea building. Someone would leave the back door open, and French, Deegan, and Anthony Stathopolous would enter at the "second half" (at night) to burglarize it. While there, French would execute a contract.

However, Joe and the Bear planned to eventually kill French. They'd also shoot Stathopolous, making this multiple murder a "package deal," as Joe put it.

At 7:45 P.M., on March 12, 1965, Joe, Romeo, and Ronnie drove over to the alley in Chelsea for a look-see. Ronnie and Romeo scoped the future murder scene; Martin claimed the back door was open, as planned. They headed to the now-crowded Ebb Tide in Joe's new Olds 88. As planned, just after 9 P.M., French took the phone and talked briefly with Deegan. Then French left alone to await Deegan's pickup for the ride to Chelsea. The rest of the conspirators left in groups of two or three—Joe exited the back door with Romeo Martin, who claimed he'd a beef with Deegan, and wanted to be "in that alley."

Soon after, Romeo parked his red Olds, now carrying Joe, Ronnie, and the Bear, at Chelsea's Fourth Street at the second meter from Broadway. Stepping out, Joe and Ronnie bent the license plates to hide the numbers; Romeo's wheels were turned hard over—one step on the gas and he'd escape out into the one-way street. Nearby, unarmed, Stathopolous waited in a car on Fourth Street. Everything was ready: Joe said they all wore disguises, and as an extra precaution he'd snapped on a U.S. Army–surplus bulletproof vest. A Chelsea patrolman had performed a routine check of the alley behind the finance company, turned the lights on, and left. As planned, Romeo and Ronnie exited the Olds and entered through the front of the building. They worked their way back to the rear door and waited. At 9:30 P.M., French and Deegan walked into the alley. Moving ahead, Deegan, armed only with a screwdriver, opened the rear door and stepped inside. Wary of the bullets that soon would be flying, French held back.

"Why are you hesitating?" Deegan asked.

French placed his pistol's muzzle to the back of his friend's skull, and squeezed the trigger. Deegan went down—as he'd vowed, no one had taken him out face-to-face. Ronnie and Romeo now arrived and pumped five bullets into Deegan's body, lying on its back. Now that there was "one less Irish motherfucker," Joe decided it was time to shoot Stath. Armed with his auto-glass-shattering .357 Magnum, he and the Bear approached Stath's car. Noting the bulky forms closing in on him, Stath thought the police had arrived, and drove off. Frustrated, Joe and the Bear returned to Romeo's still-idling Oldsmobile.

Romeo emerged from the bank and hopped behind the driver's wheel. Ronnie took a seat in the back, next to the Bear. At 10 P.M., an off-duty Chelsea police captain, Joseph Kozlowski, was walking around Fourth Street and happened to notice the maroon Olds. He stepped behind the vehicle and noted the tag looked off. He walked to the driver's side and rapped on the window.

"Your plate is bent," Kozlowski said. Joe looked at the officer, in soft hat and topcoat, and pegged him as looking "Jewish."

For a response, Romeo sped into the street, making a tire-screeching right onto Broadway. Kozlowski quickly noted the man in the back was dark-haired, with a "bald spot in the center of his head." Romeo took the next left, stopped, dropped Ronnie off, and drove back to the Ebb Tide to await French.

Around 10:50 P.M. the Chelsea beat patrolman returned to the Lincoln Bank and checked the now-dark alley. The patrolman discovered Deegan's body lying near a puddle of blood. It was clad in a suit, hands in gloves, the feet aimed at Fourth Street. Just then, back in Revere, French entered the Ebb Tide and found Joe. "It's done," he said, and Joe hugged him. He noted blood on French's shirt and shoes, and told him. "I'll take care of it," French said.

Five minutes later, Ronnie and Chico entered. "We nailed him," Romeo told French, in hearing of an informant. By 11 P.M., all the perpetrators were back in the Ebb Tide, and the weapons and gear stashed, invisible, in the grasses outside the club.

Soon, Chelsea police knew Joe and his gang had been at the Ebb Tide at the suspicious intervals of just before and just after the removal of Deegan from the planet. That night, investigators picked up Romeo, as well as French, who claimed he'd been at the Ebb Tide all night. French explained the blood, still visible despite cleaning, on his sleeve and shoe, had come from two fights he'd broken up at the club.

The ripples spread from what the locals began calling "Deegan's Alley." After reading of Deegan's murder, Frankie Salemme was puzzled. As both he and Stevie were potential targets, being "hot and heavy" in the gang war, they followed all murders carefully. They needed to know who could do what—and to whom. Frankie accepted an invitation to meet the Flemmi brothers at Stevie's real estate office in Roxbury.

Frankie asked the Bear, "Why did Teddy have to die?"

"He was helping the McLaughlins," said the Bear. This may or may not have been so. In any case, Deegan had been stalking him in a contest that could only end one way. But, with a professional's assessment, the Bear said the killers had done an "awful sloppy job." Now the Bear wanted to find Stathopolous and kill him.

As for Stevie, he'd robbed bookmakers with Deegan—and he was angry at Joe and his brother both for snuffing his partner. He also knew Jerry had wanted Deegan nailed, and his own work with Deegan might come back to bite.

Inevitably, Stevie and Frankie were drifting further into the war, given the Bear's devotion to Buddy and the Hill. Eventually, Stevie realized there was a bull's-eye on his back. His already-messy life became even more complicated. Already, his existence was largely a succession of affairs and statutory rapes. He'd split from his first wife and two daughters and eventually moved in with a woman named Hussey and her three children. For safety's sake, during the war, sometimes he kept no fixed address at all.

Together, Hussey and Stevie manufactured two more children. Needing money, he constantly was investing in various businesses. When they failed, he applied the torch for insurance.

Although mere utensils of violence, Jimmy the Bear and Joe frequently visited the Office. They offered street gossip, boxes of Cuban cigars, and white stockings. This was the top for the Bear. Going almost white collar, he opened a nightclub, of sorts, in an old smoke-gray-colored edifice on Dudley Street. The first story hosted a regular store, Walsh's, but upstairs was Flemmi's after-hours establishment. It was "anything but class" and populated with hookers, pimps, thieves, bookies, and assassins, said Joe, who called it the "Bear's Haunted House."

When passing through the screeching front door, one walked into halls and rooms of peeling wallpaper and cracked ceilings

that offered shelter to blackjack tables, chairs, and a jukebox. Beyond two game rooms, there was another chamber, whose floor was
so dilapidated, the unsuspecting might walk in and fall through
into the store below—and perhaps hell itself. Outside, nearby was
the Old Dudley Lounge, which hosted a dope operation that "ca-
tered to Negroes." Given the heat the drugs caused, the Bear considered burning the Old Dudley down outright, as he told
Raymond.

The Bear was one of his own most unlucky customers, as Joe
observed. No gambler himself, Joe leaned against the wall in the
card room and watched the Bear play $100-a-hand blackjack.
Flemmi lost so badly at his own table, Joe could only watch, sad
and angry at the waste. Through his network, FBI agent Rico
eventually heard the Bear was a failing gambling addict—and he,
"therefore, should be susceptible to pressure."

Jerry Angiulo worried about being caught in the war's cross fire, and
so was playing all available sides. Remaining friendly with the
Townies, Jerry also worked with the Flemmi brothers. By now, the
FBI pressure on Jerry had become so great, even his own Massachusetts State Police contacts were unable to help him. Additionally,
an angry Bear had accused "the guineas down in the North End" of
giving the McLaughlins $500 to prolong the war. Then on April 3,
Spike O'Toole announced to Jerry that he was going to eliminate
the Dearborn Square gang, the Flemmi brothers in particular. He
blamed Wimpy for the recent hit on Punchy. But after Spike left,
Jerry called the Bear, made him swear secrecy, and revealed the
plucky Irishman's plans. Spike was a "worker," as even Joe Barboza
acknowledged. Breaking his promise, the Bear also warned Wimpy.

On April 5, Spike and another Winter Hill cohort drove to Roxbury to ambush Wimpy. A wheelman parked and waited, while
Spike hid behind the bushes in front of the Bennett house. When

Wimpy emerged, Spike fired two shots at him, but the forewarned Wimpy pulled out his own pistol and, on the run, started shooting. Hearing the shots, the driver pulled the car around to pick up Spike—but seeing Wimpy, armed, he drove on. Abandoned, Spike fled, ending up in the arms of the Boston police, who wanted to question him at headquarters (apparently, Wimpy filed a complaint). When the Bear and the Bennetts learned of Spike's arrest, they decided to kill him after his release. They stole an auto, drove that and a getaway car downtown, and parked them both in sight of the police department entrance. After waiting several hours, they realized Spike had already exited through an unseen door.

At 12:30 A.M., the Bear rushed into the Dog House and demanded to meet with Jerry. He blurted out the story and told Jerry of Wimpy's gratitude. But the fact that the Bear had shared the tip "incensed" Angiulo. The more Jimmy tried to explain, the "deeper he got with Jerry." Blabbing, the Bear admitted his friendship with a shady Boston police officer, and that Tommy Callahan and Leo Schwartz had asked him to kill Spike. After the Bear left the Dog House, someone asked Jerry about the brothers Flemmi.

"They aren't bad kids," Jerry said.

But Spike O'Toole didn't agree with Jerry about the Flemmis, and he had some stories to tell the Office. Trusting no one, Raymond told Larry Baione to talk to Spike—Larry obeyed, and arranged a meeting at the nightclub El Morocco, a second-story belly-dancing bar near the corner of Tremont and Stuart Streets. Larry signaled Jerry, who surreptitiously arrived a few hours after closing.

During the sit-down, Spike told Jerry that Wimpy was a stool pigeon—as proof, he claimed anytime Wimpy committed or conspired in a crime, the police knew about it immediately. Raymond later told Jerry he was particularly suspicious of Jimmy's relationship with the Boston cop. At some point, the Office contemplated hitting both Jimmy and Wimpy. But ultimately the don made no move on the Bear, who remained an intimate of the Office. Sort of.

Wimpy was another matter. The Bear even confided to Raymond, "I haven't made any money from him [Bennett], but I'll use him until O'Toole is knocked off. When that does happen, I'll get away from Bennett."

Worse for Wimpy's health, at some point, he began withholding payments to his football-card partner, Stevie. This was most unwise. One never knew when the Rifleman had his scope on one's back. The scheming Wimpy didn't seem worried, however—probably, he felt he could control Stevie just like he could his other underworld minions.

18

PRICE OF A LIFE

The sheer cheapness of underworld life disturbed even hardened criminals. Joe was a special object of the McLaughlins' hatred. Because of this, Joe barely avoided becoming "meat" on a number of occasions. In his poem, "Cat's Lives," he admitted many times "I've just missed death by a little bit." In crudely rhymed couplets, he recounted the various ways his enemies had tried to exterminate him. An armed Irish hood from Charlestown had once opened up on Joe, outside his apartment. Luckily for Joe, a fast duck let him escape the bullets. Another time, he found a wire attached to his spark plug—he saw that in time to avoid a bomb. A .45 bullet nearly got him, but didn't penetrate the door of the car he'd been inside. Then they'd tried to ambush him at a stoplight. Again, they failed.

The feud seemed to make nonaffiliated gangsters do even more violent and crazy things. Of course, there were the gruesome deaths of Francis Benjamin, Hannon, and Delaney. But in 1964, someone had also killed burglar William Treannie and, as if performing a mathematical exercise, divided his body into eight pieces. Life was so cheap that after an argument over nine dollars, someone shot Somerville mobster-loser Peter Cassetta in the head. The culprits then dumped him on a dirt road in Concord. The Bear, Joe, and Ronnie agreed this wasn't a "reasonable killing because of the amount involved, and that he, Cassetta, should only have been given a severe beating."

On the other hand, the Bear racked his brain for ways to kill Spike O'Toole. He thought of tapping the phone line of a friend of Spike's to help pick the best site for a hit. Then the Bear decided to snuff the ancient ex-bootlegger Sammy Lindenbaum, a white-collar German-Jewish ex-convict who oversaw a profitable betting business, with the Office's blessing. His gray hair, and five-feet, five-inch frame made him resemble anything but a gangster. However, Joe believed "he was very instrumental with regard to keeping them [the Townies] hidden" and getting them cash to rent cars and buy guns.

On May 3, Ronnie, Joe, and the Bear petitioned Raymond for approval to kill Sammy. While Raymond didn't agree to the act, Joe left the meeting convinced he was cleared. (Eventually Raymond ordered them to forget the murder.)

Later that day, Hill sympathizer Tommy Callahan warned the Bear that Spike and the McLaughlins would move that evening. After a telephone argument with Spike, the Bear returned to his apartment on Dorchester's Adams Street. The Bear ate supper every day at his home—a habit Stevie Flemmi had warned him to discontinue. The Bear called Joe, and at 10:30 P.M. left his apartment and headed to his car, oblivious to the two-man ambush behind the bushes in front of the apartment house. Too late, he saw them as they emerged, handkerchiefs over their faces: one fired a blast with a shotgun, the other, a .38. Wounded in the torso, the Bear collapsed and, turning as he fell, pulled a pistol and shot back. Still down, the shooters pumped eight double-ought and two .38 slugs in his stomach, chest, and side. Some bullets went wild, striking a parked car and breaking windows in the apartment building. The two shooters yelled, ran to the back of the building, and drove off. Wounded, Jimmy made Spike and Stevie Hughes as the shooters—and he figured Punchy was the wheelman. A local doctor hearing the Bear's cries treated him on the spot, and probably saved his life.

Later that night, the Flemmi babysitter told Joe, through her tears, about the shooting. Joe, Wimpy, and Stevie Flemmi raced to the hospital, where a detective announced, to Joe's relief, that Jimmy wasn't too badly off. An hour later, however, a doctor entered the waiting room to announce, "We don't know if he's going to live."

"What?" cried Joe, who by his own admission was now "insane." He kicked the wall, screeched obscenities, and shoved aside any would-be comforters. Fearing another bloodbath, the police arrested men from both sides of the McLaughlin-McLean divide and let them cool at headquarters. An hour later, Joe watched as the police brought in a visibly shaken Connie Hughes.

"I'm going to knock him off right here," Joe told Wimpy. Perhaps making his own calculated statement, Wimpy said he'd spoken to Connie ten minutes after the hit and so Connie couldn't have been a shooter—but he suspected Stevie Hughes was in on it.

"Jimmy is going to live," Joe told Connie. "I've an idea who was involved and I'm going to kill him." The Boston police kept the gangsters on ice for six hours before releasing them. They carefully escorted Connie out first.

Because he survived nine bullet wounds, one newspaper dubbed the twenty-nine-year-old maniac "Iron Man" Flemmi. Even the Bear's enemies were amazed. Nevertheless, the Bear was a ruin, as Joe saw firsthand during a hospital visit. Tubes ran out of his lungs, and an array of scars, flying in every direction, decorated his chest. Just under the skin, a wire net retained the Bear's innards, a doctor explained to Joe. Nevertheless, the Bear was arguing with Stevie Flemmi about a debt.

"You're all right, you bald-headed fuck, when you can start worrying about money," Joe said.

A vengeful Joe laid out plans to kill the Hughes brothers—quite a challenge, to say the least. For seven consecutive nights, Joe hid in the bushes near Connie's Malden house, but neither Hughes brother obliged him with an appearance. Before Joe could strike, he was arrested at the Ebb Tide and tossed in the Charles Street Jail. Fortuitously, he discovered that the terrified Anthony Statho-polous was in the cell next to his. Although Stath refused to emerge, he told Joe that Connie received a veteran's check on the first of every month, which he always cashed immediately. This was good info, indeed.

After F. Lee Bailey managed to lower Joe's bail, he left jail and dispatched Guy and Chico for an ambush. Joe instructed Chico to drive to Connie's bank at the North Shore Shopping Center. The two would-be killers watched Hughes emerge from the bank with his cash. Chico jumped out of the car and covered Guy's rear license plate with a rag.

Connie drove out of the parking lot and up the ramp to the Northeast Expressway to the Mystic River Bridge. Holding an M-1 rifle, Chico concealed himself by slouching in the rear seat of Guy's car, ready to fire through the open back window. Again and again, Chico told Guy to pull closer to Connie, to no avail. Suddenly, Connie took the Chelsea exit, but, noticing Guy's pursuit, instead of stopping there, sped across the center aisle and zoomed back up a ramp to the expressway. Before Connie's car vanished from sight, Chico fired, blowing out Hughes's back window but not striking flesh.

That night, Joe, with a carbine, lurked in a Chelsea alley near Havre Street. Someone passed by. "You'll leave with more than you came if you don't leave now, mister," Joe warned. After the man turned around and headed back down Havre Street, Joe realized it was Connie. Joe rounded up Chico and Patsy Fabiano and put them in one car to locate Connie, and took another car for himself, with a driver. Soon after, he saw Connie enter a car that backed down a one-way street. Joe's crew cut down Brooks Street and took a right on Chelsea Street. Just before they reached Marion Street, they spotted Connie's car emerging. In the back with Connie was Stevie Hughes.

Guns fired. Joe pointed the rifle out the window and jacked a shell into the chamber, but in his haste, it jammed. With bullets flying all around him, Joe told the driver, "Pass them while I clear the gun." Joe went by the Hughes' car, but by the time he was ready to shoot, the quarry had stopped and backed up again on Marion Street. The Hughes' car turned down a side street by a school and then disappeared. Joe noticed a bullet had cracked his vehicle's windshield, and a hole marked the center of the passenger door. A slug had penetrated armrest-deep, stopping inches from Joe's side.

No doubt about it, Joe was on the warpath. On May 10, Joe visited Raymond to discuss a pending murder. The intended target lived in a three-story house, and Joe told Raymond he'd pour gasoline in the victim's basement and set the edifice afire. The flames would guarantee the target choked or burned to death, or evacuated the house. For the third scenario, Joe would station three riflemen to wait outside to kill him as he emerged from a window or door. Joe planned to cut the telephone wires to prevent an assistance call. He'd even ring false alarms in other sections of the city to tie up available fire trucks. There was a catch, however, that Raymond discovered.

While the third-floor apartment was vacant, the man's mother lived in the first-story flat. "This apparently caused no concern to Barboza who stated it was not his fault that the mother would be present, and he would not care whether the mother died or not," as the FBI recorded. "Patriarca . . . attempted to dissuade Barboza from this type of killing as innocent people would probably be killed. It was not clear to the informant whether Barboza accepted

Patriarca's objections, but Patriarca indicated very strongly against this type of killing."

That was Joe's bad. Raymond disliked volatile "kids," and predicted Joe would become a liability. "He's a bum," the don declared once with Vinnie in earshot. "He's crazy. Someday, we'll have to whack him out." After all, Henry Tameleo had recruited Joe—not Raymond.

But Joe still had his uses—and one of them was Willie Marfeo. Joe claimed that during a telephone conversation, Henry said, "Come down Tuesday, George and I want to talk to you." Joe appeared at Atwells Avenue, and Raymond and Henry briefed him on Marfeo.

"We want this guy whacked out," Raymond said. Joe offered to remove Willie from the planet, on the house.

"Raymond, what did I tell you about this kid," said Henry, gesturing to Joe. "I told you he was a good kid."

For the hit, Raymond proposed Joe dress up like a meat-delivery man. Joe agreed, and asked to see Marfeo and to get a rundown of his haunts so he could case them. Henry gave him a tour of Willie's favorite bars; Joe selected a parking lot near Roman Gardens for the killing spot. But, just then, Henry was also playing hide-and-seek with an IRS agent (who eventually managed to arrest him). Citing too much heat, Raymond canceled the Marfeo contract. Joe obeyed.

Still in a murderous mood, Joe decided to kill Sammy Lindenbaum—this would cheer the Bear, and help him more than a blood transfusion, Joe claimed. Joe told Sammy to come by his East Boston corner at 2 P.M. so they could discuss the recent fire damage at Lindenbaum's Revere house. Sammy complied, bringing to Chiambi's his two small dogs, a Chihuahua and a mongrel. Joe and the elderly gangster spoke awhile, and then Lindenbaum agreed to take Joe to his house.

Joe's heart raced inside his tense body. "I was very somber having worked myself up to the point of killing Sammy," Joe recalled. Just then, the phone rang and Chico called Joe over to answer the call. It was Ronnie.

"Forget it and absolutely," Ronnie said. "Don't do anything. I'll explain when I get back."

Joe relaxed and, exhausted as he hung up, said, "Sammy, I have to leave right now because of that call. I'll see you later, buddy."

Raymond himself had vetoed Lindenbaum's killing, Ronnie told Joe. Raymond, however, declared that if Lindenbaum was in fact bankrolling the Hughes brothers, he'd go, too.

On June 8, Agent Rico entered the Bear's hospital room and listened to the gangster's woes. Jimmy was upset about his carelessness on the night of the ambush. "I won't be in any sort of condition until September," he said. "There's still some lead in me that can't be removed." He vented. While there were no broken bones, for six weeks he'd wear a bag to void into through an inserted drain. On the outside, the McLaughlins were waiting to finish him off.

"I heard Jimmy O'Toole plans to take a vacation when he gets out of jail," the Bear said. He mused to Rico, "My biggest regret is that I didn't kill George McLaughlin before he became [wanted] for murder." He'd wanted to strangle Georgie to death with his bare hands in the Dudley Lounge, but his brother Stevie told him to forget it. Rico gave the Bear money to pay for his family's apartment and car loan, but noted, "He declined to furnish a receipt."

Other visits and conversations followed. In one chat, the Bear said he wanted "the opportunity to meet O'Toole and personally settle their differences," Rico wrote. Jimmy said Spike "is a real nut" and it was only a matter of time before someone would catch up with him.

Hoover personally was following the metamorphosis of the

Bear into a rat. As a report noted on June 9, "Concerning the informant's emotional stability. . . . Although the informant will be difficult to contact once he is released from the hospital because he feels that [the McLaughlins] . . . will try to kill him, the informant's potential outweighs the risk involved." In his attempt to muzzle the Bear for Uncle Sam's circus, Rico would overlook the messy trail of bodies he'd left behind. Rico suspected the Bear had done in Benjamin, John Murray, Ashe, Francione, Deegan, Lowry, and the MCI Walpole inmate Garbiel. To deduce that the Bear would continue to kill didn't require a history degree.

Raymond had ordered Ronnie Cassesso to stick with Joe—although Joe couldn't stand his partner, Romeo Martin. While many thought they were best friends, Joe complained how Romeo made a "big deal" for once having chauffeured Raymond to a wedding. Like Joe, Romeo wanted to be a writer—he taught himself to type flawlessly and had even edited a prison newspaper. But his great claim to fame occurred while doing time for assault in 1951 in Walla Walla, Washington. While playing baseball outside the jail, he bolted at the end of the ninth inning. He was still wearing his gray-and-red-striped uniform. Boston police picked him up six months later and bounced him back west to finish his sentence. Romeo had a quick wit that was less than common among his associates.

Two days after killing Deegan, Romeo married a young hairdresser from Lynn—an event Ronnie Cassesso bankrolled. Subsequently, Ronnie set up jobs for them to take. Romeo also did "nickel and dime scores," whose takes were vended through one Farmer's Café. These crimes, Ronnie complained, brought too much heat, and with increasing urgency, he urged Romeo to repay the wedding loan.

In 1964 Romeo's downfall began in earnest. He and a partner kidnapped a wealthy Newton housewife and took her for over

$100,000 in cash and jewelry. Acting on a tip from Vinnie or another snitch, police arrested the culprits almost immediately. Romeo's sponsor, capo Joe Burns, sick of Romeo's bungling, cut him loose. Now Romeo was desperately in debt, and Ronnie was becoming furious. That summer, Romeo offered a score to the Office: someone was selling off a carnival with five major rides (and probably a betting and loan-sharking side business). This proposal somehow failed, and Romeo felt the suspense.

"Yes, he knew something was going to happen but you keep pushing it out of your mind," Romeo's wife said. Under pressure, Romeo had kept writing, even composing an autobiography, as well as poems, with lines such as, "Lo! Life, love and death are always one."

In fact, by July 1965, Romeo claimed he planned to visit Florida and then start some new kind of legitimate business. Romeo, as an ex-convict, had been a Boston police informer. Joe and Ronnie may have discovered this, or they might have feared he'd flip under all the heat. Late on July 8, Joe called Romeo for a meeting; Martin left just after midnight and picked someone up. Around 3 A.M., Joe and Romeo were driving in Romeo's car. Joe was probably at the wheel and Martin was in the front passenger's seat. As they headed down a steep hill on Harris Street in Revere, Joe (as he later privately boasted) produced a weapon.

Romeo managed to say, "You motherfucker, I knew you were going to do this to me." Then Joe shot him five times in a circle in the chest—not one bullet missed. Joe grabbed the brake, but the car went off the road and continued until it struck a hedge. Without bothering to shut off the engine, Joe left Romeo's body crumpled in the front seat. The headlights still glared out in the darkness, and the right directional light blinked.

The next day, Romeo's mother-in-law allowed reporters into his apartment. "He was a terrific guy," she said softly. "Please say something good about him," pleaded Romeo's widow.

At the Martin family's request, Joe was among the six pallbearers at Romeo's funeral at St. Leonard's Church. Joe even gave a large flowered wreath. Ronnie claimed he paid $1,000 for the funeral and wake. But the Saturday after the killing, Ronnie and Joe visited Raymond and explained why they had whacked Romeo. Raymond was pleased with how they carried it out. Subsequently, Raymond approached the operator of the Blue Bunny, which Romeo and Joe had been squeezing. Raymond demanded $5,000 from the Bunny as a reward for whacking Romeo, and thus ending his extortion attempts on the place, Joe said.

Romeo's demise didn't cause much grief among his former colleagues. Vinnie Teresa claimed he'd been golfing with Romeo the day before the murder. Romeo had left his clubs in Vinnie's trunk—he admitted he kept and used them for years. Joe never officially admitted he'd murdered Romeo, but did once reflect, "Whoever killed him did a good job."

The gang war was making many unaffiliated hoodlums nervous—such as Willie Fopiano, a thief who'd done time with Joe. After his parole, Willie learned Joe had killed Jack Francione as a favor to him. (After all, Francione had botched the robbery that had landed Willie in Walpole.) Now Willie, technically, owed Joe and Buddy. While acting as a pallbearer at Romeo's funeral, Joe saw Willie across the street. Joe bounded over and grabbed Willie's hand, saying, "You've been out six months and didn't come to see me." He invited him for a meet—warily, Fopiano accepted the offer. Soon after. While in the Ebb Tide, Joe seemed in a good mood, and bought Willie a drink.

As Willie took his glass, Joe said, "I took care of that favor." Joe eyeballed Willie, sizing him up, and said, "Buddy wants to see you."

Willie knew Buddy from the street and jail—and liked him, as most people did. But Willie also feared what Buddy and Joe were doing. There was no direct statement, such as, We want you with us in the war. First, they introduce a candidate to one of their friends—then another, and a third. By then, everyone thinks the candidate has taken a side. Willie decided enough meetings like that, and the McLaughlins would be around to see him, and not on a social call. Then he'd need Buddy and Joe for protection. But sooner or later, Willie knew he must see Buddy.

In mid-September 1965, an apprehensive Willie finally drove to a Winter Hill bar that functioned as Buddy's hangout and bunker. Willie came alone, aware of the jittery paranoia spreading like a winter flu through the underworld. Before Willie could park by the Hill bar, a big man stepped out in front of his car and frisked him. Then Buddy emerged from a side door and shook Willie's hand and smiled. Buddy appeared as outgoing and cheerful as always, but Willie sensed the war "had made him anxious, hard, and brutal."

After some small talk, Buddy dropped his bomb, saying, "Wasn't that nice of Joe to do that favor [the Francione murder] you asked for?"

"Buddy, I'd like to explain a few things before we go any further. Joe insisted he was going to do me a favor. He never told me what the favor was. If Joe told you otherwise, he's lying."

Buddy's smile vanished. "If you didn't know what the favor was, why didn't you let me know that in Norfolk?" Buddy became furious. "Well, now I know where you stand," Buddy warned. "This will be between you and Joe."

And that was how recruits were made.

19

TOWN WITHOUT PITY

"It is better to die on your feet, than to live on your knees, and know
  your concepts have been sound
Than to try to run, hide and scurry, out of fear, from the dirt, the earth
  and the ground."

—Joe Barboza, "Boston Gang War"

As the gang war continued, Buddy threw everything he could at the McLaughlins. As mentioned, he lined up soldiers, purportedly tried to procure grenades, and even a "typewriter" (a machine gun). An experiment using a potato as a pistol silencer left Buddy's face covered in goop; he consoled himself for the failure with a cocktail. Even the generally nonviolent bookmaker Howie Winter showed he was capable of strong-arm work. With a partner, he kidnapped a McLaughlin man, then gagged and stuffed him into a steamer trunk, which they loaded into a station wagon. Realizing a headlight was out, Howie pulled into a gas station to swap it before continuing on his nefarious way. "I mean, you don't want to get stopped for a [fucking] headlight out!" as he put it.

As a loyal McLean friend, Joe made the regular rounds at the Winter Hill fortress-bars, such as the Tap Royal. One day while there, Buddy discussed the gang war with Joe. As the McLaughlins' chief enforcers, Buddy wanted them dead perhaps as much as he did Punchy and Georgie. He'd conceived a General Sherman–like way to cripple his enemies: destroy their Shenandoah Valley, from which they received life-sustaining criminal resources. Buddy had warned a fence named "Brown" to stop aiding the Hughes brothers. Joe promised to enforce the warning.

"Don't let the Hughes brothers catch you flat-footed," Buddy warned.

Given his unpopularity, Joe traveled everywhere with Chico and Nicky acting as bodyguards. The trio would enter a place simultaneously, and the two enforcers would sit a distance away from Joe to eyeball any potential threats. For this task, the three arrived at Brown's, noting that advertisements blocked the front window, preventing anyone outside from seeing—or shooting accurately—inside.

He stepped through the door and saw Brown behind the counter, and he asked, "You do remember Buddy McLean grabbing you down at the Frolics, don't you?"

As he spoke, Joe thumped his coat pocket, which held a pistol, on the counter. Brown turned pale. Joe said, "That warning wasn't good enough, was it? 'Cause you're still fucking around with the Hugheses, selling their hot stuff and mailing them money."

"No, no," Brown stammered.

"This is your last warning. Do you read me?" Joe left and visited Buddy, who hugged him, surprisingly elated.

Soon after, Joe stopped his car at a red light near Brown's store, and was nearly ambushed. That night, someone fired three deer slugs through Brown's window. Then Joe began stalking Brown, whom he blamed for setting him up. Eventually, a terrified Brown emerged from hiding and offered the Hill information. Buddy told Joe to let the matter with Brown slide. "Okay, but I'll get that weasel later," Joe vowed.

Georgie McLaughlin's five months in Charles Street Jail had been especially unpleasant. For two months, Georgie had been forbidden to attend church or exercise outside. His sun-deprived skin was now convict-white, and he alone of all inmates was forced to wear striped prison clothes. Other prisoners and guards were forbidden to talk to him, and he received no magazines or papers.

"The treatment here for the past five months has been one of a convicted man," Georgie wrote to the state attorney general. "I have only been indicted."

The attorney general said, "I find nothing to indicate such treatment is inhumane."

As if in revenge, Punchy made himself an enormous nuisance to the authorities. Knowing the police constantly tailed him, once, from sheer cussedness, he—slowly—drove a hundred miles east until he arrived at Provincetown. Then, his police escort still tailing him, he turned around and drove back. No wonder: "He hadn't any confidence in the police since he was fifteen," said the Boston police commissioner, Edmund McNamara.

In June 1965, Raymond sent emissaries to Punchy telling him to stop the killings "as they are bringing too much heat" on everyone. Too late, Punchy said. An overture for a "peace settlement" arrived at the Hill from the Charlestown crew. Buddy reportedly turned it down. Shrewdly, Raymond concluded that only when the right man died would it "straighten itself out." He'd built a career on being decisive at the right moment; he also mistrusted the McLaughlins.

So, through a contact at a trucking firm, Raymond told Frankie Salemme that "George" wanted to see him. Frankie had an almost mystical respect for Raymond—after all, as he said: "The head of a mafia family is considered a king." After Frankie arrived in Providence, Raymond, indirectly, explained he was backing Buddy and the Hill against Charlestown. Although initially lukewarm, after the Bear's near assassination, Frankie and Stevie were fully committed to fight the McLaughlins. But Frankie knew Larry Baione was loyal to Stevie Hughes—and given his treacherous ways, might even frustrate the Office's policy. Frankie pointed out that Larry had even asked Raymond for permission to intervene in the war.

"Don't worry about that, you know," Raymond said. "All the help you need you've got with us. Don't worry about Larry." After the meeting concluded, Frankie didn't know if Larry knew of Raymond's commission. But Frankie did know that Raymond had approved a hit on Punchy McLaughlin.

On Monday, August 16, 1965, Punchy arose early to make his customary visit to downtown Canton to buy newspapers. He was certain his enemies were, as usual, watching him. Around noon, he drove his 1965 Oldsmobile toward a West Roxbury auto dealership to make a car payment. On Dedham Street, Punchy noticed a beach wagon tailing him. Hitting his brakes, he observed a man inside the wagon carried a walkie-talkie. Punchy decided to drive to the more public and safer Route 1A. For a shortcut, Punchy turned onto Downey Street, which skirted the Norfolk Golf Club.

Only later did Punchy realize the beach wagon was in contact with men in the woods near the golf course. Stevie Flemmi, armed with his rifle, perched in a tree waiting to shoot Punchy down. Wimpy, who'd been tailing Punchy, now pulled ahead of him to mark his car as the target. Then an auto pulled near Punchy and a semiautomatic rifle's noisy pops broke the relative quiet of the fairway. The first bullet shattered Punchy's windshield, severed an artery, and nearly lopped off his right hand. The weapon (or weapons), most likely an M-1 rifle, fired as many as thirty bullets, half of which penetrated the as-yet-unpaid-for Oldsmobile. Stevie claimed he got off seven rounds from his carbine before the weapon jammed.

"Bleeding like the devil," Punchy drove left-handed. Plunging over the golf course, he finally made an exit ramp, which he used as an on-ramp to Route 128. Racing north on the southbound lane, he barely avoided collision with the oncoming cars. A quarter mile down the road, he took the next exit ramp onto Route 1 south (the Providence Highway) and pulled into an Atlantic gas station.

Five minutes later, a Norwood Hospital ambulance medic found Punchy on the floor, conscious, a tourniquet on his arm. He didn't see his attackers, he claimed, adding: "And I don't know why they should want to kill me." The Norwood police chief posted guards on every hospital entrance. Punchy later admitted the chief "was very nice to me," but admitted he was "getting fed up" with the attacks and was in "constant fear." That afternoon, doctors ordered Punchy's transfer to Mass General Hospital in a private ambulance, guarded by a shotgun-wielding police chief and sergeant. That evening, lying in his bed, Punchy claimed he had nightmares about the "next time." Punchy awoke the next morning and discovered his hand was gone. "I wasn't surprised," he said. A photographer snapped his picture: the sad and weary Edward McLaughlin was looking all his years and then some, in his hospital bed.

This was another embarrassment. A Somerville policeman left a bunch of carrots at the Winter Hill Café to improve the gang's eyesight. Frankie admitted the high-power rifle bullets fired at Punchy had ricocheted and caused collateral damage in "rural areas." Rico showed up at Frankie's garage, newspaper in hand, complaining, "What a sloppy piece of work that was, other people could have been hurt."

"Paul, I don't have his address," Frankie said in the back-and-forth with Rico. "He's a tough guy to pin down. I don't know where his starting point is."

Even as the gang wars ground on, Joe and his associates spun ever further out of control. The Bear, against doctor's orders, left the hospital and, with Johnny Martorano, drove to a cabin in Vermont. The car they drove in was equipped, unwisely, both with weapons and alcohol. Hoping to bag a deer at night, the drunken duo opened fire at a pair of eyes staring from the roadside. Soon, they discovered they'd emptied a revolver and a carbine into a cow. The carcass couldn't be strapped to the car, either, as Johnny recounted. Their Vermont host told them not to discuss the shooting, since, in those parts, they'd get "more time for shooting a cow than shooting a human."

By August 23, the Bear was back in Boston. Presumably still recovering his strength, he ended an argument with twenty-two-year-old John Cutliffe by shooting him in the stomach. The Bear was arrested; after making bail, on September 3 he went "on the lam," or to be more precise, became a "lamster." Rico and Condon closed him out as an informant.

At some point, Joe knocked over a Roxbury crap game—unaware that Jerry owned a piece of it. On learning Joe was the robber, Jerry called for him to pay the ultimate penalty. However, Henry the Banker successfully "interceded" for the Animal and he survived, as an informant relayed to the FBI. But this incident may have inspired Stevie Flemmi to summon Joe to an urgent meeting at Walter's Lounge (just after the Bear became a lamster).

With two henchmen, Joe complied. "This is red hot," said Stevie during their discussion. Claiming he'd bugged Angiulo's phone, Stevie said, "I heard Jerry say he was going to have you killed no matter what it cost. Also, we found out that Jerry met with the Hughes brothers down in Haymarket Square. . . ."

Joe thanked Stevie, pumped his hand hard, and met with Henry Tameleo at the Tiger Tail Lounge.

"Don't mistake these tears in my eyes for fear because they're not," Joe told Henry.

"Calm down and tell me what's bothering you."

"Jerry Angiulo is plotting to kill me." He gave a brief explainer.

"Jerry couldn't plan a hit without Raymond's say-so," Henry said, "and if Raymond knows it then I'd know it. If Jerry does a hit without Raymond's okay, Jerry dies. . . . I'd use four favors Raymond owes me to stop a move on you, Joe."

"What am I going to do? I don't want to upset no applecart but I can't let Jerry send somebody after me."

"I'll speak to Raymond tomorrow and we'll track all this down. . . . I'll be glad when this war is over. You should have taken the jobs Raymond and I offered you in Vegas to get you out of this."

Joe didn't disbelieve Henry, exactly, but at 10 A.M. the next day, Buddy convened a meeting of capable and proven gangsters in a private room in a Somerville bar. He wanted to discover if Joe was on "the Hit Parade," as an informant (most likely Stevie) explained. Naturally, Joe was there, but absent was the Bear, in hiding, if not hibernation.

Buddy proclaimed, "I want everybody here to know that I'm sending word to Raymond that Joe is my partner. If anybody tries to kill him, I'll try with my life to stop it, and if he dies, I'll avenge his death."

Joe said he "considered this a statement by a man among men; a man who valued human friendship more than life itself." Everyone agreed with Buddy, at least to his face, and together they drafted a statement of support for Joe, with seventy-five signatures for Raymond. The group nominated Ronnie Cassesso to deliver the message. But Ronnie so garbled it that Buddy had to use a back channel with the Office. Buddy later threatened to blow Ronnie's head off. Eventually, Winter Hill and associates concluded the rumor of Joe's hit was a mischief-causing falsehood. In any case, Raymond didn't want to "tangle with Buddy McLean in any shape, manner or form," Joe claimed.

Later, Joe's own private "cuckoo," Jimmy Flemmi, called Larry Baione.

The Bear said, "Listen, only two people mean anything to me and they are Stevie and Joe Barboza."

"There's too many of us for you, Jimmy," Larry said.

"Yeah, Larry, but I promise you this—before I get it, nine of you will be dead and you might be in the bunch."

At some point, Joe confronted Jerry, and the two prima donnas resolved their mutual hate, said the Rifleman. Joe even borrowed a mortgage down payment from Jerry. Stevie never admitted to Jerry he'd warned Joe about the hit—which apparently had never left the planning stage, anyway.

Naturally, Joe—like the Bear and Mount Vesuvius—was always ready to explode. On Friday, September 10, Henry parked his Cadillac outside the Ebb Tide. Like a hunter in pursuit, Detective Joe McCain, of the Metropolitan District Commission, pulled to the curb behind the Caddy. Then Joe appeared from the two-hundred-strong crowd, followed by his gang. Joe removed his jacket, handed it to Nicky, and blocked McCain's door.

"Look who's here," said Joe. "If I ever do time again, I'll take out on your brother what I shoulda taken out on you, you mother-fucker." (McCain's brother had served time in Walpole for robbery.) McCain kicked the door open and the two brawled on the sidewalk. McCain took a foot to the head, then unsheathed his service revolver and placed it in Joe's mouth up to the teeth. Joe surrendered, but when Nicky Femia handed Joe's jacket to Chico, a .38 fell out.

This was a prize of sorts. McCain took Joe, in cuffs, to the grand-looking Revere Beach MDC station. Clearly the loser of the fight, Joe planned to charge McCain with assault and battery and excessive force. To counter this, one of McCain's partners bashed his forehead with a phone so he'd really look as if he'd been in a donny-brook. Now the MDC had Joe cold: he was indicted with assault on a policeman, possession of a firearm, disturbing the peace, and possession of marijuana. Joe felt them laughing at him.

A mischievous Wimpy told Spike O'Toole that Winter Hill sympathizer and old-school tough guy Tommy Callahan (Ballou's friend) and a third crook had put up $10,000 for the failed hit on Punchy. Soon after, armed with a silencer, Spike shot and nearly killed Callahan. Raymond admitted he respected Callahan as a man, and the attacker's use of a silencer pointed to Wimpy. Callahan mistrusted Wimpy, who was famous for offering different people varied versions of the same facts. So far, Raymond had let Bennett's snitching alone. However, in a meeting, Raymond recounted how, after Spike had ambushed Wimpy, he'd called the Boston police, left a message with a detective, and even filled out a complaint form.

"This is the last straw," Raymond concluded. "Anyone who'd call the police to help them must be a stool pigeon." Raymond loathed informants, and ordered an investigation into the Callahan hit.

20

THE McLAUGHLINS' LAST STAND

"Boom, boom and out."

—Frankie Salemme

Punchy's repeated dodging of the grim reaper's scythe suggested to some that his life was charmed. Neither Joe nor Buddy McLean bought that. Punchy himself appeared to be in accord with his enemies on this point. Punchy knew the Hill was still after him. "No, I'm not afraid," he told a newspaper reporter just before his discharge from the hospital. "I only hope there isn't anyone with me who might get hurt because those guys don't care who gets hit along with me." He said most gunmen were "loaded with goofballs," that there was big traffic in the pills and "don't think there isn't." Sitting on his bed, he recounted the loss of his hand as dispassionately as if he were "discussing the fender of a car," the reporter noted.

His Irish social delicacy provoked a mention of his family. "When they talk about the McLaughlins, they talk about Bernie getting murdered in 1961. They talk of me and Georgie. Always the bad things are talked about. You never hear about the other two brothers who were killed in the service."

Discharged, Punchy returned to hiding in Canton. Soon after, under an armed guard, Punchy visited a prosthetics firm, where nervous employees fitted him with an artificial hand. He then enlisted a police chief to drive him to a Norwood agent to pay the premium on a life insurance policy. Impromptu visits were out of the question at Suffolk County Jail, so Georgie and Eddie McLaughlin Sr. never shared a final good-bye.

Georgie's trial began in the fall of 1965. The pint-sized killer shared the docket with not just a criminal friend (Spike O'Toole), but two young housewives (with children). Georgie entered Suffolk Superior Court, his sun-deprived face noticeably pale, and sat in the right side of the defendants' box. Spike took the left side, sandwiching the women in the middle. The defendants fielded four lawyers, each more obnoxious than the next, and the fifteen-day trial became an unruly circus that threatened to disintegrate.

Punchy, minus his right hand, in a show of solidarity, became a regular attendee. "There's safety in numbers," he said. "I am not hiding." However, Punchy always varied his exact path of ascent to the courthouse's heavily guarded eighth floor. He relaxed a bit, and told reporters, "I feel fine, considering I don't have the use of my right hand." He said, "I don't carry a gun. If I had had a gun with me in Brookline in November I could easily have killed the man who tried to take me out." He said he would ensure Georgie "was getting a fair shake and from what I can see, he's getting a fair trial. It was a bum rap to begin with."

During the trial, the ever-scheming Rico visited Frankie's garage and mentioned Georgie's witnesses. "You know, it would be nice if these girls didn't show up, if somebody could talk to these girls and not have them show for Georgie."

After Rico left, Frankie told Stevie, "No way. We hope this little clown comes out. You don't want to get involved."

Naturally, Frankie wanted to finish the job on Punchy—whom he knew visited Suffolk Superior Court at a fixed time daily. But, as he said, "It's tough to walk up to a guy and snuff him right there, I mean, that's too much." Allegedly he and Stevie even played with a mock bomb at Howie Winter's Marshall Street garage—when they turned the ignition, everyone inside dropped for cover, not realizing it was a dry run. In any case, Frankie preferred a pistol and silencer to do the killing—followed by a burial in a secret spot.

He wasn't alone in that mind-set. As Georgie's trial ground on, Rico visited Frankie at his garage for a chat. When leaving, as usual, Rico patted Frankie's shoulder—but this time, he also hit Frankie's hand and kept walking. Frankie looked down, opened his fingers, and saw a piece of paper with an address. It was that of Helen Kronis, Punchy's girlfriend in Stoughton.

At 314 Spring Street in West Roxbury, the MBTA maintained a bus terminal. There, at a spot adjacent to the Veterans Administration hospital, a bus stopped, picked up passengers, and reversed direction to return to the grand old Forest Hills station. During one Friday in mid-October, schoolchildren and other locals noted a gold-colored car in the vicinity of the bus stop. A crew-cut man wearing sunglasses repeatedly walked from the car to the MBTA parking lot, wandered there, and retraced his path. A resident watched as this man trespassed through his backyard and peered in and out of his driveway. "He was an odd-looking guy," said the local. "I thought he might be a Puerto Rican." The next day, this swarthy intruder was there to repeat his performance—then abruptly, he disappeared and took Sunday off.

On October 19, Rico visited Stevie and let him know Punchy would be getting a ride to the bus station the next day. Rico planned to be golfing, and even pretended to swing a club. On the twentieth, while in his bookstore, Stevie donned a business suit, which would serve as a costume for a major performance. His girlfriend even made up his face.

That same day, as she had for the past week, Helen Kronis stopped her vehicle on Spring Street in front of a luncheonette. As usual, Punchy emerged from the car, his topcoat draped over his right hand—in his left hand, he carried a paper bag that concealed a pistol. Kronis then drove to her job at the Sylvania plant on the VFW Parkway. Punchy bought a newspaper and crossed the street to be the first commuter in line to await the bus.

At 7:45, a swarthy, crew-cut Stevie Flemmi, eyes hidden behind sunglasses, emerged from a backyard and entered the station parking lot. From his high vantage point, the bus driver looked down on Punchy, opened the bus door, and stood up to collect the fares. Before he could take a cent, he saw Stevie emerge, as if out of nowhere, from Spring Street. In his pocket, covered in a newspaper, Stevie packed a long-barreled .38 Webley and silencer. His eyes locked with Punchy's briefly before he got behind him and produced his weapon. Stevie pointed the tip at Punchy, who'd planted his right foot on the first of the two steps leading into the bus. At near point-blank range, Stevie opened fire. After two bullets penetrated his neck, Punchy ran for it, but only managed a stagger before collapsing onto the macadam. Stevie, standing only a few feet away, calmly fired four more times, distributing bullets into Punchy's legs, arms, and torso; bullets pierced his heart, lungs, spleen, liver, and intestines. So much lead flew, the bus even took two hits, making the driver on board instinctively duck.

Noting some bystanders were ready to intervene, Stevie just waved his weapon and said, "Uh-uh." The killing job concluded—beyond question at last—the gunman ran by his prearranged route. As Frankie put it, the killing was "boom, boom and out." Stevie passed through the parking lot, then the backyard that divided two houses, and reached a parked 1965 gold-colored Pontiac hardtop convertible sedan. After he stepped inside the Pontiac, the car sped down Billings Street and took a right before anyone could read the plate.

A crowd gathered around the fatally stricken Punchy. One woman drew close as Punchy uttered what sounded like a nickname, and he handed her his brown paper bag. "Get rid of it," he said. Excited, she took it, thinking it held a lunch. To her surprise, it enfolded not a sandwich and apple, but a stolen .38 Colt Detective Special revolver, serial number 713950, loaded with five bullets.

The police took Punchy to nearby Faulkner Hospital, where at 8:15 A.M., the doctors found no blood pressure or pulse; only a faint and diminishing heartbeat betrayed the fact that he lived. Punchy's physicians said his grim state appeared the work of a machine gun. From chest to toes, there were at least twelve punctures: "You can't count them—they're all over his body," noted a hospital spokesman.

Punchy gave up the ghost. Georgie heard the news before trial began for the day. His eyes watered, but he accepted no comfort from the court officers. Later, Georgie said, "One-two-three, the ball game's over." By the time he was escorted into the courtroom at 10:20, the diminutive gangster looked as relaxed and expressionless as ever and remained so through the day.

"The Assignment has been completed," Wimpy said, noting he was leaving for a few days. The next time Rico saw Stevie, he said, "Good shooting." Stevie met with Buddy at Pal Joey's in Somerville. Buddy claimed Rico had supplied him with the name and number of a boy who'd witnessed the shooting, up close. Buddy called the boy's father and explained the shooting was a private matter, "and nothing to do with you." Stevie noticed Buddy was drinking heavily, and warned him he might be hit leaving one of these Broadway bars. The Rifleman looked across Broadway at the abandoned Capitol Theater entrance; he thought it would be an ideal place to ambush Buddy.

As usual, the Bear made the most of this event. Soon after, he visited Jerry and announced he was the gunman who'd killed Punchy. While Jerry knew better and most likely thought the Bear a fool, he paid out $500 anyway.

Punchy's estranged (and now terrified) wife Eleanor returned to Boston from Prince Edward Island. She was due in court that very week to finalize her divorce with Punchy. To a reporter, crying, she recalled Punchy and "the good years we had together." On the twenty-third, she attended, with her son and sisters-in-law, the private service at a Canton funeral home—Georgie was absent, because of security.

A curate spoke to reporters who'd squeaked into the church for the funeral. "I do not know what kind of man Mr. McLaughlin was," said the curate. "But he certainly was good to young Eddie [Jr.]. He deserves that much credit; he made sure his son was brought up a good Catholic." Eddie was a "credit to his school," and "one of the nicest boys in the parish. . . ."

Soon after, Edward McLaughlin Sr., age forty-eight, gangland victim number 26 (or so), joined his parents and three brothers in the Holy Cross Cemetery in Malden.

Georgie's trial proceeded as messily as ever. The farce largely ceased after the prosecution unveiled a reasonably infallible murder eyewitness, ex-marine Herbert Josselyn. A desperate Georgie took the stand and said, "I had a brother killed coming to his trial. I tell you that the shot that killed Sheridan was the shot meant for me."

On October 26, with fifty policemen on guard, at 3:30 P.M., the eleven men and single woman of the jury filed out of the courtroom to deliberate. Except for his ten-strong police bodyguard nearby, Georgie resembled a common pale-faced, middle-aged businessman, arrayed in a blue suit, tie, and white shirt. He looked at nothing in particular, until, at 10:40 P.M., the officers returned the charts, guns, and other evidence from the jury room to the court. Just before 11 P.M., the jurors, eyes looking down to the floor, marched in to complete the ritual. Georgie cast a glance at the jury, but no one returned the look. The verdict was clear. "Guilty" whispers flitted through the courtroom.

The foreman announced: "We find George McLaughlin guilty of first-degree murder." Resembling "a paunchy and frightened choirboy," Georgie continued to stare straight ahead, although his face whitened even more than usual. Standing near him, Maureen Dellamano's face flushed, and Georgie touched her arm and clasped her hand.

"Is there any reason why the death penalty should not be imposed?" the judge asked Georgie.

"I have no comment," mumbled Georgie. The judge announced immediately he should "suffer punishment by death."

The underworld was shaking up fast. The Hill and its allies knew that creating just a few more choice bodies would end the war utterly. "Things were shaping up at last," Joe noted.

21

A CITY ALMOST STILLED

"What greater deed can a man do than to lay down his life for his friends / Winter Hill tells the tale of a strong Irish gale who was loyal and pure and was true"

—"The Ballad of Buddy McLean"

A small feud with Charlestown had elevated Buddy into something of a folk hero—to the degree a truck-driving gangster could be. Even straight citizens who were not from Somerville discussed him at cocktail parties. In the underworld, he was a god for aspiring felons. "When you want the other guys to think you really are 'in,' you claim to know Buddy McLean," wrote one reporter.

In the last week of October 1965, police noted Buddy was uncharacteristically shy. Given his brazen fearlessness, he'd never stayed out of the public eye before. But Stevie Hughes had lately appeared twice around Winter Hill. Buddy knew he was "living on borrowed time," as Somerville's police chief put it. To borrow anything in that world also required paying the vig, too.

On October 31, Joe placed an overdue call to Buddy at the Tap Royal. He asked for "Seagull," the code word the two gang leaders used when calling each other.

Joe said he was getting some good information on the "Fat Guy," meaning Stevie Hughes. Buddy said, "I wish you'd come up, you ugly Portugee. I miss you." Ending the chat, McLean warned, "Be careful and keep your right hand high, Seagull."

That night, after taking his kids trick-or-treating, Buddy went out. He parked his car—registered to someone else—on Broadway, with the headlights aimed back at the rising hump of Winter Hill. Near the car loomed the empty Capitol Theater. Its supporting ribs protruded, and the paint was peeling.

Americo "Rico" Sacramone and Anthony "Tony Blue" D'Agostino joined Buddy, and they went looking for someone— almost certainly Hughes. During the night's sojourn, Buddy visited Casey's bar, where his appearance provoked conversation. He then moved on to the Winter Hill Lounge for a nightcap, where a patrolman Kiley was on detail. It was almost midnight when Somerville patrolman Red Bavin, walking his beat, sounded his duty call from the street. Then he entered the Winter Hill Lounge for a routine check and to eject the patrons. "It's time to leave," he announced.

As the Hill crew moved to the door, Buddy, although carrying a .38 tucked inside his belt, nevertheless approached Kiley. He shined his badge and said, "That's for good luck." The trio left the lounge and crossed Broadway. Watching them from the lobby of the Capitol Theater was a single patron, draped in a black trench coat and wearing a stocking over his head. He carried a new automatic shotgun bought from Sears and watched as Buddy and Sacramone walked to one side of the vehicle. D'Agostino got on the car's other side—none of the three noticed their stalker, until it was too late. (The Rifleman had, at least, given Buddy a warning about bars, Winter Hill, and assassins.)

It was perhaps 1:10 A.M. when Officer Bavin looked out the lounge window and noticed someone "lurking" in the shadows of the theater lobby across the street. The man stepped out, lifted his weapon, and ran at Buddy and his companions, sixty feet away. Bavin drew his revolver and raced out the door just as the gunman opened fire. In an amazing and athletic feat, without once pausing, the shooter caught both Buddy and Sacramone in the head, and D'Agostino, on the other side of the car, in the arm. They all crumpled help-lessly to the street.

The assassin ejected the last shell unfired and ran back into the theater. He flew through the lobby and out back over the rubble piles, dropping the gun and the stocking. He worked his way through a maze of backyards, losing Bavin, and reached Sewall Street. There the gunman—almost certainly Stevie Hughes—jumped into a getaway car, which drove off into the night. For a few dollars' worth of bullets, the shooter had nearly torn Buddy's uncommonly handsome head in two, and just missed killing his bodyguards. D'Agostino's arm shattered when it caught a slug headed, intentionally or not, directly at his heart. Joe claimed the Hughes brothers celebrated by getting drunk—they also were marking the anniversary of Bernie McLaughlin's murder.

Ambulances descended on Broadway, and the wounded were loaded inside for transportation. A phone call awoke Howie Win-ter, and learning of the assault, he drove over to the theater, found it overrun with police, and didn't stop.

At 3 A.M., Joe was in the crowded West End Social Club, ne-gotiating a loan from proprietor Peter Limone.

Then someone announced, "Buddy McLean got shot tonight."

Thinking it was a joke, Joe smiled, and denied it was true. "I was just talking to Buddy tonight," he said. Realizing this wasn't a jest, Joe froze, stomped out of the club, and began to inquire about one of the few people he ever had something good to say about.

Under police guard, an unconscious Buddy lingered in a room in Mass General Hospital. His doctors predicted that if he sur-vived, he'd be a "vegetable." At 10:30 A.M. the next day, his body overtook his mind, which had already passed on elsewhere. He was thirty-five, and "the last of the tough guys," said the Somer-ville police chief.

"A man was dead," Joe noted.

This was strategy. Reputedly, Stevie Hughes had once said: "What good are a tribe of Indians without a chief." Joe was probably next on the McLaughlin hit parade. On November 2, the McLeans held Buddy's wake in a rose-filled room in Kelliher's Funeral Home at 67 Broadway. The casket was closed, for obvious reasons, but a large framed photo of Buddy stood on top of the lid. Buddy's wife and son managed a dry-eyed and brave front, and greeted everyone who passed by the coffin. Joe visited the Hill that afternoon, and returned at 9 A.M. on November 4 for the funeral and Solemn High Mass of Requiem. It was a low-key, working-class ritual, with Howie Winter acting as one of the pallbearers.

"I wonder which one will get it next," queried one Somerville resident, in earshot of a reporter.

When Buddy's funeral mass concluded, the cortege drove on to nearby Holy Cross Cemetery in Malden. There the remains of Buddy, Bernie, and Punchy would reside together—closer in death than the living men had been in life. A newspaper columnist noted, "Mention a McLaughlin and someone will mention McLean, even if he is in Ethiopia."

The Hill shot back on November 13, when someone let loose a fusillade of bullets on McLaughlin ally Maxie Shackleford, as he drove a car. One slug nailed him in the arm and sent him to Mass General Hospital for stitches. On Wednesday the twenty-fourth, when Shackleford, wanted for illegal procurement of weapons, returned to the hospital, the police moved on him. The arresting patrolmen found Maxie had a six-foot, eight-inch bodyguard with a City of Taunton patrolman's badge, uniform, and service revolver. A Shackleford family friend, at thirty-six, he was an eight-year police veteran, there to keep Maxie "from getting hurt." Shackleford remained in custody with a $50,000 bail, as a fugitive from justice from New Hampshire.

———

Death had permanently yanked from the stage many major underworld players in short order. Others were all but in jail. In Lyndon Johnson fashion, Howie Winter had taken over the Hill on the fly. Given their loyalty through the feud, various associates, including Joe Barboza, the Martorano brothers, Johnny and Jimmy, Frankie Salemme, and Stevie Flemmi were in the Hill's good graces. Howie had a special fondness for the Rifleman. "I thought the world of Stevie Flemmi," Howie later said. "He was a man's man."

But the police kept all the rising stars of the new murky criminal sky under twenty-four-hour surveillance. The law struck at Joe first, when on November 29 he appeared in court to answer for his September mayhem. The prosecution argued, not unreasonably, that Joe was safer in jail than in public. Assistant District Attorney Jack Zalkind noted there had been three attempts to kill Joe in two months, and "he may not appear for trial because he will be dead." In response, the judge raised Joe's bail from $25,000 to $100,000. Joe then turned to attorney F. Lee Bailey, and the two would, over time, form what is perhaps the oddest legal pair in the state's history.

Bailey already knew Joe's "fearsome" reputation, but as a favor to Howie and Wimpy, agreed to represent him. Subsequently, the three gangsters appeared in the attorney's office. Bailey, like many others, immediately disliked Joe, telling him, "Take your hat off."

The ever-volatile Animal exploded, wanting to know why Bailey hadn't asked Wimpy to remove his hat. In response, Bailey's hand went into his desk drawer, where he kept a .38 caliber pistol at the ready for just such an unruly client.

"Wimpy is bald," said Bailey. "He can keep his hat on. Take yours off or get out."

Joe initially opted for the latter—but soon returned, at Bailey's request. "If you don't defend me, I'll go to jail," Joe said, crying—perhaps mostly for effect.

Suffering his own delusions of grandeur, Joe considered Bailey a "super egomaniac" whose superior attitude grated on him. Joe later claimed that he banged his hand on the attorney's desk, and said he "wasn't one of the robots in his office." After that, "we got along better."

Although Bailey concluded Joe wasn't much of a tough guy, he represented him, anyway. After he appealed, a judge reduced Joe's bond to $35,000, easily made.

That November, after his apprehension, the Bear was convicted of armed assault with intent to murder, and sent to Walpole. The FBI now tried in earnest to turn his brother Stevie. As a November 3 report noted, "Although the LCN [La Costra Nostra] in this area has not actively taken part in this gang war, there is every possibility that they may move into the picture in the near future. . . . It is felt that [Stevie] Flemmi will be in a position to furnish information on LCN members in this area."

Like a padrone in the mob, Rico wanted to make Stevie an important associate in His Thing, which wasn't precisely the FBI's Thing. Rico was shrewd and his sense of loyalty and duty was proportionate to anybody or anything that could promote his causes—rather like Stevie himself. Both men lived in what, to everyday people, were strange, isolated worlds that had their own odd codes of ethics. Both were willing to break those rules.

Given their upbringing in and around Roxbury, Stevie and Frankie were already tight with Larry Baione. Larry was still ready to jump into the gang war, according to Stevie. Larry even pumped $5,000 into the Hughes brothers' organization to keep it afloat. Unlike Frankie, who fawned over the Office, Stevie was prone to see it as a friend when useful, an enemy when not, and an useful sucker as the opportunity arose. Rico knew how to exploit Stevie's resentment of the Mafia. For starters, he made a "sacred" promise of silence about the Rifleman's informant status outside the FBI. Even in the agency, few ever knew about their dealings. And Rico was quite generous—when Stevie confessed he'd inflicted a hundred-stitch beating on a loan-shark victim, Rico ignored it. He'd overlook much worse to get at the Office.

22

THE HAT TRICK

"If it's bad business, it's everybody's business."

—Raymond Patriarca

Robert Palladino, age thirty-two, was a sad-faced "small-time hoodlum" facing a dead-end career, as well as death itself. He'd one feat of note to his credit. Reportedly, on November 3, 1960, while dressed as a priest, he kidnapped bookmaker Abe Sarkis's wife and children in their home. He threatened to burn them unless Sarkis opened his trap (secret valuables cache). Not surprisingly, Sarkis's family resigned itself to death—but Palladino found enough money to make it worth his while to release everyone.

Never rising above the criminal bottom, in 1965, Palladino appeared before a grand jury to talk about his onetime girlfriend, the late Margaret Sylvester. In 1964, she'd been murdered in Luigi's bar—then the property of one Andy Martorano, the father of Johnny and Jimmy Martorano. Someone in the Martorano circle had killed the woman, possibly for personal reasons. Then, apparently, the Bear had begun to dispose of Sylvester in an attic, before the police, acting on a tip, swooped down and discovered the body.

Now investigators were squeezing Palladino, and John Jackson, the bartender at Luigi's the night of the killing. In response, Wimpy and Stevie Flemmi pulled Johnny Martorano into the back of Stevie's grocery store at Dearborn and Dudley Streets in Roxbury. "Palladino and Jackson," Wimpy said.

"They're saying bad things," Stevie chimed in. Johnny Martorano realized Palladino and Jackson might implicate his younger brother Jimmy. He considered intervention an elder Sicilian son's "obligation." For just such a mission of this knight-errant, one of Johnny's lady friends had loaned him an emerald green Cadillac El Dorado with white leather seats. By Johnny's own admission, this was a conveyance appropriate for a pimp—but it served to take him and a companion to one of Palladino's hangouts.

The target was unruly the night of November 14, 1965, claimed an informer. Palladino argued with a North End loan shark, and even swung at this Mafioso, who prophetically announced, "You are dead."

Johnny corralled Palladino into his El Dorado to confront him. At that point, Palladino drew a gun and fired at Johnny's partner. Johnny claimed he then drew his own weapon and fired it at point-blank range, ending Palladino's short and unpleasant life. The killing was unplanned, and so was the disposal of the body. Johnny drove to the corner of the Beverly Street and Causeway Street exit ramp near North Station and dumped Palladino's earthly remains. No one was there at this time of the morning—except perhaps those dumping stiffs.

Palladino became memorable for two things—one, his body made a famous photograph in a national magazine. Two, he was the first of Johnny Martorano's official twenty or so victims. After Palladino, killing became easier for Johnny Martorano. "Well, it's sort of like a lawyer trying his first case," he said. "It's difficult but the next case is easier."

The morning Johnny dumped Palladino's body, a group of at least five men—almost certainly including the Bear and Joe—drove to

a Medford residential neighborhood looking for a Raymond Di-
Stasio. This DiStasio was the husband of one woman, father to
four children, and bartender to any and all who entered the
Mickey Mouse Lounge in Revere. He also was an insider to the
gang war and "very friendly" with the McLaughlins. DiStasio even
helped Punchy hunt for Buddy in the summer of 1964, Joe claimed.
Worse, DiStasio had once been on duty while Joe was in the Mouse.
After Joe left, someone fired three shots at him. Immediately, Joe
suspected DiStasio had set him up.

Today, believing it was DiStasio's day off, Joe's crew waited in
the schoolyard next door to his house, planning to shoot him
when he stepped into his car. After realizing DiStasio had already
left, the men reentered their car and drove to Revere.

In Revere, sometime after 4 P.M., New Hampshire native John
O'Neil left the cold behind and entered the Mickey Mouse
Lounge for cigarettes. A young husband and father, O'Neil had
recently rented an apartment on Revere Beach, perhaps a hundred
yards from the Mickey Mouse, and began frequenting the establishment. He wanted to become a salesman in the factory where he
worked. O'Neil didn't even know what a loan shark was. But he'd
also been cozying up to bartender Raymond DiStasio—who happened to be working this day.

O'Neil ordered a beer and managed to get half of it down when
DiStasio noticed there were two armed visitors. Knowing he was a
dead man if he remained, DiStasio ran to the adjacent dance floor.
One gunman with a .38 shot him in the head, and DiStasio collapsed facedown. The shooter approached DiStasio, stopped, and
shot him again.

Hearing explosions, O'Neil fled across the dance floor to the
glass door, screaming hysterically: "I don't want to die!" The assassins chased him, stopping only long enough to pump a couple of

more shots into DiStasio's head. The shooters put two bullets in O'Neil, stopping him feet from the exit door. A third bullet in the head finished him off; he'd left a trail of blood behind him. The killers blamed O'Neil's own hysteria for his demise.

"Why? Tell me why?" asked the suddenly widowed twenty-four-year-old Irene O'Neil. "If I have to go to the governor, I will," she whispered.

The answer was simple: "It just isn't good policy to leave unfriendly witnesses alive," as Joe once observed. The papers blared the killing.

As Joe recalled it, one paper said the "Animal" and one of his "beasties" had walked into the Mickey Mouse Lounge and shot O'Neil.

He would sue, he told Wimpy.

"Forget it. This is a good shot in the arm for our side. Now that Buddy is dead, people have you taking his place."

"Fuck you. I don't want to take nobody's place."

Neither Joe nor the Bear was much troubled by O'Neil's abrupt exit. Joe falsely claimed O'Neil was a gunrunner.

Public outrage ran high over this hat trick. So far, the bodies, whole or otherwise, so sloppily littering alleys, harbors, streambeds, and other locations, had belonged to known criminals. "To now, it was more or less a joke . . . gangsters killing off each other and saving police the trouble," noted one commentator. But not now. Anyone could be next.

The same day that O'Neil was buried, a squad of state police and Boston police detectives descended on a Brookline apartment. They found the thirty-year-old Bear, a fugitive, hiding in a closet—certainly an apt place for so nightmarish a character. Also present was twenty-four-year-old James Martorano, whom they arrested as an accessory after the fact. The Martoranos were doing the Bear a favor by hiding him. Johnny Martorano concluded that Stevie Flemmi, sick of paying the Bear's tab, had given his own brother up.

Later that day, a judge ordered the Bear caged on $100,000 bail. His counselor said Flemmi had been ambushed twice and asked for a reduction in the price. No, said the judge, explaining, "you admit the man's life is in danger. . . . Out in the street he would be worse off. . . . The people you are unfortunate to be mixed up with make it unsafe for you to walk the streets. What is happening in this city is an outrage."

After interviewing the Bear, a psychiatrist told the court the strain of his "frantic attempts" at hiding from his enemies had "unhinged his memory." The "fluctuating memory impairment will make it impossible to communicate properly with his counsel." A judge ruled the Bear incompetent to stand trial and sent him to the ominous Bridgewater State Hospital, a psychiatric facility out of a nightmare. The Bear survived Bridgewater, as he did all else. Released and found competent, on March 9 a judge sentenced him to another four to six years for attempting to kill John Cutliffe and six to eight years for jumping bail.

On January 6, 1966, Joe came to trial for his assault on Detective Joe McCain the previous fall. With Bailey representing him, he was found guilty merely of disturbing the peace. "Big Deal!" Joe boasted. He received six months at Deer Island, a spit of land just far enough out in Boston Harbor to make a good jail site. Soon after, facing a traffic charge of speeding from the police, Joe returned to the mainland for court.

Defending Joe was feisty attorney Al Farese, who told the judge: "He changed his name to Baron so he can change his life."

"Mr. Farese, when Barboza changes we'll all be living on the moon." The gavel came down as the judge imposed a $35 fine. The court laughed, but police immediately arrested Nicky and Chico, who were in attendance, wearing brand-new stolen coats.

"Those two can't even let me do time in peace," Joe screamed.

While at Deer Island, Joe lodged with Anthony Stathopolous, whom he tried to poison with a sandwich. Then Stath made peace with Joe—and increased his odds of survival.

After Joe returned to Deer Island, Guy, Chico, and Nicky oversaw his lending operations. Chico's girlfriend worked at the Boston bar, the Attic, and Chico patronized the establishment. The East Boston crew befriended several thugs of varying IQs and capabilities: Arthur "Tash" Bratsos and Tommy DePrisco, as well as Johnny Martorano. When Joe left jail, he joined this extended social circle, and absorbed Bratsos and DePrisco into his crew, while Martorano became an ally. Joe's initiates were not high-echelon material and, like their skipper, tended to solve everything by violence.

DePrisco, an ex-ironworker, was "dying to put his first notch on his gun," as Joe put it. He earned that right after blowing away his first victim—merely because the man resembled a Puerto Rican pimp whom DePrisco resented. Tash had darker and greater ambitions. He was the younger brother of a slain thief—executed, as everyone believed, by Larry Baione. Joe sensed Tash wanted Larry dead—and hoped Joe would do the killing.

Eventually, the bustling Attic became Joe's money-lending base. One night the police raided a club and arrested Joe—because they'd found a gun in the bar's office.

Chico said, "Where are you going?"

"To my second home," said Joe, not exactly exaggerating.

Chico turned on the police as they carried his boss off. "You can't leave him alone, can you? You won't be satisfied until they find some of you on the street with your heads blown off." The police weren't happy about this threat and chased Chico outside, causing him to sprain his ankle. It was not as if the police needed more incentive to chase down and corral the Animal.

"You and your big mouth," Joe later said to Chico.

In spite of legal woes, Joe earned $4,000 a week (by his own reckoning), and life was sweet with that kind of pay. Joe purchased a new home in an upper-crust Jewish neighborhood in Swampscott, on Boston's North Shore. In a sense, he was a regular suburban breadwinner now, and Claire blended in just like any other of the local housewives. With the success of his enterprises, Joe, who'd spent most of his youth in jail without automobiles and women, now invested in a major toy: a 1965 luxury gold-colored and accessory-laden Oldsmobile. It had an embedded smoke-screen device, and so, was dubbed the Barboza "James Bond car."

Also, Joe liked paintings, but only of the "right kind." He commissioned several, including one of a girl, "not a special girl, just a picture of a girl in the darkness with a light glowing around her head and torso." Others in his collection were one of a matador (later stolen), and another of a girl, but now holding a cat.

Given his financial status, he could even vacation in parts south. In winter 1965, Joe visited the Cadillac Hotel in Miami—and this was "not bad for a Portugee named Barboza from New Bedford," he noted.

23

THE BIGGEST SQUEEZE

"I have ahold of the reins, but I don't know where the horse is going."
—Raymond Patriarca

Uncle Sam's bony but powerful fist was crushing even Raymond's and Jerry's freedom—though, of course, the freedom they enjoyed was not that of ordinary citizens. In 1966, Boston and Providence lawmen applied so much pressure on the underworld, even respectable crooks were unable to ply their trade. "In all my years, I've never seen so much heat as I have in the past few weeks," Henry Tameleo told Vinnie that February. Boston police officers had shaken him down twice in the past several weeks, and this required a change in modus operandi. Despite the thousands of dollars in cash flowing in, Henry confessed he was "financially distressed." He'd recently borrowed $8,000 from a loan company, and Raymond had fronted him $30,000.

The don hadn't pressed him to repay it yet, but Henry was "extremely fearful" Raymond would "become aggravated" with him. After all, the straight-laced don didn't sanction heavy drinking or gambling among his inner circle. Becoming desperate, Henry told Vinnie he'd accept any tip for stolen merchandise that could yield a fast profit, and would take chances with any punk that came along. He tried running a fake diamond scheme; he vouched for a crooked card game and took one-third of the sucker's $9,000 in losses. Ever the gambler, through 1966 Henry lost thousands on horse races that he desperately and hastily tried to fix—to mixed success. Sometimes he gave outright bribes to jockeys. One racer was so heavily doped it began to sweat suspiciously, and authorities scratched it from the race. Henry once even listened to a pitch about an electric shock device that, sewn into a horse's leg, could be remotely triggered to boost the animal's speed. Vinnie suspected that given the velocity at which Henry was unraveling, Raymond might have to put him "to sleep."

To avoid the Boston heat, Henry sold Vinnie his money-lending operation there. He even appointed Vinnie as his emissary, empowered to collect money and carry messages. Jerry now received Henry's fiats through Vinnie—rather as God had conveyed his words to the Israelites through Moses. Thus, Vinnie's orders were Jerry's law, and this rankled Angiulo. Also, as Henry's right-hand man, Vinnie could settle beefs "of a minor nature." The fat man's Solomon-like ability so pleased his Uncle Henry, he proposed to make Vinnie as soon as possible. But Henry had warned him already with sayings such as, "The Office comes first above your family and everything." Given the commitment required, Vinnie later admitted he'd no intention of being made. Yet because the FBI thought Vinnie seriously was in line for rebaptism, it ignored his own infractions and kept paying him tip fees. Vinnie assured the agents he had to "keep up the front" to get Henry's sponsorship. Given he was "financially hard pressed," Vinnie requested a monthly $500, on a cash-on-delivery basis.

Going around Henry, Vinnie told Raymond, "I'd be glad to perform anything for you." This was a dangerous boast—Raymond just might have handed him a contract on Henry. Pleased, the graying don promised he would "find a spot for him in the organization."

In addition to Vinnie, Larry Baione was on the rise. He'd been a "wild kid" before going to jail but had calmed down and become more businesslike. Since his release from prison, Larry had taken over a major North End barbooth dice game, and it wasn't clear if Jerry was still his boss. Certainly, it was good for Raymond that Larry kept Jerry in check. After all, Jerry was the "most despised member of LCN inasmuch as he [is] extremely arrogant and dictatorial," explained Vinnie to the FBI.

The McLaughlins, buried in earth or jail, had left the Townie throne vacant. So the Hugheses, with targets on their backs, occupied the shaky perch. Connie currently was out of jail on personal recognizance, facing charges of larceny and conspiracy.

The brothers laid low until Tuesday, March 15, which they spent drinking beer at a house in Revere. After midnight, they arrived at Connie's house on Hancock Road in Malden. The story here becomes garbled—but we do know that a gun opened fire, breaking the morning quiet. A bullet hit Stevie Hughes in the left side of his chest. After he collapsed to the driveway, both he and Connie continued shooting off pistols. In the dark and confusion, Stevie took five shots in the stomach.

"Where are you? I'll get you," someone said.

"It's me, Stevie."

At that, Connie's sleeping wife awoke, and she emerged screaming from the house, just in time to see a car speed off. Although unharmed, Connie fled the scene, leaving his stricken brother behind on the ground. The Malden police rushed the dying Stevie to the hospital, where surgeons extracted lead from his abdomen and thigh and saved him. It took him a month to recover for the next time. Naturally, the Rifleman was a prime suspect in this near-fatal monkey business. But he claimed innocence, and said Connie shot his brother—either accidentally, or in a Cain and Abel scenario, possibly over a sexual affair.

During spring 1966, the thirty-six-year-old Connie mostly just hid, although he popped up briefly in Dearborn Square, presumably lining up Stevie Flemmi for a hit. On May 25, possibly on the hunt for Howie Winter, Connie visited the Stork Club, a Charlestown bar near the Mystic River Bridge. Leaving just before dawn, a Hill sympathizer (possibly the young bank robber Brian Halloran) made a phone call. As Connie drove from the bar, he picked up a tail. Connie paid his fare at the Mystic River tollgate and drove to the Northeast Expressway.

There, at a very dizzying height over the Mystic River, as a car hummed the mile or so to the end of the span, it was locked into its lane. Iron rails barred even a quick exit off the roadway to the certain death the cold water below offered. It was there that a car speeding from behind drew abreast of Connie—perhaps with Winter Hill lord high executioner Joe McDonald as a shooter and ace driver Jimmy Sims acting as pilot. An M-1 rifle and a shotgun loaded with deer slugs opened fire. In seconds, fifteen bullets penetrated the car—two of them catching Connie in the head before he reached the Chelsea city line. The car, now driverless, careened over the center strip near the Chelsea line, struck an abutment, and burst into flames. A motorist saw the conflagration, stopped, and pulled the driver out. He soon realized he'd saved the corpse of one of Boston's most bloody men.

That night, Connie's bodyguard John Locke barged into a Charlestown tavern, armed. A blood donor to Stevie Hughes after his near assassination, Locke had been with Connie right before his murder. "Just tell me who took care of Connie and I'll take care of him," Locke proclaimed. He opened fire at a Winter Hill sympathizer, who shot back. Neither wounded the other seriously, and two of the bar's patrons then beat Locke with baseball bats and deposited him outside. Soon after, Locke appeared in public with his head wrapped in a turban of bandages, and with two vicious German shepherds on a leash.

The news that half of the Hughes team was gone reached Joe on Deer Island. The next evening, the Animal lay on his bed smoking a marijuana joint, glad the gang war was wrapping up. The papers claimed Joe had issued the contract on Hughes. But, as Joe said: "I was so happy Connie was dead I didn't care what the newspapers said about me." Besides, he had an alibi: the night of the killing, he'd been eating a filet mignon stolen from the warden's fridge.

Yet, Joe wasn't content to be just the Achilles in the gritty working-class Boston *Iliad*. He aspired to be its Homer, as well. He eventually composed a poem, "The Gang War Ends," that celebrated Connie's demise. Joe noted how Hughes habitually drove slowly, to make sure he wasn't being tailed. This was a flawed and "foolhearted plan" that was going to fail, with Hughes driving drunk. Then, as Joe summed it up: "Two cars swiftly went by, firing and riddling him with lead."

During a chat on June 1, Stevie Flemmi explained to Agent Rico how Connie had been stalking him. He admitted that to him "the fact that Connie is now deceased is not displeasing."

"Do you have any idea who committed the murder?" Rico asked.

"I have an excellent idea who committed the murder, but it would be better if I don't say [anything] about the murder."

On the other hand, playing the diplomats, Jerry and Larry visited Connie's wake. Larry spoke to Stevie Hughes and, in the Italian fashion, gave him $5,000 for Connie's family.

It was 6:45 A.M. on Sunday, April 24, 1966, when a nursing supervisor crossed the connecting road from Squantum, Quincy to Long Island Hospital. She noticed something lying in the road near the gatehouse. She slowed just long enough to recognize it as a body. Soon after, police arrived and identified the corpse. It had been a criminally inclined shoe-factory worker from Dorchester named David Joseph "Baby Face" Sidlauskas. Early that morning, someone had beaten and shot Sidlauskas to death; he'd crawled along the road and died halfway between an alcoholics hospital and a sewage treatment plant.

Perhaps on that same day, one Anthony Veranis, a twenty-eight-year-old punch-drunk ex-boxer and thief, borrowed money from Tommy DePrisco. Soon after, DePrisco tried to collect the loan at an unfriendly South Boston bar, from which he was tossed outside in embarrassment, without his money. (Apparently, the tough Veranis also beat up Jimmy Martorano.) On April 26, Johnny Martorano and Tash Bratsos attended the opening of an after-hours club across from Walter's Lounge. A drunken Veranis materialized in the crowd and introduced himself to Johnny. He referred to the incident with DePrisco the day before.

"Fuck him and fuck you, too," Veranis said, and reached for a pistol. Once again, Johnny was the fastest gun in Beantown: He drew his .38, and soon the ex-pugilist was down for the eternal count. (Some evidence indicates, however, that Veranis took a bullet in the back of the head.) The bar emptied, and Johnny gave his and Bratsos's dates taxi fare. As the proprietor started scrubbing brains off the floor, Johnny and Tash moved Veranis into Bratsos's Cadillac, then low on gas. Soon after, they dumped the corpse in the bottom of a twenty-five-feet-deep embankment in the Blue Hills reservation on the Quincy-Randolph line. It was only when Bratsos refilled his gas tank that he discovered he'd lost his wallet . . . back to Blue Hills. He retrieved it where it had fallen by Veranis's corpse. Not an hour later, a jogger discovered the body.

Sometime early in the summer of 1966, a onetime Boston bookmaker named John Sweet contacted his old employers, the Bennett brothers. Now a balding middle-aged real estate agent, Sweet had relocated to Florida. There he took his place in the stud stable of one Irene von Maxcy, a local socialite. Eventually Sweet and

Irene decided to eliminate her wealthy husband, orange grower Charles von Maxcy—for which they would pay $41,000. Receiving the contract, Wimpy took $20,000 off the top and split it with his brother Walter. They offered the balance to Joe Barboza, who declined it. Walter then started shopping the contract around at his lounge. An annoyed Rifleman turned it down, claiming a proffered $25,000 wasn't nearly adequate a wage to whack a legitimate person. Another prospect was a hanger-on in the twilight zone of the lounge named William "Billy" Geraway.

Baby-faced and "bear-like," Billy was a hoodlum with a well-earned reputation as a loud and dishonest troublemaker. He was a not-so-tender shoot that had sprung up between the sidewalk cracks of Worcester's ghettos. Despite a high IQ, young Billy dropped out of school in the seventh grade and immediately drifted to crime. From age nine on, Billy played with firearms and could modify them with accessories and homemade silencers. He grew to be a six-footer with a barrel chest, thick hair, and fleshy, youthful face. A self-admitted "immoral bastard," perhaps his only decent soft spot was for his older sister, Louise, a "sort of a big brother" and "comrade" who'd fended off would-be bullies.

He started his record in 1948, and although tough, he mostly worked as con man, thief, and counterfeiter. This "ruthless clown" was a relentlessly incompetent criminal, and managed to do time in nearly every Commonwealth prison available. Billy migrated to Boston, became a regular at Walter's Lounge, and married a criminally inclined teenager. Using a stolen press, the couple launched a counterfeiting ring to print and cash payroll checks. He possessed white-collar capabilities (he could appreciate the delicate details of a dollar bill, so impossible to properly forge). Yet, Billy never rose above the gutter, and always carried a pistol for protection from his friends and enemies alike. During a poker game, Geraway complained he was winning counterfeit cash but losing real money. A friend then drugged his beer, and an unconscious

Billy crashed his 1966 Mustang into a wall. Later, he realized the only thing that had interposed itself between him and the grim reaper had been the strong X-shaped car frame.

Soon after, Walter Bennett told Billy the law wanted him for motor vehicle charges, owning a counterfeit driver's license, and "this and that." As a sop, he told Billy about the von Maxcy contract, and the "romance" behind it.

"Have they thought about divorce?" Billy asked the venerable crook.

"These people will be worth an awful lot of money," Walter said. "It will be easy." Billy declined. (Eventually two criminal misfits took von Maxcy out.)

After taking a pass on the Florida job, Billy Geraway took another collar. The police also seized his latest financial engine, a printing press, from his Boston apartment. Subsequently, he headed west for a brief romp with a fellow Dorchester con man. Busted for passing phony checks, Geraway represented himself in court and managed to make bail—the partner remained in jail. Geraway worked his way east by shortchanging waitresses, generally for five dollars at a whack.

Once home, he launched a new counterfeiting campaign with several thousand dollars' worth of checks. On June 23, 1966, the police in elegant and staid Portland, Maine, cornered Geraway, arrested him, beat him savagely, and maced him for his bad manners. (He'd told one of the officers his wife was getting anally serviced by a black man.) One nasty constable even kicked an unsuspecting Billy in the crotch—Billy swore revenge, but never made good on it.

Incarcerated, miserable, and facing an enormous prison sentence for forgery, Billy decided he'd either go straight or stop getting caught. Luckily for Billy, on September 23, 1966, a federal judge in Portland gave him five years on the counterfeiting charge. Billy went to Lewisburg and entered third-floor segregation, safe from his Roxbury friends. He also became a professional witness for the state—and in 1967 even gave prosecutors evidence in the now high-profile murder trial of the late Charles von Maxcy.

On the stand, Billy interrupted someone reading through his six-page FBI dossier, saying, "I think I can help you save time. There are 103 entries on my criminal record. I'm guilty of all of them." His own brother, an ex-convict, alcoholic, and victim of multiple nervous breakdowns, surfaced to impeach his testimony. He also learned one of his "good friends," Stevie Flemmi, wanted to bail him out—but only because he desired Geraway dead.

Not long after, Billy read he'd been indicted for killing Tony Veranis. Another indictment followed for eliminating David Sidlauskas, allegedly because he had "aggravated" Billy. Extradited back to the Bay State, Billy passed through what he called "the gates of hell" of the Massachusetts prison system. His one possession was *The Rubaiyat of Omar Khayyam*.

The next trial, for killing David Sidlauskas, was quite harsh. Billy's ex-wife testified against him, calling him "a liar and a teller of fanciful tales." On February 20, 1968, addressing the jury before its deliberation, Billy said, "The taking of a life is a very serious matter, whether it is taken judicially or on a lonely road. You can give me back my life and a reason to live it." Convicted, Billy received life—if that is the word—in Walpole. While awaiting the upcoming Veranis trial, eight of Billy's friends (and potential friendly witnesses) were killed. He pressed for an acceleration of the procedure, and was acquitted of eliminating the unpopular Veranis. No matter. As *Time* magazine put it, Billy was "buried as live man can be." Every day, he thought of killing himself—but, naturally he didn't.

His nearly half-year sentence complete, Joe Barboza left Deer Island. Nevertheless, he still found life on the outside challenging, even with only half of the Hughes-brothers team to hunt. Also, Joe severed much of his partnership with the obnoxious Guy Frizzi. It was a prize business indeed, amounting to $50,000 on the street, realizing $5,000 a week in interest. Tash Bratsos bought out Guy's end of Joe's lending business—all of the shared customers defected from Guy, as well, Joe claimed.

But as Boston's gang feuds drew to a close (albeit with a glacial pace), Joe decided it was safe enough to diversify his enterprises. Protection—or more precisely, having bar owners pay money to him so he wouldn't destroy their establishments—was one such avenue. He asked for the Office's permission to start collecting from unconnected venues: He received a green light. The East Boston gang shook down the Father's Mustache, the Diplomat, Nantasket's Blue Bunny, and Louie's Room. The last two alone paid $100 a week to Joe to protect their establishments from himself.

One target was the Living Room on Stuart Street (formerly the Peppermint Lounge). "You're pretty good at chess," Joe told the owner. "You ran a chess game with the Office a few years back and won. And you went out on your own. . . . There is one thing that this game ends. Either you kill me or I am going to kill you if you don't do the right thing." Two days later, five of Joe's men, including Chico, walked into the establishment and unleashed mayhem.

The owner, and his Mafia-connected Cleveland partner, soon after settled the matter with Joe and Henry Tameleo. That left only a black pimp who was plying his trade at the establishment. (Of him, Joe later told Congress, "And the pimp, I don't know what he wanted.") Joe settled for $7,500 as an up-front payment, and $200 a week thereafter.

The oldest profession also beckoned. Joe claimed Louie's Room served as a grazing pasture for the "cows," whose body parts were so attractive to their johns. Joe didn't mind squeezing a "Mr. Pimp" for his ill-gotten gains, and with Bratsos, he put the arm on fifteen of them for a weekly hundred dollars apiece. Joe felt dirty about it and refused to talk to the girls or their handlers—but he claimed the cash would let his gang eat better.

Growing in ambition, Joe looked north of Boston and saw dollar signs in the decaying Merrimack River basin. He now planned to invade wide-open Lawrence, a factory city, and demand tribute from all the bars and nightclubs. To start this blitzkrieg someone detonated a bomb, outside a bar, powerful enough to blow out its windows and "put fear into the hearts of some citizens." Then Joe led a three-Caddy caravan, eight-men strong, to the entrance of the Holiday Inn. The gang entered the lounge to display raw power; there, Joe shook hands with his local partner—who was squeezing the Lawrence bookies. Joe's partner claimed that news of this "show of strength" would flow through Lawrence. "The valley is yours," he told the Animal. The Portugee from New Bedford was at the height of his career, where the oxygen ran thinnest, and the fall was the farthest.

The end came like a slow tide for Joe's plans—and at an unlikely place, a Revere club called the Beach Ball. Joe was an informal ruler there, since the owners feared him too much to interfere. Anyway, the gangsters did at least attract beautiful women with distorted self-images. These ladies drew men, such as Everett native Arthur Pearson. He stood six feet, four inches, and weighed an athletic two hundred pounds. "Couldn't he fight," said a friend. "Nobody but nobody could handle Arthur. He was too big, too fast. The only way they could stop him was with a knife."

On July 24, Pearson was playing volleyball at the club and catching the ladies' eyes. When Pearson argued with a doorman, Joe, Chico, and Nicky took notice and materialized nearby. Suddenly Pearson felt something sharp against his back.

"We don't like you, guy," one of the trio said.

When Pearson left the club, he found Joe and his friends

awaiting him, and not to say good night. Knives appeared, and while his companions watched, Chico sliced Pearson from the belly to the chest, and left him. On July 28, Assistant District Attorney Jack Zalkind visited Pearson, now a mess of tubes and stitches, in the hospital. He told the ugly story, adding a coda, "Two people came up and told me not to say anything or I'd be killed."

Municipal, regional, and state police were waiting for this opportunity, and soon Joe and his crew were behind bars. The gang posted a $35,000 double-surety bond for release. Joe now faced a series of shakedowns, and only his corrupt law enforcement contacts kept him ahead of them. One state police squad arrested Joe on a driving-to-endanger charge and led him to the state police headquarters at Commonwealth Avenue. (They would have gotten him with an M-1 rifle, but he'd been forewarned.) Joe walked in with his black mohair coat over his head, looking down to see the sidewalk. The troopers didn't lead him into a telephone pole, as Joe feared they might. Even at 1 A.M., it seemed like daylight with all the flashbulbs going off. Joe lost his license and sold his car to his attorney, John Fitzgerald, for a thousand dollars—the lawyer inherited the payments remaining on it, as well.

"No doubt about it, I was hot," Joe later reflected. Certainly, it was a step up from breaking the street signals in New Bedford. Nevertheless, he habitually spat at photographers and cursed the trailing reporters who made him the center of the public's gaze. Newspaper photographers snapping pictures of his and the Bear's victims asked not to get photo credits.

That summer of 1966, a bold gang of thieves repeatedly knocked over dice and other games connected to the Office. Because of the gang's clockwork precision, it obviously was working with an insider who identified the marks. Then, the gang hit a Saturday dice game on the corner of Morton Street and Blue Hill Avenue in

Roxbury. Its members didn't even bother with masks and were clearly of "Italian extraction." Subsequently, Peter Limone summoned Chico to the Dog House to discuss his future health. Jerry described the jobs to Chico, noted that customers were now "leery" of the games, and said that these thefts must cease. He also said Chico's description fitted one of the culprits.

"If it is you, you're in trouble," Jerry threatened.

"It isn't me and if I'm in trouble, well, I've been in trouble all my life," Chico said.

On June 9, Joe, fresh from Deer Island, told Jerry he wouldn't stand for such "shit." But Jerry already had zeroed in on the actual culprits, and told Joe to offer Chico his apology. As Joe explained at DiSeglio's later murder trial, Newton gangster Rocco DiSeglio was the insider fingering the games for the stickup men. Joe knew and liked "Rocky," an ex-welterweight he'd boxed with. Considering him a "good kid," he'd even loaned Rocky money. But once Jerry knew DiSeglio's role, it was easy to track down the rest of the conspirators and match them to eyewitness descriptions. The other stickup culprits were Richard "the Pig" DeVincent, Marino Lepore, and Bernard Zinna—an odd crew that included a street enforcer and an auto-transmission mechanic.

Jerry corralled the three men in his office and discussed the robberies, Joe said. At first the three conspirators claimed they didn't know those dice games were the Office's enterprises—but Jerry didn't believe in such coincidences. Then, in classic Mafia fashion, he said, "Either you take care of him [DiSeglio] or I'll have all four of you taken care of." They did the math: One life was worth three—especially if they weren't that one.

It was 10 P.M. on June 15, in Chiambi's when Joe noted the presence of Lepore, DeVincent, and Zinna. Joe knew Zinna from Concord in the 1950s; DeVincent had once sent the incarcerated

Joe a radio. Joe chatted them up. "We have something to do to-night," Zinna said to Joe. "We're up to no good for our own good."

"Yeah," said DeVincent. "We're going to take care of business. We'll show you how it's done. You'll read about it in the paper tomorrow."

Soon after, Rocco DiSeglio arrived in his wife's maroon Thunderbird to pick up the trio. Zinna took the driver's seat, while DeVincent the Pig sat in the back. DiSeglio took the middle space between the bucket seats—which was an uncomfortable position, Joe observed. Lepore explained Rocco wouldn't be there for long, and took the front passenger seat for himself.

The next day at 11 A.M., Zinna and his two mates entered Chiambi's and announced DiSeglio's abrupt demise. The night before, they had driven DiSeglio to a dark street in East Boston and stopped. Lepore stepped out, as if he were retrieving a stolen car. That's when DeVincent shot the distracted DiSeglio in the back of the head. The quartet drove north and deposited DiSeglio's body in the Topsfield woods. The trio claimed they had done Joe a favor by taking the body out of East Boston so he wouldn't "get the heat."

"Thanks. Remind me never to let you guys sit in the backseat," Joe said. They put their heads down and looked away.

Upset, Joe claimed he personally tipped off an East Boston detective to look for his onetime friend's body in the Topsfield woods. That evening, a state trooper pulled up to Lover's Lane and flashed his beam into the darkness; a car's taillights reflected back. The trooper walked into the woods and up to the abandoned car, where inside he found the boxer's corpse on the bucket seat, blood on the face (now missing a substantial chunk) and head, and a perforation behind the ear. The two holes in the car's windshield and glass particles inside indicated he'd been shot right there at Lover's Lane.

Soon after, during a visit to the Dog House, Joe mentioned DeVincent to Jerry. "He's shooting his mouth off," Joe said. "He's a big man now. He put a bullet in Rocky's head."

Jerry admitted he didn't trust the bragging the Pig. But apparently, shooting DiSeglio was a good career move, because the Office started using the treacherous oinker on other jobs.

Willie Marfeo had "lived a charmed life," as the Office had noted in frustration. Willie even had bragged "They won't get me" in earshot of a Raymond flunky. Marfeo had had also been stinging bookmakers (the "Jew Downtown") by refusing to pay his betting losses. But that summer of 1966, he'd been living in terror, sleeping with a loaded and cocked .45 under his pillow—several times he'd pulled it on his own wife as she entered his room. Willie never went out without a weapon, claiming, "The only time they'll be able to get me will be in the daytime."

So it was in broad daylight on July 13, 1966, that someone with a paper bag over his right hand walked into the Korner Kitchen restaurant. The eatery was a block from Coin-O-Matic, and full of Raymond's shills. The stranger, who wore a straw hat, gloves, and work uniform, was clearly armed. He told the patrons, "You, you, and you get into the back and lie down." To Willie, he said, "Not you, stay there." He corralled Willie in the telephone booth and asked him for the bag—the one in which he carried his money. Willie didn't have it; the visitor then shot him to death and fled.

Soon after, Willie's wife called Raymond and said she didn't want any trouble for herself and her children. No trouble, Raymond promised. But Willie Marfeo came from a large tribe, with brothers as hardheaded as he. At least one of them swore he'd kill Henry Tameleo for Willie's murder, so for a while the underboss holed up in Providence and avoided trips to Boston. The murder would yield worse results.

24.

WORST-LAID PLANS

"As I said, it's kill or be killed."
—Frankie "the General" Salemme

"Little" Stevie Hughes (as he'd been called in Charlestown) was the final McLaughlin charter member to elude the grim reaper's scythe. He'd even recovered from his wounds sufficiently to do muscle work. Lately, people had noticed him near Sammy Lindenbaum's house in Revere each Friday. Soon, it was obvious he was acting as collector and bodyguard for Sammy's highly profitable treasury tickets business. This was not wise in an actuarial sense for Sammy—Joe claimed Sammy even brought him an offer of peace from Stevie.

"Tell him to go fuck his mother," Joe answered.

Raymond ordered Frankie to warn Sammy about the dangers of Stevie Hughes, twice. When Sammy persisted, Raymond told the General: "That's it, take him out." Raymond then borrowed $75,000 from Sammy, Joe claimed. For this job, Frankie climbed a pole and used a phone tap (provided by Wimpy), and the rest was easy.

Around midafternoon on September 23, 1966, Sammy Lindenbaum and Stevie Hughes left a restaurant near Lowell, got into a rented 1965 Pontiac, and drove south on Route 114. The highway was little more than a narrow street that snaked through a half-dozen nondescript towns, woods, and swamps in north Massachusetts. The sixty-seven-year-old Lindenbaum carried hundreds of policy slips in a paper bag and $1,200 in cash. Stevie Hughes carried a .38, $55, and a newspaper clipping about his shooting on March 16. Sammy's two small dogs occupied the backseat.

At about 1:45 P.M., a "long, black sedan" carrying perhaps four people—including a woman or someone wearing a wig—accelerated abreast of the Pontiac. Both vehicles were about to crest a hill in the small wooded town of Middleton, near the Three Pines Inn. Just then, a "pole like object" emerged from the sedan's right window—a .30 caliber rifle. An automatic weapon also protruded and fired armor-piercing shells. As the black sedan passed the Pontiac, the gunfire suddenly opened up, loud enough for drivers in other cars to hear it.

Ten bullets hit the Pontiac, smashing all the driver's-side windows and penetrating the door. Some even reached the passenger side. Shells tore a hole in Lindenbaum's round, venerable head and severed the fingers from one hand—but the digits remained wrapped around the steering wheel. Other slugs tore open Stevie Hughes's neck and chest. The Pontiac careened off the highway, took out a hundred feet of post and wire guardrail, plunged down an embankment, and came to rest on its side in two feet of swamp water. The assassins' black sedan roared on and vanished, a pinkish-beige car following.

Down in the muck and water, the old Jewish gangster and the middle-aged Irish one lay huddled together dead, one on top of the other, bleeding over the front seat. Two hours later, a tow truck pulled the heavily damaged Pontiac-hearse from the swamp. The medical examiner at the scene pronounced both men dead, but found Sammy's dogs were inside the car, alive.

Soon after, the Rifleman told Rico that since Stevie Hughes's murder, "the entire city is much more at ease." Sammy "should have known better" than to associate with Hughes. But the killing's ferocity was shocking to some in the underworld—Sammy had been, basically, "a nice quiet old man." But Raymond and his allies were cutting corners.

Now, the once-fearsome Charlestown gang was "practically decimated," as Joe noted. He celebrated the last shooting as being "identically the same" as Connie Hughes's had been. He depicted the murder of Stevie and his friend Sammy in verse, noting that it signaled the end of the gang war. Only a few men were left on the run or hiding: they were going to die, too, because the "Grim Reaper wasn't denied."

The men who survived were of proven ruthlessness—killing machines, actually—and it was unclear just who would control them, if anyone. "The boss in the Office was afraid of these independent operators," Joe claimed.

While the Bay State appeared to be calming down, in early October 1966 Raymond's diabetes was proving particularly troublesome. Running Rhode Island alone was a full-time job, preventing him from spending adequate time on Massachusetts. Frustrated, he also was "sick and tired of being tied down." He told Henry he might step down as the Boston family head. Raymond already had a replacement in mind, but it was dubious the prospect would want such a job.

Obviously, the Providence Mafia throne was shaking—and it was particularly unwise to further unnerve its occupant, sickly and irritable to begin with. That Joe's reckless, obnoxious, and unloved gang was one of the few left standing (more or less intact) didn't recommend it to the Office and its regents. Joe was still only an associate, as he realized when Henry commanded him and Tash Bratsos to stop harassing a victim. This created "some ill feeling" in Joe, according to the FBI. (One story claimed that Henry ordered Joe to keep his hands off a mark—so Joe bit the wretch's ear, instead.)

Larry Baione in particular cast a wary glance at the Eastie crew. Although himself crazy, even Larry feared Joe as a "loose cannon" with an oversized gang. He also knew that Joe's lieutenant Bratsos wanted revenge for his murdered brother. Hearing the Office members discuss matters Animal, the Rifleman presciently concluded the Eastie crew was headed to the top of the Hit Parade.

With Joe and his ilk in mind, the Massachusetts legislature passed a habitual criminal law, which applied Prudential tower–sized terms to repeat offenders. It was inevitable Joe's grand schemes would push him into collision with this sledgehammer of a statute. On October 6, 1966, while on bail for the Pearson stabbing, Joe drank with Nicky, Bratsos, and Patsy in the Intermission Lounge on Washington Street. Two detectives entered, and Joe pretended to frisk one of them; the detective then frisked him back. "We got a big laugh out of it," Joe said.

Less funny, the surviving Marfeo brothers believed Joe had killed their sibling, Willie. Subsequently, Joe heard they'd put a contract on him, using a member of the crew belonging to professionally certified psychotic Romeo Gallo of New York. Now Joe was suspicious: Raymond could have squashed the rumor that Joe clipped Willie, but hadn't. Joe concluded Raymond had decided to allow the lunatic Gallos to eliminate him—which would also appease the hotheaded Marfeo brothers quickly and on the cheap.

"Well, fuck Romeo Gallo," Joe told himself. "He could die like anybody else."

Hungry, the East Boston crew piled into Bratsos's gray 1965

Cadillac for a ride to Swartzie's in Revere. Driving down Washington Street, the Cadillac immediately acquired a vice squad tail. Having heard that a hit was in the works, Boston mob detective Sal Ingenere boasted he'd personally dispatched this patrol. Noticing the lights trailing their car, Joe told the boys to get rid of anything hot. Joe himself tossed out three joints and papers with two new addresses from Detroit and Florida. By the time the tail stopped them on Congress Street, Joe assumed the car was clean.

A detective approached Bratsos's Caddy and said, "All right, what's your name?"

"Go and fuck yourself," said Joe.

"I'm only doing my job."

"Go down to the South End and break those nigger junkies' balls."

"I'm booking you all."

Leaving the car parked against the curbstone, the police arrested the East Boston gang at gunpoint. Once herded into the paddy wagon, Bratsos managed to burn some papers on the floor. At headquarters, upstairs went the Animal for fingerprinting.

Sadly for Joe, the police uncovered an M-1 rifle and a knife in Bratsos's Caddy. Because of his various pending court actions, Joe's bail was $100,000 double-surety—or $200,000, so he'd need $100,000 to make the street. That Wednesday, openly and in court, Garrett Byrne called Barboza one of the "real killers" in the Commonwealth. His comment made the front page of the papers. The law (with a possible assist from the Office) squeezed the local bondsmen to keep Joe in jail. Finally, a New Jersey outfit offered to craft a bond. The Office promised to make up the difference of whatever his crew couldn't raise. However, someone warned Bratsos that even if Joe walked, he must avoid Boston, as he was "nothing but trouble to everybody." The organization wasn't going to "to bail out a problem."

With the determination of windup toys, the crude and bullying

Bratsos and DePrisco exerted every means to free their chief. They even shook down North End mobsters, acting as if the Office owed Joe the bail money. One North Ender, Joseph Salvati, refused to pay a debt of his someone had sold to Barboza. (When Joe heard about this, he listed Salvati in his revenge notebook.) Foolishly, Bratsos also made his own private revenge plans against Larry Baione public in Enrico's, Johnny Martorano's favorite hangout. When Peter Limone and Jerry befriended Bratsos and DePrisco, the duo should have realized something was very wrong. After Bratsos told Johnny the North End wasn't really that bad, it was obvious the Office was "lulling him to sleep."

Once, during the fund-raising, Bratsos flashed a thousand-dollar bill at a colleague and asked, "Did you ever see one of these before?" Doing the collection rounds, DePrisco argued with the manager of the mob joint the Coliseum, and even pushed him in the face. Far worse, during their reign of terror, Bratsos and DePrisco broke the legs of a well-liked, soft-spoken Irish bookie from Dorchester. Now the wrong people were very truly upset.

By mid-November, Bratsos told Joe that he'd amassed all but $28,000 in bail money, and he'd spring him in two days. As part of the fund-raising, on November 15, 1966, Bratsos and DePrisco visited the Nite Lite, where its owner, Ralphie "Chong" Lamattina, held court with Larry Baione and other men connected to the Office.

The small but ferocious reputed Mafioso Ralphie was a constant discipline problem for the Office—for Jerry in particular. Certainly, Ralphie was a very dangerous man to cross. Tonight at the Nite Lite, there was something of a plan afoot—possibly Ralphie's, Henry's, or Larry's, or a combination thereof. The made men told Joe's crew to go out and raise some more money and that the Office would supply the rest. DePrisco and Bratsos obliged. Next,

Larry, by his own admission, "threw everybody out of the joint," including the bartender. The Nite Lite was nearly empty when Bratsos and DePrisco returned around midnight—and disclosed they now had $70,000. That was far more than their lives were worth, as someone proved when a pistol came up.

Without a warning, in seconds, Joe's two feared bruisers were on the ground thoroughly dead: Bratsos carried two bullets in the brain; DePrisco, four. Someone even kicked DePrisco in the head (after all, he "agitated people," as Joe observed). The killers furtively dragged out the bodies and stuffed them in the back of Bratsos's gray 1965 Cadillac. Someone drove the car to South Boston and parked it at the junction of A and West Fourth Streets. There, bloody handprints covering the roof and rear door, it blocked a parking lot gate.

A few hours later, a truck driver investigating the Cadillac-tomb found, on the floor, Bratsos's corpse on top of DePrisco's. The driver had initially thought they were sleeping through the morning chill. On a tip (possibly from Wimpy), Boston detective Sal Ingenere and members of his elite task force headed to the Nite Lite. There, just outside the club, they interrupted a man washing blood off the sidewalk. Inside, they found Ralphie Chong and a helper laying a new carpet down while a workman was installing a mirror behind the bar. The police removed this mirror. They discovered a bullet had passed through a mirror underneath, and the wall behind that, and had fallen down into the room beyond. The slug was still in one piece and matched another bullet found in one of the corpses. A search of the Nite Lite uncovered bloodstained pieces of the old rug Ralphie was replacing. Although Chong told the police he was the club manager, they couldn't find his name on the payroll.

Naturally, news of the killings spread through the North End like a winter cold—and the locals responded with their usual gregariousness to police inquiries. But not only were mouths stopped at the presence of the authorities—so were the usual games of chance that were the Office's lifeblood. This was a mess for many reasons. Jerry was incensed at the crush of the police and how these "amateurish assassinations" had "embarrassed the Italian organization." Now, he never drove alone, anywhere. Publicly, Henry said this was a "bad move" and the "people of Boston are getting fed up with this." Even the less than delicate Larry Baione offered a lament: "It shouldn't have happened inside his [Chong's] joint. No reason for it. . . . Once they get on the sidewalk, crack them and fuck them and walk away."

Raymond issued a meeting summons. On the morning of Friday, November 18, Vinnie picked up Henry and drove him to the Nu Brite location, where Jerry and Peter Limone already waited. Together, they entered Raymond's office. The killing was the result of improper supervision, Raymond explained.

"I wasn't around and can't be blamed," said Jerry.

Not so, Raymond said. As the group leader, Jerry should exert such control the members would never do something like that. He also criticized the inept handling of the mess. "Everyone suffers from the heat from the local police," Raymond pointed out. He then called in his personal executioner Rudy Sciarra, and Vinnie left the room. Presumably the blame was on Ralphie—who was a suspect now. If he didn't straighten this mess out, he might be next on the Hit Parade.

Knowing it was safer to submit to the law than Raymond's judgment, Chong surrendered to arrest as accessory after the fact. Jerry promised Ralphie he'd pay $24,000 for a three- to five-year sentence. The grand jury was squashed, and the cash outlay worth it, the Office decided. But when Vinnie told the FBI about the secret transaction, the deal collapsed.

Some enemies now made friends and vice versa. The Office began to squeeze one of Bratsos's companions for an outstanding loan made to Tash. Additionally, Larry told Stevie to "keep control" over the Bear so he didn't make problems for the Office. Given one of his brothers worked with Jerry, Guy Frizzi was left alone.

But Raymond decided the Office's course was irrevocable and that the East Boston crew must go. He summoned Wimpy, the Martorano brothers, and Frankie to poll them where they stood. Johnny Martorano admitted he'd liked Tash and DePrisco and left it at that. This probably saved his and his brother's lives and positions. Then Raymond announced he was taking out Joe's crew, and asked how Wimpy felt about it. Ever the trimmer, Bennett voted to be Switzerland. Then Raymond let them all go.

25

THE OFFICE DOOR SLAMS

"I always say make sure if you clip people, you clip the people around him first."

—Jerry Angiulo

Apparently, the remaining East Boston crew prepared to hit back at the Office. An army of policemen, including a bomb squad, descended on the two-story brick-front building that housed Chiambi's. They found nothing, at first. But when a thirsty officer looking for a drink opened the fridge, he found several loaded M-1 ammunition clips. The police also found three guns in a paper bag, nestled in a hole in the ceiling of the men's room. They also uncovered a club, bat, blackjack, bayonet, small arms slugs (including .38 caliber "dumdum" bullets), a loaded .38 automatic, a Luger, steel-jacket bullets, and several .30 caliber armor-piercing shells.

Mere hardware was useless. And with his crew severely winnowed, the message to Joe was clear. The Office was severing their marriage in a painful divorce. He blamed this betrayal on Jerry and Raymond's love of money. He knew some of his $70,000 in bail went to Raymond, and "they cut up the rest." The Office had even begun to siphon from Joe's club-protection money. Joe wrote to Wimpy, saying he'd get "30 men whether they were innocent or not." If he ever got out, Joe was ready to shake the

Office's entire roster from Prince Street to the foot of Hanover Street.

In the meantime, all he could do was suffer, a criminal celebrity with no street power. On a much-needed trip to the dentist, reporters hounded his cortege so badly he refused treatment. Back to his cell he went, jaw still swollen.

Seeing how dire the situation was, Chico Amico called a meeting of "our friends," as Joe put it, in a South Boston poolroom. James Kearns, Wimpy, Stevie and Frankie, and the Martorano brothers attended. The participants spoke, threatened, and felt one another out.

Fed up with the "crap," Chico asked, "What are we going to do about it?"

"Nobody wants to take on the Office," said Wimpy, who already planned to sit this ugly dance out. "Not right now, anyway."

Seeing Chico's look of disgust, Wimpy took him to one side and told him how he could rally the Baron allies. He said the Office's only two killers were Baione and his sidekick, Phil Waggenheim. "If you'll kill Larry, I'll arrange to take care of Phil. . . . They'll [Joe's friends] be with you after you make the move on [Baione]."

Obviously Wimpy knew Larry's unnatural and abrupt demise would be blamed on the East Boston gang, which was doomed already. Now Chico began to shadow Larry, hoping to find an exploitable weak spot in his routine. Chico even peeped through the windows in Larry's Franklin farmhouse.

Although the plan made some sense, Chico wisely mistrusted Wimpy. Larry didn't like Wimpy much—calling him "The Man's Spy" (meaning Raymond). Wimpy had a vested interest in Baione's elimination. In a smuggled letter, Chico told Joe, "I'm going to do my best, Joe, but if I die I want you to cut that motherfucker's [Wimpy's] head off and put it on my grave."

———

The longer the Animal remained in his prison-cage, the more the ranks of his pack outside thinned. Reputedly, Chico Amico realized he had a bull's-eye on his back and, terrified, holed up in his Princeton Street house in East Boston. The evening of Pearl Harbor Day, Amico was in the El Morocco nightclub. With him was the large and brawny James Kearns, a twenty-seven-year-old bartender and "sadistic bastard." A good fit with Joe's crew, Kearns could boast arrests for rape, forgery, and assault. Kearns's "main virtue was that he would not murder his friends." He went about well equipped: Inside one of Kearns's stolen cars, police had found a bat, 150 master auto keys, a switchblade, several wallets, spent .45 caliber shells, a police transistor radio, a set of license plates, and two wrenches.

That December night, a witness heard Chico pleading on the phone. "Please, straighten it out. It's my life," he said. "You've got to straighten it out." A messenger visited Chico at the bar and proposed that he make a cash pickup in Revere. Kearns was openly suspicious—the messenger nervously downed six scotches.

"This better not be a setup," Kearns said, and punched the man in the face. The scuffle caused the police to materialize, but Kearns said, "We're leaving and we don't want any trouble." Then Chico and Kearns drove to Squires, a "swinging joint" in Revere. Sal Ingenere, with an elite squad of tactical police force (TPF) patrolmen, tailed them. Ingenere sent two of his men inside to talk to Chico. One officer had seen what Amico's cutlery skills had wrought on Arthur Pearson, and now his legs shook. Chico occupied his typical spot, at a table by the end of the bar, with Kearns and Guy Frizzi. After two frisks, the TPF men reached Chico, who declined Ingenere's invitation to come chat. He bought an officer a drink, stood up, said he knew about the contract, and told him to thank Sal, anyway.

Not disguising their hatred, Kearns and Frizzi just eyeballed the officers who now headed back to the waiting car. The TPF men took position again in the cruiser with Ingenere. They watched as Chico and Kearns left Squires and entered a green sedan. At the wheel, Kearns pulled onto Route 1, and a black sedan pulled out from the other side of the road in pursuit. The two cars turned onto Squire Road, and after a two-hundred-yard chase, the black sedan overtook its quarry. In the chase car's passenger seat was an assassin armed with a .30 caliber army-surplus carbine. He opened fire on Chico and Kearns with armor-piercing bullets.

The slugs made shards of the rear windshield and riddled the trunk and windows. Six bullets passed through the front windshield, with three entering the back of Chico's head. His forehead blown out, he slumped dead on the right front seat. A bullet grazed Kearns's left cheekbone, while glass flying from the rear windshield slashed his face. He lost control of the wheel. The car hit an embankment before slamming into a telephone pole, which snapped as it checked the vehicle's progress and stove in its side. The killing job done, the black sedan vanished, leaving a trail of semiautomatic shell casings along Squire Road.

Too late, the pursuing TPF squad exited the ramp from Route 1 and pulled up to the wreck. Steam poured from under the car's hood as Ingenere jumped out and ran to the driver's seat to get Kearns. Another TPF man opened the passenger's-side door, and Chico fell out from the blood-spattered interior into the street. Out came Kearns, his face badly cut, his shirt bloody, and his foot injured. He remained standing, a smile playing on his lips, and Ingenere angrily ordered his arrest.

"What am I being arrested for?" Kearns yelled.

"Accessory before and after. You set Chico up." This shocked Kearns, who was soon after rushed to the hospital. Later, he went to jail.

At 3 A.M., guards awoke Joe in his Charles Street Jail cell and took him downstairs to the lawyers' conference room. Two Boston police detectives waited. "We've got some bad news for you, Joe," one said.

Immediately, Joe knew a loved one had checked out—but discovering it was Chico left him stunned. "No matter who died, it affected me, but Chico's death affected me the worst. He was like my son, my brother, my partner." Joe said, "Get Patsy Fabiano off the street."

The detective agreed, and a glum Joe returned to his cell and broke the news to Nicky Femia. When Fabiano turned himself in, a court judge raised his $1,000 bail to $75,000. He went to Charles Street Jail to live in a miserable, if safe, isolation.

The Office gloated. "This is what happens when they step out of line," boasted Larry Baione, who'd already been offered Bratsos's client book. He told Stevie Flemmi the city needed some peace.

The week after Chico's murder, Kearns stood quietly in Chelsea District Court, wearing a bloody shirt. Bandages swathed his stricken and unlovely head. Angry that Kearns refused to cooperate with investigators, the presiding judge said, "It's only a matter of time before they [the feuding criminals] will all eradicate each other and that will be a good day for Massachusetts."

From his cell, Joe could see everyone in the guardroom, and who entered and left. After a bandaged Kearns arrived, Joe managed a conversation with him. He decided Chico's demise was Jerry's handiwork then and spotting attorney Joe Balliro, he arranged a meeting.

"You tell Jerry he's not getting away with this," Joe told Balliro. "Anything goes."

Balliro asked Joe if he really wanted this message passed to the underboss.

"You're motherfucking right I want you to tell him."

Two days later, Balliro returned with the response: Jerry had claimed innocence. In fact, Bratsos had owed him $26,000, and it was a "terrible mess."

Joe concluded, accurately, "That's the only thing he's concerned about—his money." The Animal (possibly with guidance from the Rifleman) concluded it had been Jerry who'd soured Raymond on the East Boston crew. Frustrated, Joe began running off at the mouth, claiming Raymond was a "fag" and other silly, life-shortening things. When he discovered Raymond had issued a contract on him, Joe took the threat seriously. Despite his public defiance, he wrote a letter to Raymond and gave it to his attorney John Fitzgerald, who handed it, unsealed, to Vinnie Teresa. Fat Vinnie claimed he shared it with Henry first. In writing, Joe promised, "I'll never give you or anyone else trouble." Also he begged, "Just let me live." He was sorry if he'd offended Raymond, and asked him to cancel the hit. He admitted sometimes he couldn't control his temper, and he apologized if he'd offended anyone in the Office.

Having read the message, Henry instructed Vinnie to reply, "Don't worry about it, Joe." Then, he said, after Joe left jail, "We whack him when he least expects it." However, when the two presented the letter to Raymond at his house, the don exploded and refused to answer it directly. If Joe got away with what he'd done, it would undermine the Office, Raymond claimed. "He's gonna get killed in or out of the can. You send the word to him—and that's all there is to it. I want him to know, to spend every night shitting in his pants, this bastard. Who does he think he is? He'll kill this guy and that guy. I'm a fag, he says. I'll get him. He talks that way about me. I'll straighten him out." Vinnie passed Uncle Ray's message to one of Joe's friends.

A wary Raymond also took aim at a loan shark who'd taken over managing Joe's territories. Raymond issued a warning to him not to cut into the Office's territory. He also told Henry to kill this loan shark immediately if he got out of line. In a calmer mood, Raymond again promised to make Vinnie—that is, if the books, then currently shut, ever reopened.

In his garage, Frankie Salemme observed a conversation between Stevie Flemmi and their joint accountant, Peter Poulos. Frankie realized something was amiss when Stevie pulled out a pistol and pointed it at Poulos's head. Stevie explained the joint card business he ran with Wimpy had come up short. And he wanted to know why.

"I gave Wimpy the money to give to you," said Poulos.

Frankie intervened, suggesting they summon Wimpy and then decide who was lying. "It's your business really, not mine," Frankie said.

It was all about business. By now, Stevie had become Wimpy's right-hand man, which was useful for multiple reasons. It gave the Rifleman a certain stature with not only Rico, but also the In-Town Angiulos. As one Bennett descendant claimed later: "Steve played the Italian Mafia off against my uncles and both of them off against the FBI. He was a con man. . . ." Clearly, Wimpy's usefulness was over, and he'd messed with one of Stevie the "spontaneous reactor's" two priorities in life. Someone as shifty as the Fox should have seen this coming—but then again, the Bennetts had taken in Stevie like a son, and they were good family men, if nothing else.

The next day, January 19, after trying to see a Boston policeman, at 6 P.M. Wimpy pulled up to the garage in his Cadillac. With Stevie and Frankie present, Poulos said to Wimpy, "I gave the money to you, you did it before."

Before a flustered Wimpy could speak, Stevie shot him in the head. Wimpy's cleverness had reached its limits, and he was now dead. Flemmi took the forty-seven-year-old body to the Hopkin-ton Sportsmen's Association, thirty miles west of Boston. When Stevie first arrived, a policeman asked why he was there—to shoot, the Rifleman replied, almost truthfully. Soon after, in daylight, Wimpy entered his resting spot. Frankie's business partner, George Kaufmann, sold Wimpy's Cadillac for $6,000.

The days since Wimpy's last public appearance became weeks, and they in turn merged into months. It was clear Wimpy was dead, and not of natural causes. His family reported him missing in March. His brother Walter Bennett "became obsessed" about him, and his suspicions grew.

On January 25, 1967, a jury found Joe guilty of carrying a gun and a knife. A judge awarded him two four-to-five-year concurrent sentences, among other punishments. To Walpole the Animal went—where, as in old times, he could pal with the Bear (now a celebrity with his own dozen-strong jail crew). Joe would also man-age the kitchen, and as a prison runner, travel anywhere in the facility at his leisure.

Still tight with the Bear, Joe told him he was "boiling mad" at what he thought the "sneaky weasel" Bennett had been doing. "Wimpy is a treacherous sick buzzard," Joe said.

"Don't worry about it," the Bear said. "You'll be happy soon. Just watch."

Word reached the Bear about Wimpy's demise. Soon after, the Bear entered the maximum-security TV room, where Joe was with some cronies.

"Joe, I want to speak to you," said Flemmi. "Alone."

They took a walk. When the two reached the end of the block, the Bear divulged the glad tidings about Wimpy taking a bullet just under the eye. "The fox that bit us is dead," he said.

The Fox was also invisible—in a pit, and covered in lye. Later, the Bear offered a detective $10,000 in $1 bills if he could find a single tooth of Wimpy's.

With this slaying, Stevie Flemmi's and Frankie Salemme's stars seemed ascendant. Frankie claimed that this rise was "spontaneous." As a fig leaf to cover his treachery, Stevie claimed the Office would have hit him if he hadn't killed Wimpy. But the tailgate thieves who usually hung around Frankie's garage now were "leery" of the two, and they vanished. One night in July 1967, the duo met with a drunken Larry Baione and Peter Limone in Giro's. Limone put an arm around Frankie and with the other grasped Stevie. He announced he was proposing them for membership in "our organization." Ordinarily, to become a member, Limone said: "You would have to make a hit and I would have to be with you as your sponsor to verify that you made the hit and report on how you handled yourself. But, with the reputation you two have, this may not be necessary." Neither accepted the offer—yet. But Frankie wanted to be made very badly, Stevie observed. He claimed that these days, Cadillac Frank was acting pushy, and even mimicking Larry's distinct accent.

On February 8, Ralphie Chong appeared in court with his attorney to plead in the Nite Lite slayings case. When the lawyer said "not guilty," Ralphie said "guilty." The amazed lawyer looked at Chong, who nudged him to be quiet. This way there was no trial or embarrassment to the organization. The police had even skipped taking Ralphie's fingerprints or photograph. Not only would he avoid getting whacked, presumably, he'd receive only three to five years. However, that arrangement had quietly changed after authorities had acted on Vinnie's tip that bribery had bought Ralphie a soft cushion.

Because of an investigation, Ralphie instead received two long sentences of five to seven years, instead. This was a loss of face for the Office, and Jerry was baffled how the plea deal had become public. But there were bright spots in this gray sky. Wimpy was gone, the gang war was at least at a standstill, and only Joe and his shrinking crew remained as a nuisance.

There were plenty of people who would see to Ralphie's well-being in Walpole. Joe was there, too, waiting for him.

26

THE DON AT BAY

On Friday, February 17, 1967, Frankie learned "George" wanted to see him, and he and Stevie drove to Nu Brite Cleaners. The Nu Brite headquarters was just across the street on Atwells Avenue from Coin-O-Matic. Raymond stayed in an apartment upstairs. While there, Raymond rambled about different subjects, not getting to the point, and asked Stevie from where in Italy the Flemmis came. Stevie asked if Raymond could assist his almost-legitimate car repair and resale business. But as the two Bostonians were leaving, Raymond said, "Hold up a second, Steve. Frank, I just want to explain something to Stevie here."

"Go ahead," said Frankie, who left the room.

Raymond said, "Listen, your brother's coming down here, he's coming down here with Barboza. I don't want him down here anymore. . . . Tell your brother to stay out of here."

"I will."

He also told Stevie not to mention any business dealings they might have, as Jimmy couldn't "keep his mouth shut." Then Raymond gave him $5,000 to sustain his auto operation. Stevie never returned to Raymond's office. No matter. On February 8, 1967, Rico had already made Stevie a Top Echelon spy for Uncle Sam.

Tension kept rising on Atwells Avenue. A newspaper reporter entered Raymond's office and asked about a Senate investigative committee. "You go out and try to prove that I do wrong," Raymond said. "Then come back here and tell me about it." Raymond stood up. "Now get the [fuck] out of here."

But on March 12, during a forced visit to the Office, Vinnie heard Raymond's announcement that the FBI had planted a microphone in his stronghold. Now "extremely mad," he planned to have his Coin-O-Matic old office, and the new one (under construction above Nu Brite Cleaners) swept for microphones. He told Vinnie to associate with only trustworthy men and to never bring anyone into his office. If Vinnie came with a driver, he must wait outside while Raymond spoke to Teresa, alone.

Henry counseled Raymond to remain calm, as all bug evidence was illegal and unusable. Nevertheless, the device's existence vexed Raymond to the point of craziness. How the FBI had planted it was a mystery: a burglar alarm had been installed in Coin-O-Matic, and Raymond always could rely on the locals to finger any strangers on Atwells Avenue before the strangers could do mischief. Enraged, Raymond vented at the head of security, his brother Joseph. "You dumb son of a bitch," he screamed. "I oughta hit you in the head for this. For Chrissakes, we could all go to jail."

Raymond stopped using the telephone just about completely. For meetings, he turned a radio up so loud it nearly drowned out his voice. He also installed an electronic device—marked "Anti Bug"—to counteract any hidden microphones. The device had a switch and a dial similar to an amp meter. Vinnie said it acted as a scrambler, emitting electronic beeps—but the noise made it difficult for those in the office to understand the discussion.

In Roxbury, a ferocious Larry Baione was still moving up, absorbing booking enterprises from independents. Blocking Larry's takeover of Roxbury was Walter Bennett, who continued to brood over Wimpy's absence. He blamed Larry for the killing, but deduced it had been Stevie who'd done the job for the "Guineas." He vowed revenge, and with his wife Barbara Ann, he plotted Larry's demise. Walter threatened to plant a bomb in Larry's car, or take out Larry's Franklin house and create multiple victims at one swipe. Preparing for a hit, Bennetts even held a vigil in the family station wagon in the Jamaica Plain parking lot across from Larry's house. A criminal bungler, Walter wasn't secretive, either, renting rooms near Jay's Lounge to line Jerry up and "take him out, too." Foolishly, Walter asked Frankie to help him set up Stevie.

With the Office's backing, on April 3, Frankie sprung a trap. Poulos picked up Walter at his house in Dorchester and chauffeured him to Frankie's garage at 6 P.M. Walter climbed the staircase to the garage office. There, he reached both the end of the stairs and his life, when a waiting Stevie shot him to death. Frankie put the body in a car, drove to Hopkinton, and buried it next to Wimpy's. That night, after Walter failed to materialize for dinner with Barbara Ann, she began searching for him. On behalf of herself and their fourteen children, Barbara Ann reported Walter missing on April 10. Someone eventually found his car in a Logan Airport parking lot. Jerry reportedly was "delighted" his nemesis was gone.

Of the Bennett brothers, only the fifty-six-year-old bartender William remained. A nonviolent, regular sort, his options were few, and government protection wasn't one of them. Bennett kept on, trying to keep Walter's Lounge afloat; when Frankie and Stevie asked to buy the bar, William figured they were the culprits. And, after two months of waiting, Rico and another agent paid a call to Bennett at his house, and not exactly to commiserate. "If you don't want the same thing happening to you that happened to your brothers, you'd better give us the books [of loan clients]," one told William.

His son (and namesake) had eavesdropped on the chat. Alone, he asked his father, "These are supposed to be the good guys?"

"No, no, they are not good guys," William said.

On Wednesday, February 8, 1967, Ralphie Chong finally arrived in the prisoners' intake in Walpole. Joe found Ralphie standing in T-shirt, shorts, and socks, looking as gnomelike as ever. Ralphie affirmed he was Joe's friend, and said, "What happened wasn't my fault. I had no say in the matter. Why, they even used me to take the beef."

"Ralphie, I know you're my friend. I don't hold no grudge," Joe said, although he trembled with rage. They met again in the TV room, where Joe claimed, "I just want the beef straightened out so I won't have no worries later. . . . Look, to show you I'm your friend, I'll tell you a secret. I've got some powerful tasteless poison. I've also got a zip gun [jury-rigged pistol]. You let me know who is bothering you or who you want killed and I'll take care of them."

Apparently frightened, Ralphie threw Joe a hard look and thanked him. Laughing hard on the inside, Joe thought, "I'd have this little bastard brought down to his real level by the time I was ready to pounce on him." The next day, in the kitchen, Joe tried to pass a couple of pork chops to Chong, on the side.

"Look, Ralphie, I saved you two nice big ones," he said.

"No, thanks, Joe, I'm not hungry."

A cat and mouse game went on for a few days, with Ralphie

trying to avoid anything Joe served. Then starving, at last, he'd accept food, but say: "No, not that big piece. Give me this little piece on my plate in the corner."

After Joe served him, he looked sad, as if Ralphie had "loused up" a poisoning. Ralphie started avoiding the kitchen completely, and Joe decided to visit his cell. Well informed by his spies, Joe picked his time, 3 P.M., carefully—that was when the guards were rotating shifts, and the cells were unlocked. Ralphie was enjoying his afternoon nap as Joe entered the cell. When the Animal moved between the sink and the top of the bed, Chong awoke and recognized him. Ralphie's narrow eyes widened when he saw Joe's cleaver.

"Don't flinch or move your hands," Joe warned, knowing Ralphie's lethal reputation. "I know you got a knife under your pillow but before you can get it, I'll sink this cleaver into your greasy head."

"What's the matter?"

"Tell me what happened at the Nite Lite." Ralphie started talking, explaining he hadn't wanted the murder to happen. He'd planned to play cards with Bratsos—but the duo had come in drunk and talked about shooting different people. Joe didn't know how nasty Bratsos could be . . . and so on.

At conversation's end, Joe said, "I'm going to kill you but not now. I want you to worry, but I swear I'll kill you." He spat in the smaller man's face and left the cell. On February 18, Joe claimed he watched Ralphie, carrying his gear in a laundry basket, walking the corridor. Chong was transferring to the onetime Norfolk Prison Colony, "two miles down the hill." He said that as Ralphie passed him, he put his eyes down and picked up the pace.

The state was squeezing Joe ever harder. Now he faced a habitual-criminal indictment—this meant a potential eighty-something-year sentence. If the Office didn't clip him, Joe would spend the second half of his life (and then some) in jail. Admittedly, perpetual incarceration for Joe had always been something of a foregone conclusion. But now the legal mechanism was finally in place to enact it in one simple transaction, instead of piecemeal. Even Joe, after a lifetime of gorging on his own bad luck and stupidity, found this prospect distastefully hard to swallow.

Joe realized he needed powerful friends to extricate him from the current legal mousetrap ensnaring him. Joe also knew the more of his fellow mice he pulled into the trap, the kinder his captors might be to him. Stevie Flemmi and Johnny Martorano periodically visited Joe and the Bear in Walpole. Johnny would sit and talk to Joe, while Stevie chatted with the heroin-addicted Bear. The Flemmi brothers' conversations were far from happy; sometimes their arguments escalated into fisticuffs. During the confabulations, the quartet would switch partners. But Johnny noticed that the members of the Flemmi-Barboza trio sometimes whispered conspiratorially among themselves. It appeared they might be hatching a plan.

FBI agent Rico claimed Joe had first wooed him and Condon; Joe maintained it was the other way around. In any case, on March 8, 1967, a corrections officer paged Joe to the Cedar Junction control room, and explained two FBI agents wanted to chat.

"Tell them to go and fuck themselves," Joe said. He walked fifty feet, then turned around and said, "I'll see them." He found the agents waiting in the visiting room. One said, "I'm Paul Rico and this is Denny Condon."

"I've met you before, Rico. At the track. Do you go there often?"

"No, I don't gamble," said Rico, telling a lie from the start—as did Joe. He told the agents he was willing to talk if they didn't testify against him about what he said.

"If you want to talk in confidence, we would respect your confidence," one of them said.

"I've always tried to make a living outside of the law and . . . if anyone could prove I was doing wrong, I was willing to pay the consequences," Joe said. "I want protection for my wife and children." Once the agents agreed to help, Joe baited his hook. He claimed the FBI thought they knew the truth about the gangland slayings. But he, Joe, really knew what had happened in "practically every murder" in the area.

He told the agents that a big sentence would drive Claire to leave him, and he would "probably commit suicide." As for the Office: "They know they'd have to kill me when I got out and . . . they know I'd take plenty of them with me," Joe said. "That old fool in Rhode Island misinterpreted my respect for fear. Fear him? I didn't fear tougher guys than Raymond Patriarca." He'd also learned, through watching his friends disappear, one after the other, during the gang war, to accept dying.

He'd suffered "20 double crosses" and now there was revenge to consider. Rico noted the loss of the $70 thousand or so bail money in the Nite Lite bothered Joe more than had the murders of Bratsos and DePrisco. Besides the theft of money, a Winter Hill mobster had tried to lure his brother Donald to a hit. The Office had threatened his women. Joe said, "I want to double-cross them for their double crosses." The means: "I've got nothing left but my mouth with which to fight now. . . . I'll bring them in the can with me since I can't get out to them, and when I get them here we'll get on with it."

Once his verbal dam broke, Joe unleashed a Mississippi of gossip, rumors, and slander on the agents. By conversation's end, Rico and Condon had planted a seed that would grow into a rather vile bush. They kept Hoover informed with daily updates. Joe informed the Bear, whom he vowed to never "fry," of the proceedings. Like

Hoover, Flemmi gave the project his approval. On March 21, Rico and Condon transferred Joe to the federal building in Boston for an interview. To the agents, Joe divulged he'd told the Bear about getting Patrick Fabiano to cooperate. The feds moved Joe out of MCI Walpole and the county itself. The war on the Mafia had begun, belatedly, noted a Boston newspaper.

The Bear then told his brother Stevie about the Animal's plans to flip. Stevie informed Raymond—and then told Rico and Condon about that tip-off. This complex and treacherous four-way trunk line allowed the agents to apply "imaginative direction and professional ingenuity" in guiding their turncoat. In turn, Stevie told the Bear to convince Joe it was Jerry trying to put him away for life. Even as Joe spun his yarns to Rico and Condon, he planned to double-cross them. On April 6, an attorney, presumably John Fitzgerald, told Vinnie Teresa that Joe had a message for the Office: He'd skip testifying against Raymond if the don showed him some favor.

"Tell him to drop dead," Raymond replied. Tell the messenger that if Joe "hadn't been in jail, he wouldn't be alive today." In an almost unheard of move, Raymond threatened the lawyer: "If he [the attorney] doesn't be careful, he'll be in trouble, too."

In the many years he'd known Raymond, Vinnie had never seen him be so upset for so long. Raymond's anger never lasted more than a day or two, until now.

On April 14, Joe, still facing a gun-carrying charge, was arraigned in Suffolk County Court for being a "habitual criminal." He told the FBI that Jerry wanted him "buried in jail" and planned to use the district attorney's office to "crucify him." Joe said, "If I ever testified, you people would have to find me an island and make a fortress out of it."

One agent asked, "Don't you feel it would be fair in the interests of justice if you testified against them?" Wrong question: Joe said he wanted the right lawmen to know that he was cooperating. He gave up Raymond, Henry, and Ronnie on the Marfeo hit, and even fingered his pal Johnny Martorano for taking out Veranis.

27

THE NOOSE TIGHTENS

"I'll rip my nose off myself & spite myself."

—Joe Barboza

On April 24, 1967, Joe was convicted on another charge: carrying a weapon and a dagger in a motor vehicle. He now completely acquiesced to the government's prosecution arm. He told his codefendants, Nicky Femia and Patsy Fabiano, he was cooperating; through Fitzgerald, he broadcasted through the underworld that he'd testify. Joe was transferred from the state prison to an isolated cell at the Barnstable County House of Correction on Cape Cod. He believed Raymond, after indictment, could certainly get someone to poison him, at the least. One of the underworld "suckers" would kill him for free, in expectation of Raymond's future favor.

Joe began to work with two prosecutors: Kennedy family friend Paul Markham, the U.S. attorney in Boston, and his assistant, Edward Harrington. Both lawmen knew Joe had crossed state lines to conspire with the Office to kill Willie Marfeo. This case offered a potential test of the new federal interstate crime law, one that Bobby Kennedy himself had sponsored. However, while Joe was safely in Barnstable, his family was exposed seventy miles away in Swampscott. The loyal Claire was ready to leave her friends and relatives to hide with Joe on the Cape. Instead, at the head of a U.S. Marshals detachment, John Partington presented himself at the Baron residence. Blue-eyed and lanky, Partington might have modeled for a Norman Rockwell painting. He hailed from Cumberland, one of a number of nondescript farm and factory towns that ringed Providence—and thus, firsthand, he knew about Raymond and his grip on the region. After a stint in Korea, in 1962 Partington had joined the U.S. Marshals.

The prior January, Bobby Kennedy had visited Rhode Island to attend the funeral of a local congressman (and Raymond pal), John Fogarty. With Partington driving, Bobby and a U.S. judge headed to the Mass in Providence. "How do we get that bum on the Hill?" Bobby asked. He suggested the government create a special program to protect a witness and his family from harm, give him a new identity, "and a new start after he testifies against his mob bosses." Soon after, Partington accepted a job as the head of the new Witness Protection Program.

Partington was a cop's cop, and now the success of Joe's mission was on Partington's head. Obviously, Joe was safest behind bars—but he could provide the prosecution more if he lived normally—or to be more accurate, if he lived a facsimile of that domestic life he'd tried to enjoy between jail sentences. Partington assumed, possibly accurately, that men like Joe went through intense "emotional shit" when they ratted out their former partners. "I had to keep him pumped up, keep his mind charged so he'd testify," he said. "Otherwise we'd lose everything we'd spent months pulling together." Partington also knew if Raymond killed the Baron family, Joe would attempt to massacre the entire Office in a bloodbath. And if Raymond kidnapped Joe's women, there would be no testimony.

So Partington and his men protected the Barons round the clock. On his first day on duty, Partington sat in Joe's kitchen with Claire.

"What is expected of me, and what are you going to do?" she asked him, arms crossed self-defensively.

"I don't know." Daughter Stacey entered the kitchen, her curls and smile reminding Partington of Shirley Temple's. After asking the marshal why he was there, she climbed into his lap. Oby, the family's Siamese cat, joined her there—despising felines, Partington brushed Oby off.

"You hate my cat!" Stacey yelled, bawling, and ran with Oby into the next room. When another marshal entered the house, Oby escaped through the back door.

Partington ordered a rescue detail, and out the reluctant marshals went, calling, "Kitty, kitty, come back." Later Oby returned with a dead mouse, which he dropped at Partington's feet.

"He's sending you a message," quipped Claire.

The presence of Partington and his men spurred Joe to complain that the feds had made his $3,000 dining room into "their clubhouse." But Partington had forbidden his marshals from even using Joe's bathroom. He also advised the detachment not to bond with the Barons. But given that Partington worked in Swampscott sixteen hours a day, he ignored his own recommendation. In fact, the marshal paraded Claire like a surrogate wife, and at times Partington dared wonder if she wanted more than mere protection. He also did things his superiors would have frowned on, allowing the stunning Claire, in a bikini, to visit a nearby beach. Stacey Michelle even called him "Uncle John" when he arrived in the morning; he read her to sleep at night.

After Joe's testimony produced indictments, the Baron women needed to go underground and join Joe. Before young and dainty Claire's reunion with her cruder and more antisocial other half, she demanded a Saturday night out—but at the Ebb Tide. Partington agreed. "You got to have balls in this business, and I wanted Patriarca's men to know we weren't scared of them." Later, Claire took a private walk with Partington on the nearby boardwalk.

"All of this was make-believe," Claire said. "It's been peaceful without him."

"Mrs. B, the United States government is on your side."

"You don't know him [Joe], John. You think you do, but you don't."

May was harsh on Patriarca, Inc. Louis the Fox, facing income-tax-evasion charges, had, with Raymond's permission, requested all the FBI-bugging logs pertinent to his case. On May 19, 1967, a judge ordered the requested logs publicized, and agents produced ten days' worth of notes on the Office's activities—bookmaking, stolen goods, hidden racetrack interests, and other assorted examples of sleaze. The big dailies published page 1 articles detailing the intimate and fluid connections between organized crime and the upperworld of businessmen, politicians, and judges. Now his "amazed" underworld colleagues knew about the bug, something Raymond had concealed for months. In Revere, tongues wagged in Vinnie's mob hangouts—and the criminal consensus was that Raymond had goofed mightily in the Fox's defense. Raymond and the Fox eventually became bitter enemies—and it was just a question of who would hit whom first.

Worse, official Boston was locked down. Given the uncertainty about how much the FBI knew about Raymond's secret network in government and law enforcement, friendly pols were running from their contacts in the Office. Raymond had lost major face—hoodlums saw he hadn't been infallible, after all; he hadn't outwitted the FBI. Now, not even Henry Tameleo was such a "big man"; crooks stopped bragging about him. Police took shots at him: In the space of a year, Henry had faced three collars for petty crimes, including conspiracy to violate Massachusetts's small loans act. Cops had even nailed him for driving without insurance and made him surrender his auto plates. The legal fees had cost him $23,000, and, apparently, he and Raymond were both "all washed up."

Raymond, no fool, was aware that the underworld could erupt completely—and, in a second, bury him in a Vesuvius-like flood. A month before, Vinnie had observed Raymond acting unnaturally calm. But, on May 22, during a conference, Henry and Vinnie found Raymond "acting like a wild animal" and "making extremely illogical statements." Raymond verged on a nervous breakdown, confused and crediting everyone but himself for the bug revelations. Later that day, Vinnie spoke to Henry and LCN flunky Danny, who both called Raymond "obscene names and blamed him." Several days later, a now-placid Raymond announced he'd outlast the problem by waiting for the publicity to drop and the heat to die down. In the meantime, he didn't want anyone hanging around him.

One challenge came from Rudolph Marfeo, a Providence wise guy, and brother of the slain Willie Marfeo. Age forty-one, hard-headed Rudolph had, more or less, revived Willie's dice game, which raised the Office's envy and objections. An annoyed Raymond personally visited Rudolph at his house in Johnston, Rhode Island, to command an end to the game. Rudolph shouted and cussed at Raymond, claimed an eavesdropper. A local tough guy, twenty-six-year-old Anthony Melei, was at Marfeo's house. Raymond asked who he was.

"He's with me," Marfeo replied.

"If you're going to be a gangster, you're going to have to learn to die like a gangster," Raymond told Melei.

Fulfilling Raymond's fears, a gunman even fired on his bodyguard, Rudy Sciarra, on Atwells Avenue. While no one was hurt, Raymond was "visibly nervous and upset" when the Providence police took him in for a statement.

———

On May 16, Rico and Condon visited the Boston U.S. Attorney's Office to meet with Ronnie Cassesso. Due for a grand jury appearance, Ronnie was about a hundred pounds lighter and working as a prison electrician. The agents told Ronnie that if he were of "material help," they'd let the right people know it.

"People in prison are telling me I'm a member of La Cosa Nostra," Ronnie said. "It seems to me that if such an organization existed and I was a member of it, I would know it. . . . I used to think standing on the corner well dressed and making the night spots was a big deal," he said. Now he felt that lifestyle is a "sucker's game," and he planned to "go to work" when released. Knowing Joe had arranged this meeting, Ronnie claimed he said: "You go back and tell Joe Barboza that he fucks his mother!"

As the ship of the Mafia began to take on water, panic spread, steadily, relentlessly. Henry had given Joe several murder contracts at Arthur's Farm; Joe and Raymond had discussed some of these killings in Providence. Henry particularly fretted over what Joe might say about the premature and not-quite-accidental demise of Willie Marfeo. "That dirty fucking bum!" Henry proclaimed. "I knew he was a weak bastard!" Henry told an associate, "It's that fucking scumbag Barboza who has been whacking all of those kids in Boston on the sneak. That weak dirty piece of garbage is ratting on everyone, including me!"

Worse, Henry had been Joe's sponsor: The Office blamed him for these woes. Now like a "wild man," Raymond claimed Henry hadn't been careful enough and that if he hadn't trusted everyone they wouldn't be in trouble. The ever-indelicate Jerry mentioned that if Henry had let him kill Joe as he'd wanted to (for the stickup of his game), these problems wouldn't exist. Understandably, this didn't set well with Henry, who had said, not inaccurately, Joe was a "stand-up guy," and had suggested he be left alone. He blamed

Jerry and Raymond for pushing Joe into the witness box. The entire organization was eroding with mistrust—its edge was gone. Members of the Office wanted to flush out any stool pigeons. They even started releasing falsehoods to different sources to see if the FBI or other lawmen repeated them. Then they'd know who the traitors were.

As Markham had planned, the interstate telephone calls and drives from Boston to Providence satisfied the federal requirements of the case. On Tuesday, June 20, a judge issued warrants for the three conspirators: Ronnie, Raymond, and Henry (Joe was an unindicted coconspirator). Henry found it unbelievable that he couldn't manipulate federal lawmen as he had those from Rhode Island.

Nevertheless, pretending to be "Henry Thomas," Tameleo went underground at the Wakefield's Statler Hilton Motel on Route 1. However, Vinnie divulged the location to his FBI handler. Moments after the bench warrant was issued, waiting agents collared Henry, just outside the motel. He was with a young black-haired woman; Henry admitted she'd spent the night with him but that she was a "good kid." The gallant Tameleo would only offer her name, and said he hoped she wouldn't be "in any difficulty." Once in the FBI car, the agents explained how Henry didn't have to make a statement, etc. "By this time I am well aware of my rights," Henry said. As he explained, one question was leading to another, and he ended the chat there. The mistrustful and baffled Uncle Henry didn't blame Vinnie for the pinch, but rather his personal driver. Vinnie wasn't about to disagree—and to remove any suspicion, he flew to British Antigua to pick up $7,200 in Raymond's casino-skim money.

Even as Henry received his irons, seventy miles away agents descended on Raymond's Providence headquarters. Danny Raimondi greeted them inside. "What can I do for you?" he asked. They explained. "Come on back here," Raimondi said, and led them toward a kitchen, where a woman was preparing food. "Raymond," Raimondi called. The agents gave Raymond his first collar in two decades. Looking grim, the fifty-nine-year-old don appeared in manacles before the U.S. commissioner in Providence to waive a preliminary hearing. Released on $25,000 bail, on Monday, June 26, Raymond appeared in a gray-blue business suit and silver tie for arraignment in the federal courthouse in Boston.

With his typical stealth, Raymond entered the building "virtually unnoticed," using the Devonshire Street entrance. The state processed him and Ronnie in the twelfth-floor courtroom, now filled to capacity with onlookers. At the judge's command, the don himself stood, and said in a weak voice, "Not guilty, sir." Raymond was missing the strength he'd displayed for prior courtroom performances, as the FBI noted. Ronnie pled likewise, and the arraignment was over in minutes. Raymond ascended to the fifteenth floor to add a new portrait (by way of a mug shot) and fingerprints to Uncle Sam's archives. With his attorney, Charles Curran, Raymond then waited for the courtroom to clear before leaving the building. The Office knew if it couldn't break Joe's testimony, the executives were going away.

By July, Joe's legal status was worryingly vague: The witness-immunity bill that could protect him now languished in Beacon Hill's inscrutable bowels. And the wily Raymond and Henry also planned their countermoves. Jerry suggested they select one of Joe's chums and "take him out," just to send a message.

Attorney Fitzgerald began playing his own dangerous—and illegal—game. That spring, he had dinner with Henry, who asked, "What is the story on Joe?" Henry had been close to Joe and given him advice. The two had always talked through their problems. "Why would Baron want to hurt me?" Henry asked.

On July 6, Fitzgerald met Raymond and promised to do "everything in his power to aggravate Baron," as Vinnie told the FBI. The agents asked Joe if he'd testify against Fitzgerald—he would, Joe said, but didn't want to if the lawyer was filing a motion on his behalf.

Raymond put a private eye on the payroll for $200 a day to check on Joe's background. The operative claimed Joe had peddled drugs, fathered two illegitimate children, and simultaneously pimped three "cows." Worse, Joe's mother had been a streetwalker. True or not, Henry and Raymond planned to drop these tidbits during Joe's cross-examination in court and provoke him to "jump off the stand and attack" them. This would deliver a mistrial, at least— and any chance to prolong their freedom, and thus increase the chance they could snuff Joe, was worth it.

Larry Baione helped out. He obtained state prison and Boston police documents on Joe. He even polled the Animal's girlfriends for love letters (one was from Lowell, the other Medford) that would offer additional proof of Joe's dementia. Personally, Larry had no fears about Joe's mouth. But he needled Jerry and Limone by say- ing, "We are all going to end up in the can over Joe Barboza." A man of action, he wanted to head right to Barnstable and plug Joe in his cell.

Henry defiantly made a good time of it, dining out and gam- bling extravagantly. He borrowed $10,000 from Raymond (which he subsequently blew at the horse races), and kept laying heavy bets on ball games. For proper wagering, he needed two phone lines in his room in his house to get all the national basketball game point spreads. In contrast, the sober and somber Raymond was resigned to his fate. He even decided to appoint Jerry in his stead after the inevitable jail term deposed him as don.

Although he'd been a regular Judas to Raymond for years, Vinnie liked the don. He even urged him to flee to Haiti, whose maniacal dictator, François "Papa Doc" Duvalier, was a former partner of the Office. Papa Doc even offered Raymond a thousand acres of beachfront property to develop, and a twenty-year tax abatement. Raymond stayed put, anyway.

On August 8, police wielding machine guns and shotguns sealed the sixth and seventh floors of Boston's Suffolk County Courthouse. Along with ten witnesses, Joe discussed Rocco DiSeglio's murder. Afterward, the state police formed a six-car caravan to escort him to Barnstable. Back in the courthouse, the jury returned secret indictments naming Jerry Angiulo as conspirator to murder and accessory before the fact. The documents also fingered Lepore, DeVincent, and Zinna as conspirators and murderers, and detectives arrested all three that night. With this testimony, Joe had all but concluded his fruitless, Byzantine negotiations with the Office.

The next day, Wednesday, August 9, at 9:30 A.M., the forty-seven-year-old Jerry arrived at the Suffolk County Courthouse with Joe Balliro. Facing the electric chair, Jerry dressed impressively in a white shirt, black suit, and blue-black striped tie. He shielded his eyes with dark-rimmed glasses, and his silver hair rolled straight back from his forehead. The elevator doors opened at the eighth floor, and Joe Balliro led Jerry through the crush of newsmen to Garrett Byrne's office. Jerry looked straight ahead, ignoring the crowd until a photographer flashed a strobe light and halted him.

"That's too close," Jerry said, before moving on. The chief investigator for the Boston police, John Doyle, immediately arrested Jerry, who now entered the state's legal machine. Denied bail, Jerry went directly to Charles Street Jail. Prepared, his black briefcase carried toothpaste, toothbrush, and a shaving kit. But the prison fare of mashed potatoes, fried bologna, and stewed corn prompted his complaint. When an attempt to bribe a guard for tastier chow failed, Jerry noted the stool pigeon Barboza ate his choice of food.

The guards soon caught Jerry making hand signals from a jail window to his fiancée, situated across the street. So officials sent Jerry sixty miles southeast to the Plymouth County House of Corrections, where the rustic surroundings were pleasant. In this new facility, Jerry frequently ordered takeout food and shared his meals with the guards themselves, who set up a dining area for the underboss, complete with tablecloth. To increase his popularity, Jerry even distributed fifty World Series tickets, worth $50 apiece, to the prison staff.

Jerry met daily with his brother Danny to exchange messages. With Jerry's mailing address belonging to the state, an embold-ened Larry Baione decided "the day of the independent [football] cards is over." All these operators would work with Limone or other appointed middlemen. Befitting his status, on Mondays, Larry also joined the regular 10 P.M. North End Mafia card game with soldier Nicky Giso and family consigliere Joe Lombardo.

Despite Joe's early success in repaying the Italian organization, by August he was frustrated. Claire's weekly meetings in the Barn-stable jail lasted only an hour—not enough to justify the long trip from the North Shore. Worse, he couldn't stand being called a stoolie, and even wrote a semiliterate letter to *The Boston Herald Traveler* entitled, "Why I decided to tell all." He declared, "All I want is to be left alone. Leave my family alone." He went on, not-ing how many young inmates think that by working for Raymond they could become "big men." He wrote, "The office likes them to believe this, because then they can bleed every single favorable ef-fort from these disillusioned kids and men—and then throw them a crust of bread. . . . And it goes on and on in one complete cycle of evil and viciousness while the office sits back, laughs, and reaps the harvest."

Joe also addressed a litany of complaints and passive-aggressive poses in a letter addressed "To whom it may Concern." He asked why he was being punished for doing something nobody had dared to do. The authorities had spent hundreds of thousands of dollars hunting down Raymond and came up lame. The promises to Joe were lies and he wanted to know what favors were coming his way. His life was unpleasant: He was going "stir crazy" and facing the worst pressure he'd ever endured. It would be easy to kill him where he was a "sitting duck." The authorities couldn't be bothered with addressing this. He complained that the food in Barnstable was inferior to that in Walpole. Before moving to the Cape, he'd been able to see Claire twice weekly. Clearly, ready to go into hiding, Joe said he'd lose $4,000 if he sold his house.

He noted he hadn't wanted Pearson stabbed—presumably, he hoped to wriggle free from that charge by his cooperation. Then he threatened to stop collaborating: a recurrent theme in all his dealings with prosecutors and authorities.

"Believe me before I'll be used & played for a Mickey the dunce I'll refuse to testify. . . . I am no threat to the law in New England in or out because I'll be too busy running."

While stewing in fear and anger (and facing a separate gaming indictment), Henry showed Vinnie a newspaper article where Joe denounced one of his friends for playing around with underage girls. "He will be gone in a week," Henry said. Vinnie passed on the veiled threat to the FBI, and Joe's guard detachment increased. Joe claimed he couldn't sleep in the mornings—he knew there was a jail personnel shortage, but he was sure between 9 P.M. and 5 A.M. someone could get at him from the front of the jail.

But Joe also entertained illegal opportunities, real or imagined. Lawyer Al Farese showed him a letter from the Office that pledged a refund of the stolen bail money, among other treasures. The price list dictated that Raymond's innocence was worth $75,000, Pearson's life, and the freedom to testify against anyone else Joe wanted. The Animal claimed he watched the lawyer pocket this promissory note and considered taking it from him by force.

Instead, Joe said, "You talk about your dead parents' grave and church and novenas and you are plotting things like this. You are really a mouthpiece."

There wasn't much honor these days. Rico and Condon continued to play their hands like masters through this lethal and epic poker game. In addition to their small cadre of informers, the two G-men had Stevie Flemmi in their corner. Through him, they owned the Bear, whom Stevie played like a pawn on a chessboard. During their meets, Stevie gave the Bear drugs or money; often the brothers would argue. However, the interactions allowed Stevie to plant ideas in the Bear's brain about Joe. Contrarily, he could glean information from the Bear about the Office's plots to discredit Joe's testimony. As an added touch, Stevie could plant notions in his brother's head, knowing he'd relay them to a trusting Joe as if they were the Bear's own.

For instance, after Larry Baione asked Stevie to get the Bear to destroy the Animal's testimony, Stevie refused. He told Rico of Larry's artifice and instead promised to warn the Bear that discrediting Joe was perilous. Indeed, in a heartbeat, the Animal could finger the Bear as an accessory to Deegan's murder. (It was a bit awkward: While the Bear didn't mind seeing Raymond and Henry suffer, he owed Jerry $10,000.) Poor Vincent could do little more than passively accept Joe's "gift of life." Yet in the summer of 1967, the Bear told a stunned Joseph Balliro that he didn't trust Joe "for one moment." He admitted to being the "fellow in the backseat." If Joe gave him up, he wanted Balliro as attorney.

Stevie also tipped off Rico that Larry would probably ensure Stathopolous "will not be around to corroborate Barboza's testimony." No matter. Between a vigilante MDC detective and the now-dreaded Roy French, Stathopolous's life was already constant terror. On September 15, while Stathopolous visited Old Orchard Beach, he thought he glimpsed French pursuing him. "To hell with this, I'm going to turn myself in," he told a companion. He entered the Maine State Police barracks and offered to sign any statement that would put French away.

Additionally, a grateful Rico covered the Rifleman's flank from rivals and lawmen with brigade-strength FBI paperwork. The wily Spaniard also could smear anyone Stevie chose to in his reports to the Jupiter of law enforcement, J. Edgar.

Frankie Salemme glimpsed a few strands in this complex web of deceit, but never asked Stevie or Rico directly about it. As Frankie once said, "If someone volunteers something, that's fine, otherwise, you don't ask."

Once again, a mob attorney visited Joe and relayed a personal message—from Raymond's own purplish lips. The don promised no one would harm Joe's family, and he'd be welcome, after leaving jail, to visit the Office. Joe concluded the story was bogus: this counselor only merited telephone conversations with Raymond. In any case, none of these schemes flitting about ever materialized.

Joe did stand with Vincent Flemmi, though. Conspiratorially, Doyle took Stath to Barnstable to discuss his upcoming testimony with Joe. Stath asked Joe about where the Bear stood. "I'm going to keep him out of it," Joe said. "He's a good friend of mine and the only one that ever treated me decently."

28.

BARON'S ISLE

"Everybody wants something for nothing & cheap as possible. . . . My life is ruined, even if I was freed. Because I have to run all my life."

—Joe Barboza

Before October came round, Joe met with the "Fibbies" (Rico and Condon) thirty times. He even carried the home phone number of Condon—of whom he once wrote, "yes he has the most class but has viper blood in him too!"

His grand jury testimony done, Joe's guards drove him via Congress Street to the federal building. As the caravan entered the Callahan Tunnel, Joe noticed a tail. While it turned out only to have been a car full of reporters, the marshals wanted to know how Joe had noticed. "It's my business to notice such things," Joe said. He spent the night at the marshal's offices and then returned to Cape Cod, to prepare for the trip to his new home.

Just before midnight on September 19, an armored police van arrived at a private airfield on Cape Cod. State troopers stood guard as the van doors opened and an unshaven and disheveled Joe emerged from inside. Awaiting him were a Coast Guard PBY seaplane, John Partington, and a deputy. Despite the darkness, Joe wore black sunglasses, and a fedora crowned his greasy black hair. The collar on his trench coat was turned up, and a cigarette dangling from his lower lip completed the expected portrait of the "Neanderthal" tough-hoodlum look, noted Partington.

"Hey you, where are my bodyguards?" Joe asked, moving to the plane.

"Lose the cigarette," Partington retorted.

Joe blew smoke at the marshal and mimicked him in a sing-song voice: "Put the cigarette out, put on your seat belt. Who are you, the goddamn warden?" he asked. No response. "I said which one are you?" Partington identified himself, and they climbed into the plane. Joe said, "Oh, you're the prick who's been taking my wife to the beach in her bikini. . . . What's your angle?"

The conversation was a dead end. Soon after, the plane landed at Logan Airport, and the passengers boarded a helicopter that flew them over rocky and rugged Cape Ann. The sun's early rays revealed a fifty-acre speck, looming just about a mile offshore. It was the rocky and treeless Thacher Island, the site of an unmanned lighthouse and two houses.

"You gotta be shitting me," said Joe. "You expect me and my family to live on this shithole?"

"It's either here or a ten-by-twelve-foot cell," said Partington.

After the copter landed, the ground view of the landscape didn't improve Joe's opinion of the island. Claire and Stacey Baron were waiting for Joe in the smaller of the two houses. The other building quartered the sixteen marshals guarding the Barons. Besides Joe, there were other predators and killers here, including rats, snakes, gulls, and poison ivy plants. "It was a real hellhole," said Joe. "It didn't take me long to learn to hate the place."

Soon after his arrival, Joe guided Stacey as she rode her bike (a marshal's gift). When Joe concluded the session, she asked Partington: "Uncle John, can I ride my bike some more?"

Partington said, "Sure, ride it all you want."

She tried to climb back on the bike as Joe grabbed her. "I don't like you," she said to Joe. "I want John as my daddy."

An hour later, Joe was walking on the rocks near the water when Partington approached for a chat. Joe sucker punched him—just as a helicopter, carrying the Fibbies, buzzed over the island. After the chopper landed, an agent noted Partington's bloody lip and asked, "Is there a problem, John?"

"No," said Partington, who could have charged Joe with assault—which brought a minimum ten-year sentence.

Later, Joe said, "Thanks for not ratting me out."

"I'm not a rat."

"Yes, you are, but you are a good rat."

This exchange made Joe friendlier. The marshal observed his ward over time—he watched the Animal patiently teach Stacey the alphabet and colors, or brush her hair, for hours at a time. Craving diversion, sometimes the Animal played cards with the marshals, or he and Partington strolled the small prison-island. They talked for hours together, sometimes comparing their professions. "He explained to me about how he killed people," said Partington. "He was teaching us his tricks as a mob hit man so we would do our job and keep him alive." Over time, the two shared their worldviews. The launch of *Sputnik* provoked jail philosopher Joe to tell Partington there was life on other planets—and humans were pretty meaningless in the cosmic scheme. During one walk, Joe looked up at the sky and asked, "John, fucking what's up there?"

But Joe wasn't mellowing. Because Partington didn't always remember everything Joe wanted him to, Joe dubbed him "Amnesia Head." And when annoyed, Joe would threaten, "I'm gonna eat your liver."

"Joe, you don't fuckin' scare me, you know."

In a boxing demonstration, Joe broke three of a marshal's ribs with one punch. One marshal picked up a dog for Joe at the local pound. For the next two weeks, Joe began teaching it—using, no doubt, unpleasant Pavlovian techniques—to attack the marshals at his command, via hand signals. The marshals returned the dog immediately to the pound. Joe got others.

The bored marshals even tried to kill a beached seal. Naturally, Joe eagerly signed on to this project, grabbing a baseball bat and butcher knife. After the Animal slipped a noose around the seal's neck, it reared and knocked Joe in the water. The deputies had a good laugh. Joe also tried to stone a seagull to death, but it survived, limping about: He adopted the fowl and nursed it along. After stuffing Oby the cat in a sack, he threw the beast into the sea. The cat survived until rescue, and Joe declared Oby a "stand-up" feline. Joe also adopted a stray feline, Carrots. Each day he'd lock the door to his room with Carrots outside. When he returned, by some mysterious means, Carrots would be waiting for him in the room. After once staying awake for twenty-four hours, Joe at last discovered that Carrots crawled up a fireplace and entered through the chimney and, from there, padded to his room.

Finally, using the Deegan murder as a sight, it came time to aim the governmental cannon at the Mafia hierarchy. Rico and Condon, along with Doyle, began interviewing Joe in mid-October to locate the best legal targets. This was tempting: As a Portuguese Jew doubly excluded from the Mafia curia, Joe resented the Italians' racial snobbery. He could now repay his perceived mistreatment, along with as much vig as he could tack on to the bill.

So, Joe assembled a list of almost exclusively Italian culprits, including Louis Greco, Peter Limone, Henry Tameleo, Ronnie Cassesso, Joe Salvati, and Romeo Martin. He also created a new story (naturally, with the same ending for Deegan), but with the players' names altered to protect the guilty and punish the somewhat innocent. His specific reasons for each man's selection varied a bit. Apparently, he held his ex-partner Ronnie responsible for DePrisco's and Bratsos's murders. Nor had Ronnie followed Joe into the testifying business to back him up. Additionally, Ronnie had, deceitfully, passed himself off as a made man—and Joe hated Mafiosi.

French had, in fact, been the primary Deegan shooter (and reportedly had once punched Joe out in the Ebb Tide). Henry may have been the father Joe had always wanted to kill—certainly assassination is a form of flattery. He'd hated Romeo and killed him. Greco had delivered a haymaker at Nicky Femia in East Boston—because of this, Greco said he had a good idea why Joe "threw my name in the hat."

For some reason, Joe also wanted to punish Joe "the Horse" Salvati, a mere mob hanger-on. It may have been over the $400 Salvati owed to Joe—when Nicky Femia had tried to collect this bit of "chump change," the Horse had rebuffed him. And besides this snub, Salvati's height and build resembled Vincent Flemmi's—and so Joe replaced the Bear with the Horse in Romeo's backseat.

As a lifelong liar, Joe routinely mixed fact with fiction to sound credible. So now he threw in true tidbits, such as the bent license plates on Romeo's car and the appearance of Officer Kozlowski. Combined with Stathopolous's testimony as a backup, the prosecutor had a potent case. In Joe's new version, on January 20, 1965, Peter Limone (whom Joe loathed) had offered him $7,500 to kill Deegan. After all, Deegan had murdered Anthony Sacramone and robbed the office bookmaker with Delaney and Hannon. Joe claimed Henry personally granted the Office imprimatur. After Joe took the contract, Louis Greco asked to join, needing money and wanting to kill his wife. Then, on March 11, Limone expanded the contract to include Anthony Stathopolous. The bill for this "package deal" was $10,000. After committing the murder most foul, Joe said Limone paid him his fee on March 13.

Two months of babysitting the Animal had left even Partington's nerves fraying. One night, during a card game that he was losing, Joe said, "Whoever has the ace of hearts fucks his mother in the ass."

"Joe, what if I tell you I have the ace of hearts?"

"Then, John, you fuck your dead mother in the ass, you asshole," Joe said without a flinch. When Partington lunged at Joe, his deputies separated them. Soon after, they apologized, so to speak.

Predictably, it was a gloomy season for the Office and its regents, as Vinnie observed. During one meeting at Atwells Avenue, Raymond conducted business as usual—but Vinnie saw the pretense. The cheery front Raymond offered didn't hide his despair about state and federal indictments. Indeed, Raymond appeared disheartened over "things in general" and believed Henry's and Jerry's cases were hopeless—they faced jail, or even the chair.

Perhaps worse, the fear he'd once inspired was gone, and his grip on the underworld was loosening. The New England Mafia faced a return to its roots as a mere street gang. Cowboy punks were making scores without permission or tribute, and mere anarchy loomed. Henry the Referee had to reprimand someone who'd tried to whack a victim without top clearance. Then he heard a debt collector had visited a debtor's house to recover a loan, with his family present. It was "wrong to enter a man's house with a gun and threaten to kill him as a man's house is his castle," said Henry. He instructed the collector to desist.

But, like declining Rome, the Office had tradition and discipline and reserves, so it wouldn't vanish immediately. If only Raymond knew where Joe was, he could get to him. And should Joe visit Rhode Island, the Office could certainly strike. *The Boston Globe* gave the Office a break on October 21 by publishing an article called "Secluded Isle Baron's Roost." This gave Raymond a map. "How sick can you get?" Joe asked. His conclusion: "I think all reporters are punks!"

A coast guardsman based in Gloucester received an ungrammatical letter at home, typewritten on white paper. "We desire the layout of the Cape Ann area," it said. "We can make it worth your while. Will be in touch." Not thinking the epistle mattered, the mariner destroyed it. Then, realizing better, he told the FBI; his guard unit also received a special danger briefing.

Trials approached. The law heard that five professional killers planned to await Joe outside the Suffolk County Courthouse on October 25, the first day of testimony. A sniper would lurk in a nearby office building. A tip sent the Lynn police to a sixteen-hundred-pound cache of recently stolen dynamite and a thousand-foot roll of primer. Reportedly, the mob even debated killing Garrett Byrne, but voted down this most unwise proposition. Nevertheless, Byrne assigned a police Medal of Honor winner to guard his locked office door.

Authorities took draconian measures in the courthouse: Three policemen protected the grand jury room, and lawmen sealed the eighth-floor room that contained prospective witnesses. The jury lounge on the fifteenth floor became an armed camp. The vigilance of Joe's protectors, who included bomb-sniffing dogs, was world-class. So, for nearly two hours, a healthy and intact Joe spoke of Deegan's killing to the court, and there were indictments. Soon after, police picked up Roy French across the street from his house in Everett. After his arrest in a Cranston cleaning shop, authorities let Henry stew in a Providence jail, pending a fugitive-from-justice hearing. On it went, with Peter Limone, Joe Salvati, and Lou Greco all taking collars.

Hoping to forestall the damage, Raymond instructed Vinnie Teresa, "You take Pro Lerner [a reputed assasin] up there and case the [Thacher's] island. See if you can get Barboza." Obviously, Vinnie got the word to the feds. By the time his yacht reached Joe's roost, Partington had disguised Joe as a marshal and armed his men with carbines. Maurice "Pro" Lerner, although a skin diver, concluded this mission was suicide. That night, Stacey Baron safely knocked on the marshals' door for some Halloween candy.

The marshals moved the Barons (and their small menagerie) to a millionaire's estate at Freshwater Cove, on the other side of Gloucester. The new site was a plot of land that occupied a peninsula, accessible only through the grounds of a Coast Guard station. Inside a surrounding fence stood four large houses arrayed around a central cobblestone garden. The interior furnishings were worthy only of a slum, Joe noted. But it was safe: The marshals installed an electronic detection system with spotlights and ran barbed wire up from the ocean's edge. In the adjacent woods, flare bombs were attached to trip wires. One night, a seagull set one off; the light show resembled the famous Bristol, Rhode Island, Fourth of July fireworks, said Partington. None other than Cardinal Cushing's house stood across the water from the compound. And, "like an altar boy," Joe waved at the many nuns who waited on His Eminence, said Partington.

The Baron compound also hosted Joe's three German shepherds, including two named "Zero" and "Minus," and various other animals. The bitch Minus was "cuckoo like all females," claimed Joe. If anyone yelled at him or Stacey, Minus ripped their pants off, as two marshals discovered. Given the pets' tendency to eat or kill one another, the roster of the Baron zoo fluctuated. Joe retained his pet seagull, although it walked with a limp. Oby ate Stacey's two canaries (given to her, apparently without irony, by the marshals); a Doberman later devoured Oby. Feline-wise, that left only Joe's beloved stray cat Carrots.

For new kicks, Joe pitted one of his shepherds against a stray dog. When the stray got the advantage, Joe bit its ear, forcing out an unforgettable howl. Joe also wasted time fishing or cooking in the compound's shared kitchen, where he specialized in Portuguese food. Partington knew his men disliked seeing Joe with a knife, but the Animal was honorable as chef.

Although, on principle, Joe hated all lawmen, he occasionally gave some marshals a grudging respect. On the other hand, he cut the car tires of one marshal—"the most no-class creep of them all." Another time, catching a marshal drunk, Joe chased him up a flight of stairs. He came just short of a "deep breath" of stabbing another who took a book from his bedroom.

On Thanksgiving night 1967 Partington saw something moving across the courtyard. He searched the estate and found Joe in the kitchen, by an open window, about to jump. "You motherfucker," Joe said softly, and turned. His mouth was foaming, and his eyes were as big, dead, and black as a shark's. Walking to within inches of Partington, he said, "If you ever see me this way again, John, get the fuck away from me. I'll fucking kill you. Don't you ever forget it."

The Animal was always counterscheming and inventing absurd plans—he was more dangerous to himself than to his enemies. Joe bragged that his wife kept a large handbag with a .45 hidden inside. While at the estate, Joe decided to kill a Boston attorney (possibly Bailey or Farese). He tape-recorded an argument with his wife, planning to play this over and over again and make it appear as if he was in Freshwater. He might have executed the scheme, but he failed to steal a vehicle.

Somehow, Partington managed to protect the maniac under his wing as if he were a president. Partington sometimes formed automotive caravans comprising three "inconspicuous" vehicles. The drivers never took one-way streets, given gangsters were skilled at applying hijacking roadblocks. Once, Partington and Joe drove to court in a bright red sports car, with caps on their heads and mufflers around their necks to disguise them. Another time, Joe rode in a mail truck so the marshals could deliver him to the post office of the federal building. Partington also arranged a night-time voyage on a Coast Guard cutter to the dock by the foot of Hanover Street. To return, Joe boarded a fishing boat at a South Boston pier. In an imperial touch, Joe and a cadre of machine-gun-toting guards even flew in a helicopter to the roof of the court building.

The marshals, who often slept with Joe in the courthouse, were risking their lives—one bold man acted as his official food taster. At least once, a deputy masqueraded as Joe and rode in an armored car, sirens wailing, to the courthouse. The actual Joe, to the degree there was one, entered a side door; when Joe left the courthouse, Partington deployed decoys. Once, dressed as a marshal in the midst of the squad, Joe couldn't resist saying, "All right, Barboza, you asshole, keep moving." Even the newspapermen laughed.

Yet the Office's indefatigable hands appeared everywhere: thugs spooked a writer who volunteered to pen Joe's biography; one assassin got arrested to see if he could hit Joe in the courthouse; yet another operative stole a police officer's uniform. Again, Raymond dispatched Lerner to kill Joe. After enduring a rainstorm in the woods trying to line up a rifle shot into the compound, Lerner gave up, again unwilling to trade his life for Joe's. And Pro Lerner was "no run-of-the-mill mug," Vinnie noted.

Undaunted, Raymond tried other means. The Office unsuccessfully offered $50,000 to a convict to confess to killing Deegan. To further spook Fitzgerald, Guy Frizzi visited the lawyer's Everett office and introduced himself as Peter Limone's partner. He cryptically told the office manager, "I've killed before and I'll kill again and I won't stand for this."

Fitzgerald then visited the Bat Cove and asked if Limone could stop Guy from going to his law office—if that was what Limone wanted. Limone promised the visits would stop. Then a duo (including, possibly, Henry Tameleo's brother) in their fifties came by the office and asked if Joe Barboza's "brain trust" was there.

With all this attention, Fitzgerald figured they might just make him disappear.

"You're playing with dynamite," Larry Baione warned Fitzgerald, in public. Fitzgerald tried to reactivate his captain's commission for the simmering war in Vietnam. That failed, and he waited stateside for a bullet.

29

CHANGE IN OWNERSHIP

The "skittish" William Bennett had kept a few steps behind his brothers when it came to their rackets. But now, as the Bennett heir apparent, he obsessed with finding his lost siblings. Hoping to move on Frankie and Stevie, Bennett enlisted two underworld friends, Hugh "Sonny" Shields and Richard Grasso. Despite William's plots, Stevie told Rico that his own Dearborn Square gang had "much better connections and information on Billy Bennett's activities than he has on their activities."

The faithless Grasso told Stevie about Bennett's plans and, with Frankie, he formed a counterplot. The scheme required luring William out of his house and easing his way into the "Bennett Burial Site," as Frankie dubbed the Hopkinton disposal ground. The pawn would be the baby-faced Grasso, a nonentity who was just the right man to lull the wary Bennett. As planned, on December 23, 1967, Grasso and two other men, including Shields, drove to Bennett's house in Mattapan. Bennett entered the car, wearing a shoulder strap carrying a pistol under his jacket. According to testimony, five minutes later, while driving on Harvard Street in Dorchester, Shields produced a pistol and shot William four times in the head and chest. As he died, William uncooperatively made for the door, which opened and let him drop into the middle of the street. Grasso panicked, pulled over, and left the car running in a driveway. Soon after, Peter Poulos managed to collect Grasso and Shields and made for Frankie's garage—where the General awaited them so he could dispose of the body. When Poulos arrived, he now saw no Bennett, and the "clowns" were in a panic.

"He fell out," one of them said.

"What do you mean he fell out?" Frankie asked. He shot up the street in his car and drove past the body, which lay in a snowbank on the roadside, near a meat stand. While Frankie swung around to pick up the corpse, a cab arrived on the scene, high beams glaring. Now unable to stop, Frankie continued, and soon after, the police arrived. Seeing Bennett's shoulder strap and weapon, investigators were worried the victim had been a cop. After learning he was just a half-assed criminal, they were relieved.

The now panicked Grasso was in Poulos's car when, to calm him, someone produced a pistol and shot him in the head. This killing was almost in the line of sight of a Boston police squad. No official response. With Grasso's body inside, Stevie drove Poulos's car away—accidentally triggering a specially installed siren. Again, this attracted no attention. Grasso soon after reappeared in the trunk of his own car, then parked in Brookline. There were two bullets in his head; the car had been ticketed; there were no arrests.

Until now (claimed Joe), the Bear had liked to joke that "Wimpy and Walter are together playing whist." When the Bear learned of the third Bennett's ultimate exit, he said, "Dammit. I wish they'd buried him with the other two so Wimpy and Walter could have had a referee when they play whist. Nothing like keeping it in the family."

Clearly, Rico could guess why the Bennetts had such a high mortality rate, but the agent did nothing tangible. In a February memo, he declared, "Through informants of this office, it has been established that this [Stevie] individual enjoys a reputation of being a very capable individual and that he will now be the leader of the group formerly headed by Edward 'Whimpy' Bennett." The Bennetts were erased as a power in the underworld, and their killers laid down the new law before the third brother was even planted. After identifying William's body, his wife returned home. Before she was able to get her coat off, the phone rang. Someone told her "that if she said anything to the police, she would die and so would all of her children." She stayed indoors for a long time after that—years, in fact, said her son. In keeping with the new order in Roxbury, Larry Baione bought Walter's Lounge soon after, to remake as his own shylocking and bookmaking center.

The Office discovered attorney John Fitzgerald planned to co-author a book with Joe, and maybe even to testify. Fearing the potential trifecta of Marfeo, DiSeglio, and Deegan, Raymond summoned Frankie to Providence. The don offered him a contract on Fitzgerald—by any means he preferred. Killing Fitzgerald didn't bother Frankie—after all, he claimed the lawyer was playing both ends against the middle. In fact, Fitzgerald, an officer of the court, continued Joe's finance business from his Everett law office. Frankie knew the identities of some of the Animal's customers, and had figured out how the operation ran. One of Joe's collectors still made the rounds at the spots in Revere, Chelsea, and East Boston to pick up the client payments. On Saturday mornings, the Barboza collector visited Fitzgerald in his Everett offices to split up the take. As Frankie observed, Claire Baron would be there to get her cut, too. Fitzgerald even drove Joe's gold Pontiac, marking him as part of the East Boston crew. In short, as Frankie put it: "He [Fitzgerald] was a lawyer, and he was also, as I like to say in the vernacular, a crook."

After some preliminary work, Frankie decided executing the Fitzgerald contract was a simple enough job. However, just before New Year's, Larry Baione came by Frankie's club and announced, "Raymond now is going to handle this. They're going to blow him up."

"Blow him up for what?" Frankie asked.

"He wants to make an example."

Given his aversion to big bangs and small cities, Frankie said he voided the contract; the Rifleman remained on the job.

On December 19, 1967, a nervous and profanely explosive Joe Barboza returned to a Boston court for a pretrial hearing against Raymond. Joe told Partington that it was Christmas, and he had to bring something back for his daughter. "Get me a stuffed Santa Claus or something as a present." (The Animal always bought Stacey a stuffed animal after a hit.) While in court, Joe faced Raymond for the first time since the Office had fired him and handed eternal severance packages to the Eastie crew. Raymond fixed his famed icy glare on Joe, and at testimony's end, made a fist, extended his thumb, and drew it across his throat.

"You rat," Raymond called.

"You fuck your dead mother in the mouth," said Joe, lunging at the don. With a little luck, he later boasted, he could have saved Uncle Sam the cost of a trial. But Partington and another marshal grabbed Joe off his feet as he rose, and carried him away.

Later, arriving at the Coast Guard station, Joe strode onto the deck of a ship equipped with a helicopter landing pad. The sight of the Cro-Magnon convict out in the open, carrying a large stuffed Santa, provoked the crew to laugh. "You motherfuckers wanna laugh at me?" Joe asked. "You want a fuckin' shank down your spine?" The mirth ceased.

The winter of 1968 was mistreating the LCN of New England. At the opening of the DiSeglio trial in early January, Joe composed a telegram for Jerry. With his wife's help, he quoted a line from the book of Daniel: "Mene, mene, tekel upharsin" (which was a prophecy a kingdom would fall). He signed it "The Animal."

Informant Vinnie Teresa sat in his catbird seat and watched how the players reshuffled, like so many cards. The tribulations of the Angiulos were a special delight. Incarceration proved expensive for Jerry and his moneymaking machine. Since his arrest, Jerry had lost "a great deal of prestige" and his brothers were "bungling" the operation, the FBI noted. A sentence of six months to a year could even mean the revocation of all the franchises Jerry ran for the Office. But, the Angiulos had brought this on themselves with "sloppy management," as Vinnie told the FBI. For the interim, Raymond officially appointed Larry acting head of Boston, a promotion that might stand, even if Jerry eventually returned to the street. A Baione-led Boston branch of the Office was fine with Vinnie, since Larry had "the faculty of making everyone with whom he comes in contact with feel important."

The Office still hoped to snuff Joe before he could testify against Jerry. Reportedly, four Mafia shooters covered the Suffolk County Courthouse's four doors. So, one morning at 2 A.M., Partington squirreled a uniformed Joe into the building, secretly embedded inside a twenty-strong marshals' contingent, whose members all wore hoods with eye slits.

When the prosecutor ordered Joe to the witness stand, the entire courtroom stirred. A "bevy" of attractive mob groupies had assembled, just for a glimpse of Joe Baron, as if he were a rock star. The pale-faced Animal met the court's expectations: Wearing a suit, his black hair coiffed in a neat pompadour, he could have been a banker—or a caveman. Getting ready for a kill, Joe walked with a slight swagger, and his rare smile lacked humor. Passing by the prisoners' box, he ducked his head, ignoring the four men his accusations had seated there. While testifying, Joe clasped his large boxers' hands tightly, and his pinky rings looked "girlish and dainty on both little fingers."

Then he testified, often in the coded language of gangsterese, peppered with his own double negatives. The prosecutor often had to translate for the jury. Whenever Joe finished speaking, he'd look at his former colleagues in the dock as if they were garbage. The accused stared at Joe with undisguised hatred. Resembling a "nervous bartender," Jerry thrust his head forward as if he were trying to catch every word. By Joe's second day on the stand, he remained calm, even if his odd look and speech unnerved the jury.

The defense threw everything at Joe. When reciting Joe's encyclopedic criminal record, one attorney asked the Animal if he'd broken into a poultry store and illicitly taken a rooster.

Disgustedly, Joe said, "I don't remember stealing any rooster, Your Honor."

Before the trial, an enraged Joe had planned to get in striking range of Balliro and break him up with his own hands. Perhaps sensing this anger, sometimes Balliro turned his back disdainfully at Joe, hoping to provoke an explosion. At one point, Joe pointed a finger accusingly at Balliro and shouted, "I'm up here telling the truth, and I'm not motivated by any capital gains . . . I'm not ashamed of anything, Mr. Balliro."

Eventually, Balliro forced Joe to admit he was trying to sell his biography. "There would never be a need for a book if these guys hadn't killed my friends," Joe said. Balliro mentioned as possible author Truman Capote, who'd penned *In Cold Blood*.

"Ever read it?" Balliro asked.

"No."

Smiling, Balliro said, "I think you'd like that book, Mr. Barboza."

The courtroom mood was sometimes grim: The color photos of DiSeglio's ruined face made one female juror blanch. But the revelation that Joe once performed "public relations" for Fishbein Insurance caused courtroom snickers, which the judge rebuked. When Joe's testimony concluded, some in the court were relieved.

"Personally, I was glad when he was off the witness stand," said the jury foreman. "When he was there I worried there would be trouble."

The defense continued to sharp-shoot Joe's testimony, hoping to pick off its most exposed and vulnerable parts. There was some crucial argument about where DiSeglio had given up the ghost. Counsel insisted the murder had occurred in Topsfield between 1 P.M. and 7 P.M. on the sixteenth (a Topsfield witness had heard three shots at 5 P.M. that day), and not in East Boston the prior evening. Experts debated the workings of rigor mortis, and Balliro insinuated Joe had killed DiSeglio himself.

On January 18, the jury left for what proved to be a mere two-hour deliberation—the surprised judge had to interrupt his lunch to preside over the verdict reading. Of the defendants, only Jerry, clutching the dock rail, biting his lip, and swallowing continuously, showed emotion as the foreman said "Not guilty" over and over again. Jerry sagged, and several times blinked back tears. The now-unaccused stampeded: Zinna headed to the public entrance without even retrieving his belongings. When the ex-defendants reached the eighth-floor corridor, they ran into a crush of pleased supporters, friends and family, and reporters.

"I don't want to say anything right now," declared Jerry. "I want to see my old mother. She's 73 and this thing has been bothering her." Proclaiming his World War II service, he said, "Now I know what I was fighting for." Paraphrasing boxer Rocky Graziano's customary radio victory address, he said, "Well, I won, and I'll be right home, Mom."

Joe appeared to be guilty of the not guilty verdict. The jury foreman said: "He was an animal himself. How can you accept whatever he says?"

But Joe blamed the district attorney's office for bungling the job, instead.

"See what ya get for trying to do the right thing?" he asked Partington.

30.

THE BOMB

On January 30, 1968, attorney John Fitzgerald parked the James Bond car in Everett, near what would be his office for one last day. He and Farese were parting ways. It was raining, and for reasons he forgot, Fitzgerald didn't activate the alarm after locking his car. Then he walked to the office to finish the paperwork to sever his partnership. Knowing his unpopularity with some of Farese's clients, he carried a licensed pistol.

That same day, after taking a phone call at Frankie's club, Stevie Flemmi drove to the Sharma Tavern to meet Larry Baione. Joining two confederates, the Rifleman headed to Everett to fulfill Raymond's contract, said Frankie, who claimed he sat this dance out. After Stevie's crew located John Fitzgerald's distinctive automobile, it took perhaps as few as sixty seconds to plant a dynamite bomb. Stevie was back in Frankie's club before suppertime. Now all the conspirators waited for Fitzgerald to activate the bomb.

Just after 5 P.M., Fitzgerald stepped out into the dark and entered his Pontiac. Imitating a television stunt, he opened the door and sat with his left foot outside, and his right foot on the accelerator. The door still ajar, Fitzgerald pressed down on the pedal. Although later he couldn't recall if he turned the key, there was a loud noise and an enormous force rose up from under him.

"Oh my God, they have put a bomb in the car," he thought. As the first charge detonated, the car's windows shattered; the lawyer pulled his now-shredded legs up into the vehicle before throwing himself out. He landed on his back and elbows on the cold, wet ground—just before a second charge went off, generating much greater force than the original one. This explosion broke the hull of Joe Barboza's onetime prize toy and ejected the front windshield from its perch and through the rear windshield. As Fitzgerald watched, windows on a house across the street shattered as wire and debris ascended, severing the electrical wires overhead.

A nearby policeman ceased directing traffic and ran to Fitzgerald, who, conscious, cried for help. "Call Rico of the FBI," he said. The attorney's face was bloody, his clothing burnt, and parts of the car seat were "sort of molded to his body." An ambulance rushed him to nearby Whidden Memorial Hospital, where surgeons performed a five-hour operation. Since his right leg was ruined, they amputated it—which required pumping Whidden's entire supply of Fitzgerald's blood type into his veins. And Fitzgerald still owed $2,300 on the now-ruined Pontiac.

On hearing the news, Joe became "insane with fury." He warned Partington to worry less about the Mafia killing him—than for Joe to escape and go after the Office.

On the other hand, Larry Baione was angry the bombing had fallen short of obliterating Fitzgerald. Consoling him, Raymond let Baione know he believed the Office had sent its message, nevertheless. Indeed it had. Someone had actually struck at a lawyer, one of the connective tissues that knitted upper and under worlds. Since the criminal rank and file knew that the "cocky" don had approved the act, it waited for the inevitable counterreaction. Knowing the publicity might hurt his legal fortunes, Raymond even requested a postponement of his trial and its removal to New York. However, the authorities kept the trial in Boston, where the veneer Raymond had so carefully painted over himself and his corporation had worn thin. A legal tide was moving in, powerful enough to take him out, just as a rogue ocean swell had removed downtown Providence in the Hurricane of 1938. Seeing the peril, in March, a desperate Raymond even met with Rudolph Marfeo, in the latter's house basement. Raymond then claimed Willie Marfeo's murder had all been Henry's doing. The don told Rudolph he wanted one of the Marfeo brothers—legally clean—to testify he, Raymond, had been friends with Willie, with a trouble-free relationship. Rudolph agreed to think about it—if Raymond arranged the murder of the man who'd hit Willie. Raymond wouldn't go that far, but gave his imprimatur to Rudolph to do it. On and on the two haggled, but the negotiations went nowhere.

In dismay, feeling the public sentiment against him, Raymond stopped discussing the trial. Henceforward, his mood swung between mad rages and silent depressions.

Now Stevie saw great opportunities—the despised North End mob was nearly crippled. The Rifleman told Rico he and Larry Baione had reconciled—and, dishonestly, he claimed Larry boasted he'd murdered Wimpy. On the other hand, Stevie also admitted he wanted to kill Larry and pin it on the Martoranos.

As for Jerry, since beating the DiSeglio beef, he appeared to have "flipped his lid." Jerry now constantly talked as if he were a movie gangster. Of late, the newspapers were revealing his seedy role in throwing a gubernatorial election against a fellow Italian. The FBI noted that although Jerry could recall his glory days as a capo and underboss, he'd concluded that "no power is worth the aggravation and tension that he went through in the state murder trial." Nervous, he sold Jay's Lounge and suggested he might become an advisor like Joseph Lombardo, retire safely with his millions, and hand over his operation to Larry. But Jerry and Larry concurred that Joe Barboza must die an unnatural death—and the Office pledged $150,000 to make it happen.

For the Marfeo trial that March, Partington flew Joe into Boston via helicopter to the Hatch Shell stage at the Charles River esplanade. Eight men with rifles exited the chopper and entered a caravan of tinted-window Cadillacs. For three days, Joe and Partington inhabited a cell in the courthouse. Investigators uncovered a cache of five hundred pounds of nitroglycerin intended for Joe's car. "Hey, J. P.," Joe told Partington, "that'd blow your bony ass right down to Providence."

In court, Joe was once again the star. On the sixth, he entered the courtroom in the "middle of a square" of twelve marshals. Joe strode to the defense table, smirked at his former colleagues, and then walked away. Partington studied Raymond, arrayed in a cheap suit with a dark necktie; he noted white socks showing above the wingtip shoes. Raymond's "deeply lined face made him look like he'd been hired as an actor to play mob boss." Bereft of his customary cigar, Raymond curled up his torso and put his two thin arms on the table in front of him. In contrast to the "saturnine" Raymond, Ronnie and Henry "could have passed for grocery clerks dressed for Sunday church," said a reporter.

At last, Joe finished his testimony, allowing one of the prosecutors, Paul Markham, almost inaudibly, to rest the government's case at 2:27 P.M. "Barboza's no angel," said the prosecutor. "But"—he said, pointing at Raymond—"if you didn't have the Raymond Patriarcas, you wouldn't have the Joe Barbozas. Who's worse?"

On March 8, after only four hours, the jury announced all three men guilty. Hearing this, Raymond leaned on the courthouse railing, and gripped it until his knuckles whitened. After two decades on the street, Raymond was returning to prison. Reporters asked him for a comment. "I'm an old man," he said.

Partington ran back to Joe's cell. "Guilty, all counts!" he shouted.

"We did it! We did it!" Joe screamed manically. Despite this, Joe was "very disappointed" with Raymond's prosecution and resented that Markham never personally thanked him. Joe wrote: "While these people don't want to show their appreciation, I am sure that Joe Balliro . . . would show his appreciation in me, and I am sure that if things don't work out, that I can at least end up with $150,000 from Balliro."

Emotionally unstrung, Raymond seethed with contempt for Joe and the FBI. This verdict must have shocked Henry, who had bragged he'd beat the case, and had even arranged a trip to Miami. Soon after their convictions, Raymond, Henry, and Ronnie each received a five-year sentence and a fine of $10,000. To the court, Raymond stated: "Your Honor, I've got something to say. It may be out of line. I had my witnesses here, but counsel said it wasn't necessary to use them. If we had used my witnesses it might have been different."

The verdict was a long shot. Bookies who'd taken bets on a not-guilty outcome now had to pay out as much as five to one. As lucky hoodlums collected through their shock, the Providence LCN all but trembled that the FBI would engineer yet more convictions.

Late that March, Joe claimed Claire was intermittently ill, there was no daytime matron, and he was up "against an impossible situation." Joe even wrote to Robert Kennedy and complained about his treatment. No matter—nothing came of it. Nevertheless, unintentionally, Joe had started something much bigger than himself: the witness protection program. Its existence made organized crime permanently vulnerable.

It still was a volatile criminal underworld on the streets. On Saturday, April 20, 1968, Rudolph Marfeo, with his muscle, Anthony

Melei, performed a weekly shopping ritual in Pannone's Market on Pocasset Avenue. Now, today, after two masked men carrying sawed-off shotguns entered the store, there was just enough time for Marfeo to draw his .38. The gunmen opened fire, blasting Marfeo's left side apart; he fell near the front door. Melei, catching double-aught buckshot in the face, died near the ice cream freezer.

On May 21, in Suffolk Superior Court, Joe pled guilty to two counts of conspiracy. He was now a committed witness, and even told the Fibbies he was looking forward to testifying in the Deegan trial. On May 25, the third and most high-profile of all Joe's witness stints started. Once again, the Office fielded a legal army, with Joe Balliro the first in a crowd of ruthless and amoral defense attorneys.

Once again, Rico, through his informants, knew most of the defense's strategy—both in and out of court. He discovered Jerry and Larry wanted to "reach" prospective jurors and defense witnesses. Jerry would pay Zalkind $200,000 for a guaranteed "not guilty."

In the midst of its dark days, the mob got some good news on June 5. Robert Kennedy's life and career had ceased abruptly during a brief encounter with nonentity Sirhan Sirhan. Hearing this, a distraught Joe vanished into even deeper seclusion, and, for a brief time, nobody saw him. But Kennedy's mission against organized crime continued, and new deputies arrived at Freshwater to keep Joe safe.

Joe's presence was not the only absurdity at the Deegan trial. Among the exhibits were: toy .38 and .45 caliber pistols; a toy M-1 Garand rifle; a character mustache; and a Charlie Chaplin mustache. To demonstrate his escape from Deegan's alley, Roy French dropped to the courtroom floor onto his fingertips and toes and, using a "crablike stride," made his way across the floor. This odd tone continued all the way to the dramatic high point of the trial: The Animal's testimony. After Judge Felix Forte ordered all the courtroom shades on one side of the room drawn to discourage snipers, Joe took the stand, arrayed in a green sports jacket and chinos. A seasoned witness now, he looked away from the defendants and spoke so softly Judge Forte told him to speak up.

Joe admitted his various nicknames, which included "Brandy, Seagull, Rainmaker, Xavier, and Farouk." He also denied that the reason he changed his name to Baron was because he felt he deserved feudal tribute. Now, to replace the Bear with Joe "the Horse" Salvati, Joe stated Salvati's disguise included a flesh-colored wig that made him look bald. "I could see Joe [Salvati] putting on this wig and hear the snapping of the elastic. . . . [The wig] had hair around this way and it had [a] few strands over here. It gave you a very high—there are a few strands in front that went back here and you were bald."

In sweltering heat, the cross-examining defense again opened on the Animal, now virtually caged on the witness stand. Joe pushed back. One lawyer sticking pins into a murder-scene chart asked Joe to help him place one. Joe asked, "You want me to tell you what you can do with that pin?" Joe denounced another lawyer for bad breath. Balliro was especially abrasive and asked Joe why he'd wanted Deegan gone. "The money meant nothing, nothing," Joe said. The most important thing was that "I elevate myself with the Office."

Balliro made a face. "What's he looking at me like that for?" Joe asked.

"May the record show that it was a look of disgust," said Balliro.

"No it wasn't, Joe [Balliro]. You're trying to irritate me."

Then, on Joe's third day on the stand, the defense, going for the throat—or to a lower region—produced Joe's love letters to a mistress. From one of Joe's love epistles a defense lawyer quoted, "I don't care whether they're [the accused] innocent or not. They go." Joe knew that Claire would hear of his adulteries, and his cool broke.

On the stand, the hulking Louis Greco looked nervously out from behind his dark-rimmed glasses. This was a sad spectacle. A seventh-grade dropout, unlike most gangsters, he was a World War II hero of sorts. He limped from a permanent wound suffered during the second landing at Bataan. But Greco could also be a "vicious vicious guy" with a frightening temper, said Vinnie Teresa—and only his close friends dared call him by the nickname "Gimp." Words were difficult for him to manufacture into logical sentences; when he became frustrated and unable to speak, he just walked away. Or he might strike. Vinnie uncharitably thought him a "bumbling idiot."

As a civilian, Greco had worked as a car repossession man, landscaper, and heavyweight fighter. A brief career as Revere restaurateur ended in fall 1958, when someone (possibly at his behest) firebombed his eatery. Thereafter, for a time, Greco became a chicken farmer in North Kingston, New Hampshire. Greco liked flowers, and would go on to plant them in every prison he served in.

Now he was in Joe's sights in court. "I'm fighting for my life," Greco explained. Joe was a "Judas," and he never liked him. "Don't like him today."

After the state rested its case, five of Boston's most aggressive defense lawyers denounced Joe as a "liar" and "executioner" in voices that alternated from soft and patient to loud and emotional. After fifty days, the trial, the longest of the three Joe testified in (it produced a 7,555-page transcript), mercifully ended. After two days and seven hours of deliberation, on July 31 the jury voted that the Deegan six were guilty. Immediately, Forte ordered Henry, Ronnie, Limone, and Greco to the chair and life terms for French and Salvati.

Weeping broke out among the defendants' wives. Never before in the state's history were so many men convicted and condemned to death at once. It took armed police to keep about twenty-four protestors at bay.

Like nothing else before, the Deegan trial broke the backbone of the New England mob. The bosses, said Vinnie, were in "utter panic" and confused about what their next moves should be. The death sentence made Jerry "despondent." He felt Ronnie should have been "man enough to take the fall" for killing Deegan, with Joe. The Angiulo brothers were "sick" over losing Limone, and all blamed his demise on Henry, who'd been "the connection" for Joe into the outfit.

The trial riled others, too. Rico and Condon visited Frankie's garage. Stevie Flemmi was there, and perhaps for his benefit, Condon said, "I wonder how Louie Greco likes it on death row?"

The statement puzzled and offended Frankie.

Condon asked Frankie, "If you're so smart, why don't you get on the stand and testify?"

"Who's going to listen to me? Who's going to believe me? I'll go on the stand if you do. You won't get by St. Peter in the gate, you can't. You broke one of the 10 commandments: 'Thou shalt not bear false witness.' You can't get by him, Dennis." The more Frankie "hit" him with that, the angrier Condon grew. Just then, Frankie caught Rico flashing a wondering look at Stevie. Not aware of its meaning, Frankie invited the agents to join him and Stevie for their customary lunch at a local restaurant. Condon refused: The argument about the trial was the end of Frankie's rapport with Rico. No matter: Stevie and Rico remained close. After all, Stevie was fascinated with getting away with whatever he wanted, and with giving up on "jerks like me," Frankie concluded.

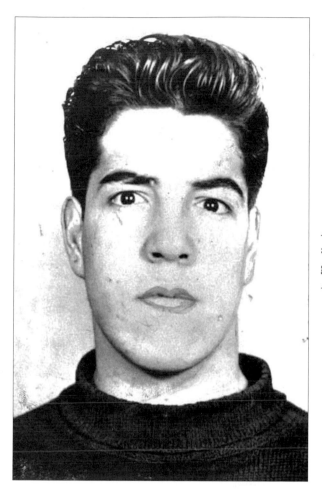

A youthful Joseph Barboza, already practicing his savage glare. (*Courtesy of the Boston Public Library*)

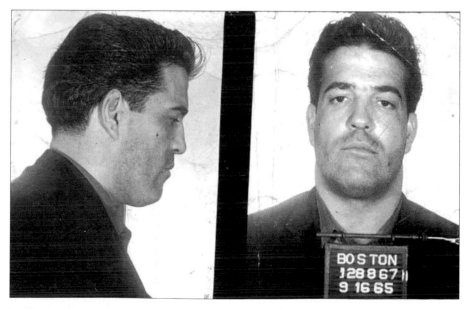

Joe Barboza's now seasoned visage, in a 1965 mug shot. (*Courtesy of the Boston Public Library*)

Vincent James Flemmi, the portrait of the Bear as a Cub. *(Courtesy of the Boston Public Library)*

Stephen "Stevie the Rifleman" Flemmi as a youth. He later proved to be the cleverest and most treacherous of Boston's major underworld leaders. *(Courtesy of the Boston Public Library)*

New England Mafia leader Raymond Patriarca, with his famous scowl. *(Courtesy of the* Boston Herald*)*

Raymond in his heyday, complete with cigar. *(Courtesy of the* Boston Herald*)*

Henry Tameleo, the clever under-boss, the glue that held the Patriarca family together. *(Courtesy of the* Boston Herald*)*

Gennaro "Jerry" Angiulo, leader of Boston's "bunch of bookies." *(Courtesy of the Boston Public Library)*

The Bear in custody.
(Courtesy of the Boston
Public Library)

James "Buddy" McLean, founder
of the Winter Hill Gang.
(Courtesy of the Boston Herald*)*

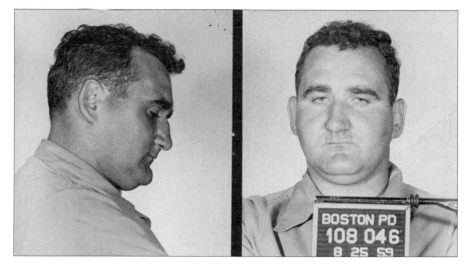

Cornelius "Connie" Hughes, one half of the Charlestown crew's most deadly pair. *(Courtesy of the Boston Public Library)*

Stephen "Little Stevie" Hughes (second from left), the other half of Charlestown's most fearsome duo. *(Courtesy of the Boston Public Library)*

Edward "Punchy" McLaughlin.
(Courtesy of the Boston Public Library)

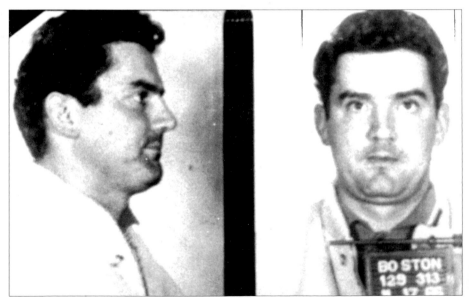

Francis "Frankie" Salemme, variously called Cadillac Frank (for his taste in cars) or the General for his prowess in criminal planning, murders included. *(Courtesy of the Boston Public Library)*

Mafioso Peter Limone (at left), whom Joe falsely accused of engineering the Degan contract. *(Courtesy of the Boston Public Library)*

William "Billy" Geraway, who played a very dangerous game of chess with Joe Barboza. *(Courtesy of the Boston Public Library)*

The bloody aftermath of the assassination of Buddy McLean, on Winter Hill. *(Courtesy of the* Boston Herald*)*

Connie Hughes's automobile after his dramatic shooting. *(Courtesy of the* Boston Herald*)*

Joe Barboza attempting to hide his famous visage. *(Courtesy of the* Boston Herald*)*

A reluctant Joe struggles with his minders. *(Courtesy of the* Boston Herald*)*

31

THE ANIMAL LOOSED AGAIN

So eager was Joe to keep testifying, he gave up Johnny Martorano for yet another crime: killing a grand jury witness, John Jackson. However, by now Claire was too miserable and tense to remain a witness's spouse. "I never realized this was going to drag on as long as it has," Claire said.

"What would have happened if the FBI hadn't gone to talk to your husband in the first place?" one Fibbie asked.

"The Suffolk County district attorney would have given him 99 years and I would have divorced him and been rid of him." She'd nearly left him the past summer, and she openly advertised her readiness to leave now.

On Saturday, October 5, 1968, Joe had at least one piece of good fortune, indirect though it may have been. Sometime around 1 A.M., his onetime victim and accuser Arthur Pearson left the 416 Lounge (formerly the Nite Lite) in the North End. Two men approached Pearson's car and threw a brick through its window. A fight started, knives flashed, and someone stabbed Pearson seventeen times in the stomach. Ambulance drivers pronounced him dead before he even reached Mass General Hospital. A friend said only a knife could have stopped Pearson in a fight. But as the pall-bearers hauled the twenty-five-year-old's pearl-gray casket out of Our Lady of Grace Church to the hearse, some observers shook their unbelieving heads. In private, Jerry admitted he was fed up with the gang that had apparently stabbed Pearson.

On November 1, Joe appeared in Suffolk County Superior Court, with John Fitzgerald and his cane. (Joe now called Fitzgerald "Lucky," as he'd survived the bomb attempt.) The judge filed the dreaded habitual-criminal indictments against Joe—for now. He faced only a few more months in jail.

Heartily, Joe said, "Thank you, Your Honor." He and Partington checked into a Boston hotel for their last night together. Joe, now merely another criminal nonentity, warned Partington, "Just wait until tomorrow. You're gonna see the real Joe Barboza, not the rat fink. You bring your big shiny badges, bring your big shiny guns, because you're gonna need them." To prepare for the show-down, Joe stayed up all evening boxing alone, his muscles bunching up threateningly.

That morning, Partington told his men he'd visit Joe alone, carrying his walkie-talkie. "If I click it twice, I want you to come in shooting," he instructed. The marshal entered Joe's room, lay down on the couch, pulled his cap over his eyes, and announced they'd leave in ten minutes.

"Where are the others?" Joe asked.

"Do you think for one minute, after all you've done, after all we've been through, that I would let this end in a showdown? No way, Joe."

With two of Joe's dogs, the duo drove to Logan Airport, where awaiting them was the PBY that had first flown them from Cape Cod to Boston. Before boarding, Joe produced a pack of cigarettes, lit one, and deliberately and defiantly blew smoke at Partington. Then Joe put on his signature wraparound shades, drew close to the marshal, and said, "See ya, Amnesia Head." He added, "By the way, I left you a parting gift in the apartment."

On the plane, Joe gazed at Partington through a window and smiled; then the plane rose out of sight. Soon after, Joe entered the junior officers' quarters in Fort Knox to serve the rest of his sentence. There, in the protective bosom of the U.S. Army, Joe, not exactly treasure himself, admitted the nearby gold gave him something to think about.

Partington headed to a Boston hotel room to meet with a distraught Claire Baron, now ready to bail out on Joe. Somehow, Partington convinced her to continue her marriage and enter the witness protection program. Soon after, the marshal discovered Joe's farewell gift was his adopted stray dog, now abandoned in Gloucester.

The Barons had gotten off rather lightly from their connection with Deegan. But the guilty and innocent men whom Joe's testimony had convicted and their families suffered immensely. Some victims committed slow suicide with drugs or alcohol, in deaths that required a thousand cuts to complete. Greco's children could see their father only in increments. One of his sons arrived for a jail visit and noticed his father's leg was missing (an amputation from substandard care for his managed diabetes). "That was one of the worst times," Mrs. Greco later reflected.

To survive, Marie Salvati settled into a routine, collecting cards and other memorabilia from her husband and storing them in a box. She said: "And let me tell you, for like 30 years, I want to say I felt like my life was in the shoe box." The architect of the contract, Roy French, was a "nice guy," as Frankie Salemme said, applying the gangster's version of the phrase. However, Frankie added: "There's a certain amount of honor you have to have even among thugs like us. If you don't have it like me, setting up Stevie [Flemmi] would be out of the question, you know. I'd rather go down or he and I take off and go down fighting. . . . I would never do that. . . . You just didn't do those things." Reputedly, French created an altar out of the toilet bowl and blessed himself with the water.

That March, Raymond, out on a $25,000 bond, beat a separate loan-sharking charge in a Providence court. Although he kept strategically stalling, the don was inevitably heading to his one-time home, the federal penitentiary in Atlanta. Although his men were shocked and crestfallen about Raymond's looming sentence, the don had steeled himself to return to the proverbial can. He would, as best as he could, dictate policy from Atlanta, while minor beefs were Larry's or Jerry's domain. But Raymond was so angry, even his colleagues found it nearly impossible to speak to him. The mere mention of Henry Tameleo's name made him furious, since he blamed him for bringing "all the local punks around." If Henry had been more discerning, these troubles would never have happened. (For his part, Henry, locked up without bail in a Rhode Island cell, now fumed at Jerry and Raymond for antagonizing Joe until he flipped.)

As one reporter noted, Raymond now was a shell: His familiar frown, with the arms-wide, leave-me-alone gesture, wasn't as effective as it had been long ago in courtrooms in Providence and Cambridge (or when he'd exited Charlestown State Prison).

With four men on death row, a desperate Raymond said he needed $200,000 and didn't care how he got it. Providence had simmered with gang violence for years, and the don, weakened, was a potential target. One nutty drug-addled Providence gang vowed they feared neither Raymond nor the FBI. With that in mind, none other than John Partington would deliver Raymond safely into custody.

But, as always, Raymond was doing time well: As one of his guards said, Raymond was the best charge of the five thousand inmates he'd overseen in three and a half years. When Partington arrived at Raymond's holding cell, he discovered the don was chain-free. He ordered the prisoner manacled.

"I'll have you like a goddamn bug," Raymond said, snapping his fingers at Partington. The lawman managed to get Raymond, who was hobbled in irons, outside and into a waiting police car after a "skirmish." Clumsily, Raymond fell into the car and screamed at Partington. The don said he'd known the marshal's father as a stand-up guy and that Partington had no respect for his elders. The marshal's apology calmed Raymond down, slightly. After the armed party arrived at Green Airport, the plane was searched, and Raymond and Partington took seats in the first row of the coach section.

An amused Raymond called to the unnerved pilot: "Hey, Captain, c'mere a minute." The captain approached "meekly," and Raymond asked permission to smoke, without heading to the rear of the plane, as required.

"Certainly, Mr. Patriarca," said the pilot, "let me light that for you." But after Raymond produced a White Owl cigar from his pocket, he let Partington light it instead. The captain offered them two first-class seats, which Raymond accepted, but Partington declined. Nevertheless, Raymond remained relatively calm en route. During a comfortable chat, he recollected for the marshal their first awkward meeting in 1963, when Partington had served him papers. On the tarmac in Atlanta, Raymond even invited Partington to join him on the ride over to the prison. The lawman agreed, and said it felt as if they were going to a Red Sox game. At journey's end, Raymond nodded good-bye and then headed into the prison intake area. Soon after, the onetime head of criminal New England was working as a janitor, seven days a week. His brother, Joseph, more or less oversaw the family business back in Providence.

On March 28, 1969, after serving three years for a gut shooting, Vincent James Flemmi received a good-conduct discharge from MCI Walpole. On the street, he became a professional Seconal and Scotch addict, sobering up long enough to be godfather to one of Johnny Martorano's sons. The Bear became "very strong" with Larry Baione and Jerry and was ready to whack anyone they wanted. He even accepted a contract from the Office on his disciple Johnny Martorano. A drunken Bear entered a car, with Johnny himself at the wheel. So smashed was the Bear, his pistol accidentally fell out of his pocket onto the floor. Johnny picked it up and put it in the Bear's pocket and offered to give him a ride home.

The next day, Larry Baione said to Stevie Flemmi, "Your brother was supposed to kill Johnny last night but he got yellow."

The Rifleman took aim at Johnny his own way, telling Rico that Martorano was "still hustling girls outside of Enrico's." Johnny also was handling stolen merchandise, possibly drugs, as well. As for himself, Stevie claimed that neither he nor Frankie had been "doing as well, financially, as most people in the city believe and that both of them have a lot of fixed expenses and have not made any money through their associations with [Larry Baione]."

There were still lingering gang-war slights requiring revenge. In March 1969, Spike O'Toole was out of jail and looking to return to Dorothy Barchard and his daughters. He had asked Tommy Ballou to intercede for him with Howie Winter. He only wanted peace, and claimed he'd never tried to kill Howie or Buddy. Howie had replied that there were many factors involved in peacemaking. For instance, the Bear was emerging from jail, still carrying a bullet in his spine—possibly from Spike's own pistol.

Howie discussed amnesty for Spike with Frankie and Stevie—naturally, the Rifleman didn't want to "let Spike off the hook." Frankie thought the Hill should at least pretend to be friendly, for now. There was a meeting of the Hill members at the landmark Jimmy's Harborside Restaurant. All agreed Spike's public execution would hurt their gambling and moneylending careers. Moreover, Spike apologized for shooting Tommy Callahan—which, he claimed, he'd only done because Wimpy had falsely accused Callahan of bankrolling the hit on Punchy. Larry Baione said he'd intercede personally with Callahan—Raymond had prevented Hannon and Punchy from executing Callahan, and so the tough old Irishman now owed the Office a favor. In the meantime, the Office would leak it to the police that everyone was friendly. Soon after, back in Jimmy's Harborside, the Hill and Spike made a peace—which, even if only temporary, might relax Spike's guard.

Whether Stevie or Frankie knew or cared, others besides Rico were pursuing those who bombed John Fitzgerald's car. The lawmen found a break in hoodlum Robert Daddieco—a onetime partner of Vinnie Teresa's, and small-time stick up man. Daddieco was also a woman-beating "pervert," testified Frankie—and so noxious he'd barred him from Boston itself. Daddieco's fortunes collapsed during a bank-robbing spree with some "Canadian kids." During one theft, a bank guard got the better of Daddieco, put a gun on him, and arrested the whole gang. Wary of his ex-partners, he soon left the prison population, flipped, and offered to testify about the Bennett and Fitzgerald cases.

Indictments in the offing, Rico called Stevie at his Milton house, explaining that "Jack from South Boston" wanted to see him. Soon after, at Revere Beach, Rico told Frankie and Stevie they and Peter Poulos faced charges for killing Wimpy. Daddieco was also fingering culprits for the Fitzgerald bomb—and another indictment potentially loomed there, as well.

"Take Poulos with you," Rico said. "He's the weak link." After Poulos joined Frankie and Stevie, the trio drove to Chicago in a Cadillac, and then flew to Los Angeles. Frankie didn't bother leaving the airport before flying to New York City. There, from his room on Eighth Avenue and Forty-fifth Street, he watched the theater lines for *Man of La Mancha*.

On September 11, the Bennett indictments hit page 1 in Boston. The news that Stevie and Frankie had sold out to the Office shocked Joe. This was the "final disillusionment for a man who had repeatedly risked his life in the gang war for his friends."

Under aliases, Stevie and Poulos briefly rented an apartment in the smoggy City of the Angels. On the twenty-seventh, en route to New York City, Stevie decided the world was safer for him without Poulos. Near Las Vegas, on September 29, 1969, Stevie was driving with a "leery" Poulos. When he turned off the highway onto a smaller road, Poulos questioned it. Finally, Stevie told Poulos he was tired, and asked if he'd drive. When Poulos approached the driver's-side door, Stevie raised a .38 caliber pistol to Poulos's head and fired it three times. Planning ahead, Stevie had brought a shovel and rope to help him dispose of the body. Digging here was harder than Stevie had expected, so he made do with just covering the body with brush. Although a state trooper later pulled him over, he let the Rifleman proceed on his way.

On October 10, a grand jury issued indictments against Frankie and Stevie for bombing Fitzgerald's car. The next day, someone stumbled across Poulos's now-anonymous corpse by the highway. It wasn't until early in 1970 that the investigators, using the cadaver's fingerprints and gold-laden teeth, confirmed the identity with the Boston police. While at a Times Square newsstand, Frankie read in a Boston paper his accountant was dead. When

Frankie eventually met up with Stevie in New York City, he asked him why he'd snuffed Poulos.

"You know he witnessed the murder, Wimpy's murder, he drove Walter there [to his murder], he would have been a threat."

"To eliminate him like that, Steve. You know, come on."

"Oh, it had to be done, he would have been a weak link, they would have made a witness out of him."

Discussing Poulos made Stevie uncomfortable, so Frankie told himself, "I can't resurrect this kid, what's done is done."

Stevie, as "Jack from South Boston," called Rico, who kept his word with him, if not his faith with the government. Stevie left New York City (and Frankie) for Montreal, to work, under an alias, as a printer for *The Montreal Gazette*. He made as much as $400 weekly—good money—but his family in Boston went on welfare.

Officially, Condon ended (temporarily at least) the FBI's connection to Steven Joseph Flemmi.

Tirelessly, Rico pursued any avenue to further injure the LCN. Luckily for him, Red Kelley confederated briefly with the bold thief Phil Cresta and his gang. After Kelley and Cresta took a Brink's truck in a major haul, the inside-tip man squealed. Soon after, Red Kelley was arrested and, facing hard time, summoned Rico. The "Smiling Irishman" concocted a tale about Raymond orchestrating the Rudolph Marfeo–Anthony Melei homicide—which may only incidentally have been true. After Kelley appeared before a grand jury, indictments came down for Raymond, Pro Lerner, Luigi Manocchio, Rudy Sciarra, and John Rossi.

By now, despite talk of retirement, it was clear Jerry would continue as the Office's number two, as risky as that numeral might be. In fact, back in 1968, Jerry learned a bookmaker needed a $50,000 loan to keep afloat, he didn't farm him out to Larry. Instead, Jerry gave the bookie a cash infusion and made him a partner of the Office. With Raymond out as the sun of the LCN universe, Jerry's moon shone all the brighter. Jerry still needed to visit the ancient and retired consigliere Joseph Lombardo, but only for guidance in "big beefs."

Larry didn't need to be jealous of Angiulo (now a recluse) anymore. In fact, in July 1968 during a one-hour conversation on Thatcher Street, an informant watched the duo "embracing and hugging each other with their 'organization hug.'" They resembled a pair of homosexuals, noted the FBI report.

Larry Baione now served as the warped North Star of the Office's Boston galaxy. Ambitious and unfettered, he continued to squeeze every available shylock in Boston. Larry wanted them all to participate in a clearinghouse to centralize all loan-sharking administration. Despite his promotion, Larry was still ferocious. For some reason, soldier Nicky Giso struck someone. The victim appealed to Larry, who just gave him a "couple more whacks" with the warning, "You're lucky to be alive."

Apparently mending his ways, the Bear had visited the North End and expressed his sorrow to Larry for how he'd mistreated the capo. Flemmi had also apologized for falsely claiming credit for other men's hits. Although planning to stay out of jail, he admitted he'd probably start stealing. The boys passed the hat and staked the Bear $8,000 so he could buy a house in Hyde Park and open a retail TV shop.

But on December 13, the Bear stabbed two brothers surnamed Pacino. Out on bail, on January 8, 1970, he met informer James "Black Jimmy" Abbout in Jamaica Plain. While riding in the backseat of Abbout's Buick, the Bear reached down to his ankle and produced a .32. This he aimed at the back of the head of Abbout, sitting in the front passenger seat. However, Abbout heard the click of the weapon and "catapulted himself" into the rear, grabbing Jimmy's hands to "fire the shots off." After the driver jumped out, the Buick rolled on until it crashed into a parked car.

While the two fought in the back, the Bear bit Abbout's finger, wrapped around the trigger, to the knuckle. The gun fired twice, wounding the Bear in the shoulder and the top of the head. Abbout fled on foot, leaving behind a groaning Jimmy to search for his weapon on the floor. Two kindly strangers dressed the bite wounds the Bear had inflicted on Abbout and called the police. Wounded, Flemmi made his way to Chinatown, where a physician discreetly treated his wounds.

A few days later, Abbout, then in Charles Street Jail, called the Bear to patch things up. "You stupid motherfucker, I'll cut your fuckin' head off," was Flemmi's peace offering.

These threats pushed Abbout into the arms of the MDC detective Joe McCain, for whom he promised to testify. Three days after the attempted-murder trial started, the Bear left the courthouse and, upholding family tradition, became a fugitive. Despite the star's absence, the jury returned a guilty verdict. On October 29, 1970, the FBI and state police jumped the Bear in a Chicopee trailer camp as he exited his car. Two years later, the court upheld the Bear's conviction in absentia for trying to kill Jimmy Abbout. The judge doubted the story the Bear told about having been kidnapped by men who told him the trial was postponed. The Bear's explanation that he remained away because he was too scared of assassins also failed to move the magistrate. Back to the human zoo of Cedar Junction Vincent James Flemmi went, and to the consolation of the needle.

Others in the underworld continued to find their rewards—whether justly deserved or random. There was a reckoning for the sixty-seven-year-old Louis the Fox, whose name ultimately belied his blatant stupidity. On February 6, assassins armed with shotguns killed him and a twenty-six-year-old girlfriend, with the shells ripping half her face off. Then, on February 11, Thomas Ballou made the mistake of letting the wrong person get behind him. Someone shot him in the back of the head three times. Perhaps he should have taken a clearer side against Charlestown. The body lay faceup on Jefferson Avenue, an alleyway off Bunker Hill Street.

32

THE NEW LIFE

"When the victim is buried, there isn't a worry in the world."

—Joe Barboza

The federal government had decided to dispose of its now-useless tool, Joe Barboza, by physical relocation. After some preliminary inquiries, bureaucrats decided to send Baron to Australia. Officially, neither J. Edgar Hoover, a sociopath second to none, nor the FBI objected. But, on learning he couldn't take his German shepherds, Joe rejected the offer.

The fatal shore being unavailable, the Justice Department made two failed attempts to relocate Joe domestically. People kept questioning Claire on her accent; Stacey had to forget the name Baron, and she lacked any school transcripts. Joe couldn't produce a credit history or legitimate job references. Nevertheless, in April 1969 the feds deposited Joe, $1,000 in his pocket, in idyllic Santa Rosa, in Northern California. It was "a Podunk place, [a] nice place to live, nice place to raise your family," said one resident, Tim Brown, a detective-sergeant at the local county sheriff's office. Detective Brown saw Joe around town and, like other residents, gave him little thought.

"I mean he lived a regular life on appearances," Brown said.

Even when, during lunch, an FBI agent said, "I'm babysitting this man," Brown just thought it a trivial remark.

While "Barboza's Corner" back in East Boston was now vacant and boarded up, Joe had the entire beautiful Golden State at his disposal. Clearly, Joe's federal handlers overlooked the fact that he was a weapon that was no special friend to the hand that wielded it. "Bitter, I am so god-damn bitter with these people, you can't even begin to realize what I have in mind in doing to get even for the devious and treacherous bullshit they have handed me," Joe wrote Fitzgerald.

At first, Joe attempted to earn an honest—or at least nonviolent—living. He enrolled in a culinary school, joined the Seamen's Union, and in August 1969 sailed to Kowloon. En route, Joe claimed he learned Chinese cuisine, uncovering a "lot of secrets to their cooking." He also boasted that in Manila, he picked up the clap; in Hong Kong, he mutilated a seaman with a fishing knife after robbing him. While onboard, he nearly killed another sailor. (In China, he also took the time out to send Partington a postcard.) During his first (and last) voyage, Joe suffered an accidental (possibly) back injury. After graduating from a "body casket" he walked briefly with a cane and received an $18,500 insurance settlement. His nautical career was over. "Strange how well my back feels now on," he observed not long after.

In January 1970, during a Seamen's Union meeting, a New Bedford sailor recognized and confronted Joe. By that February, alleged Boston hit men Harry Johnson and Allen "Suitcase" Fidler were cruising around Northern California. The San Francisco FBI office tipped off the local police, who stopped and detained Johnson and Fidler long enough to find their false identifications, stolen handguns, and ammunition. The police then ordered them out.

Back in California, Joe also managed to find his old friend from MCI Walpole, James "the Greek" Chalmas. In 1962, Chalmas had annoyed his friend Georgie McLaughlin by dating one of his girlfriends. Facing a hijacking charge, too, Chalmas decided to go all the way to San Francisco, where he lived under the name of "Ted Sharliss." Both Joe and the Greek kept their East Coast connections fresh.

Claiming he'd been promised plastic surgery, a lump sum of cash, and a job as a cook at a Veterans Administration facility, Joe called Lucky Fitzgerald to complain and ask for money. At one point, he had only four dollars in his pocket and his landlord was selling his house out from under him. And, naturally, Joe wondered how he could be expected "to carry a lunch pail like an average person."

Aware of this situation, on February 2, Ted Harrington, one of the prosecutors Joe had worked with, wrote a letter to a U.S. deputy assistant attorney general:

> A year has passed and we have been unable to provide [Barboza] with a job. . . . He [Joe] has indicated that he will publicly retract his testimony given in the aforementioned cases and will make known to the press that the Government did not give him a fair chance to go "straight."

Given how Joe was, to put it politely, "easily recognizable," he wanted the cash to either relocate or to undergo the plastic surgeon's scalpel.

The Department of Justice responded: "The memoranda submitted do not . . . support the expenditure of Nine Thousand Bucks." Not getting the answer he wanted, ever the loan shark, Joe headed east in the first of five shakedown pilgrimages. On his first trip back, he met with Fitzgerald to tape a TV special about the gang war, before leaving with an "entourage" to visit the Combat Zone. Although his presence in the state was a parole violation, Joe contacted the strike force and threatened it, anyway. In this case (and the ones that followed), Harrington and his colleagues managed to calm him down until he returned west—minus the hoped-for cash. The visits back east weren't all business, said Joe, who claimed he paraded about in public in disguise.

He'd accumulated professional makeup kits, forty pairs of sunglasses in different shapes and styles, and wigs. Sometimes the Animal donned an "Afro" wig and colored his face and hands with pigment to appear black. Another outfit was that of a hippie, with a long-haired wig, false beard, beads, glasses, dungarees, and boots. He even rode a cab through downtown Providence past the Office—but didn't stop to look inside to see who was running things.

On a visit to Eastie, only Joe's friends prevented him from assaulting Guy Frizzi. "I'd rather he run frightened; death is too good for him," Joe concluded. That spring, Joe visited a Boston newspaper reporter, James Southwood, at his Cape Cod house. Southwood hoped that by becoming Boswell to Joe's Dr. Johnson, he might better his own shaky financial estate. The talks concluded, the writer drove Joe from New Bedford to Hartford Bradley Airport. Through the bursts of incoherent babble, Southwood managed to extrapolate a message, as he recalled later.

"I put those people in jail and I can get them out," Joe said. Although Southwood was driving, Joe also put a derringer to his head. "I could kill you," Joe promised, before claiming he didn't know how to use the weapon, anyway. After Joe's departure, Southwood received a car rental bill (for Joe's transportation) so high, he skipped paying his light bill that month.

During one trip east, Joe checked into a motel in the rural town of Westport, near New Bedford. A friendly headwaiter in his forties named Lawrence Hughes then put Joe up in his own house. Petty criminal Lawrence had met Joe in the early 1960s in a New Bedford restaurant, and something must have clicked. Now Joe had a need for such an obedient tool, because he'd hatched an ambitious, if crazy, criminal scheme.

Joe commissioned Fitzgerald to contact Joe Balliro to collect money for his extensive testimony recantation. "I got enough that will convince any court that I was lying," Joe claimed, "so we will change the testimony and we will pick up a bundle of dough and everything will be straighten [*sic*]."

As his plans moved forward, Joe convened a meeting at Lawrence Hughes's house. Attendees included Joe's brother Donald, Southwood, and Joe's cousin, the oddly named Herbert "Herbie" Jesus. This crew reprised the Cream Pie Bandits of Joe's ill-spent childhood. To it, Joe divulged he bore thousands of dollars in stolen West Coast securities, which he appropriately dubbed "papers."

Joe told the gang "to get on them, move them, that there was a lot money involved." As Joe had instructed, one of the crew contacted a building contractor named Frank Davis, an associate of Raymond's. In early May, Davis traveled to a stand of trees in the sprawling and secluded Freetown State Forest to meet Joe and five of his gang. The Barboza crew was armed, and at least one man disguised himself with a gas mask, said Joe.

Davis explained the terms. "Raymond and Jerry said if you change your testimony, you could come back to Boston and they won't bother you," he said. Davis offered a quarter million in belated hush money—Joe countered with a $500,000 price tag.

Soon after, the Office declared the deal acceptable, and Davis took some of the bonds. Joe's ambitious, if sleazy, schemes appeared heading to fruition at last. However, before leaving, Joe also told the crew about a "wise guy" named Clay back west. He said, "When I get back to California I'm going to have to straighten him out."

Ricky Clayton Wilson was a tall, lanky twenty-six-year-old unemployed mechanic, heavy equipment operator, and "speed freak." He lived in Glen Ellen, near Santa Rosa. Fittingly, he'd married a dark-haired, attractive, once-divorced, and highly troubled young woman, Dorothy "Dee" Mancini. A gangster, or what passed as one in Northern California, he rode with the Misfits biker club. Clay was constantly armed. "He was proud of guns," Dee Mancini said of him.

Two years before, while burglarizing a California house, Clayton had acquired a packet of documents. They included a birth certificate, a seventy-year-old baptism record, and hundreds of thousands of dollars' worth of stocks and negotiable bonds. Fencing them was clearly beyond Clay's humble means, so he kept the paper buried in a container by his house. There they lay until that May, when, by chance, Wilson met a stocky, dark-complexioned man from the East Coast who called himself "Joseph Bentley." This Bentley intimated he possessed East Coast Mafia connections—which was true, but not in the way Wilson thought.

When Clayton divulged he was sitting on all that valuable paper, Joe next made plans to start moving it, along with some guns. Joe visited the couple's house in Glen Ellen several times. As the trio became closer, Dee noticed Joe always wore a bulletproof vest under his clothes; he also carried an automatic pistol and a .38. Joe's house contained a closetful of artifacts, including scrapbooks with newspaper clippings about murders in Massachusetts. Later, Joe explained he was in a new federal witness protection program.

"No one burned me and got away with it," he said. A man named Salvati had stolen a mere $400 and Joe put him in the penitentiary for it. "I can do anything I want like that," Joe said. "I have the government wrapped around my little finger and can manipulate them anytime I wish." He became friendly with Dee, and not necessarily in a merely platonic way. He told her the feds would protect him against enemies. "To him, this was merely a game of chess," she said.

When Joe returned to Santa Rosa, Dee and Clay were at logger-heads. Dee felt she'd lost custody of her son because of Clayton, Joe claimed. In turn, Clay, high on mescaline and LSD, had broken down a door, beaten Dee, and been arrested. Joe claimed he patched things up between them by getting them to split. By June, the Wilsons formally separated.

Besides acting as marriage counselor, Joe continued his endless juggling acts back east. He remained at the center of a web of rumors and accusations; his constant lies prevented any valid version of the truth to prevail. On May 14, a despairing Claire Baron told Fitzgerald she was "quite upset" that Joe wasn't working, and planned to leave him and return to Boston. "He is hanging around with some rough guys," as Claire noted.

In June, while visiting a lounge, Joe accidentally dropped an address book full of the names of federal, state, and regional lawmen. Eventually, the book reached Clayton Wilson, who returned it to Joe. However, hearing of the notebook, a local thug became wary of Joe. After the biker vouched for the East Coast gangster, the thug threatened to kill Clay, Joe, and Dee. Wilson "went on a real paranoid trip & thought I was undercover & setting him up," Joe later wrote.

Dee lived in a house on Lakeside Drive in Glen Ellen with a friend of hers, a twenty-two-year-old horse groomer named Paulette Ramos, as well as Chiang, a dog. It was on July 5, by the best estimate, when Joe arrived in his Ford station wagon at Dee's house. Clay was there, although he'd recently knocked Dee down so hard she had sustained a concussion. Dee noticed Joe was, as usual, carrying an automatic pistol and a .38, neither of which he bothered to hide under his jacket and slacks. During the visit, Clay uncovered a tin box, opened it, and handed some of the hot bonds over to Joe. Soon after, Joe stomped out of the house, and Clay, in leather pants, followed. "You don't know who I am, but you're gonna find out," Joe told Clay. "I'll put you on ice later."

That evening, the two men sat on the porch, speaking loudly enough for Dee, inside the house, to catch snatches of their conversation.

At last, Joe said, "It's a beautiful night, let's go for a walk." Joe and Clay led the women into the nearby woods—and in the increasing darkness, Ramos found it difficult to find her way on the rocky path. On they went, and Ramos kept "four to five car lengths" behind the men. She overheard Joe tell Clay, "You've been hard to get a hold of."

Then she saw an orange flash, up at about the level where she estimated Clay's head was. In it, briefly, she saw the outline of a large man, and heard an explosion followed by the drop of a body. Frightened, she and Dee ran back to the forest gate, where they heard two more explosions. They didn't stop running until they reached the house. After waiting for a half hour, Dee swallowed some Seconals and passed out—without troubling the police with so much as a phone call.

With a dead Clayton out in the dark somewhere at his feet, Joe checked himself for bullet wounds. Finding none, he managed to hide the body in some bushes. Two hours after shooting Clay, Joe arrived back at the house, and found a sleeping Dee and conscious Ramos. "I have to take care of a stiff I put in the brush last night," he told her. "Let's go for a ride where we used to ride horses up the hill." He was insistent. "Something has to be done with Clay. You saw it happen so you can watch around." She noticed Joe's automatic pistol and agreed to help. The two drove off; Joe parked the vehicle and, armed with a shovel, walked to the corpse's location. "It's nothing," Joe said. "It's just a life, it can end at any time and anyway, he was a punk." Joe went behind a bush where something was wrapped in a blanket.

"What's that?" she asked.

"It's Clay."

Joe attached a rope to Clay's body and dragged it, the legs

bound, behind him. Noticing, in the first rays of sunlight, one of Clay's eyes protruding from his head, Ramos fought down her vomit. Joe covered the dead eye with the blanket and pulled the corpse a short distance up a hornet-infested hillside near Jack London Park. Removing his green jacket and setting it down, Joe started digging. He could only guess at the best procedure—for although he'd made many corpses, he'd never buried one before. Indeed, he'd rarely ever bothered to dispose of a victim. While toiling away, he saw a horse and rider pass by, and removed his weapon from his waistband and rested it on top of his jacket. After finishing the shallow, crude grave, he put the body inside and shoveled dirt over it. Then he replaced the gun in his waistband and donned his jacket again.

"He cheated me," Joe told Ramos. "Clay didn't need to be around, he was causing trouble." The two returned to the house—behind them, only a single foot of earth separated Clayton's mortal remains from the world above and from the legal proceedings that could avenge him. "Only you and I know where Clay is, and anything ever comes down, you would have to be the only one that spoke," he warned Ramos. He entered Dee's house and went downstairs, leaving his Ford in the carport. He later bragged of fornicating with Dee while there.

At 3 A.M., Clayton Wilson's mother awoke from a nightmare—in it someone had "done away with Clay," she told her husband, Jim Wilson. Refusing his comfort, she sent him over to Dee's house in Glen Ellen. Arriving at about 6:30 A.M., Wilson knocked on the door, and a half-asleep Dee emerged in her bedclothes. Wilson asked about his son; without inviting him inside, Dee mumbled vaguely that Clay was missing, as usual, but might return in a few days. Before leaving, Wilson noticed a good-looking dark Ford in the carport.

Soon after, Joe entered his attractive Ford and drove back to his apartment, reaching it at 7 A.M. Claire was awake, and upset he'd been gone all night. "I did wrong by burying him with the girls," Joe later claimed, adding, dishonestly, Dee to the burial party. (Dee said she didn't see Joe until days later, let alone sleep with him.) But he concluded, "If I had gone to the police and told my story & had his stomach pumped to show the consumption of reds I would have had a clear cut self defense. But my situation & past made me paranoid."

When Joe saw Dee a few days later, she didn't mention her missing husband. Ominously, on July 8, someone burned Dee's house down. The day after, Mrs. Wilson saw Dee—who, from a Seconal-induced fog, claimed Clay had, some time ago, left with friends in a black pickup truck.

Carrying a $2,000 bankroll from Frank Davis, Joe returned to the Bay State with the $126,000 in bonds. Joe told his crew a story about a "junky motorcycle freak" who'd tried to kill him back west. He claimed he'd bagged his life and wife, both in the same night, but in different ways.

Joe now planned to tell the Office he'd recant his testimony for the "right price." However, by admitting perjury in the Deegan trial, a capital case, he also faced an automatic life sentence in Massachusetts. The presumed solution was F. Lee Bailey. Joe thought the attorney could conjure "some magic scheme" to free his victims but "leave him with a whole skin," as Bailey himself put it. If Bailey sprung the Deegan convicts, his already-considerable fame would be assured. Davis retained Bailey as his agent.

On July 11, the attorney flew down to the New Bedford Airport. Someone picked him up and drove him to Lawrence Hughes's house. There in the Baron-lair, more machines guns confronted Bailey than he "ever saw in military service."

Understandably, Joe's gang was tense, and a trigger-happy look-out nearly shot the attorney. Bailey ascended a flight of stairs and passed a guard with a sawed-off shotgun. There, the attorney immediately recognized his onetime client awaiting him, armed with a carbine and smoking marijuana.

Bailey didn't even know Joe also packed a .25 automatic in his pocket.

"Stop these James Bond moves," the attorney said.

"I don't trust nobody," Joe replied. When they were alone, Bailey handed Joe an envelope containing $800, saying, "Somebody left it in my office." Discussing the Boston Mafia trials, Joe said his story about Raymond's, Henry's, and Ronnie's roles in the Marfeo murder "was at least, in large measure, fabricated" (with Rico's and Condon's assistance). After talking for nearly two hours, Bailey promised a future visit, and Joe shared his Santa Rosa address and telephone number.

But, that July the racial fault lines in New Bedford's West End quaked, and the city erupted into a bloody chaos. It was, possibly, the perfect environment for a serial killer. At 11 P.M. on Thursday, July 15, Joe and Herbie Jesus drove from Fairhaven over the short, narrow bridge that spanned the Acushnet River to New Bedford. The cousins pulled "adjacent to a car occupied by four Negroes at a stop light," as Hoover's own report stated. While the car idled, Jesus and Joe exchanged words and waved guns at the blacks. Joe ended the debate by pointing a .25 automatic at them. Once Joe was out of view, one of the aggrieved motorists, anonymously, called the police and reported the license plate. At 12:30 A.M., New Bedford patrolmen saw and stopped Joe in the city's North End.

After the officers identified the city's most notorious and wayward son, one policeman drew his weapon and pointed it at Joe's head. "Move and I'll blow your brains out," he said.

"Have you ever seen brains blown out?" Joe asked.

On searching the car and its passengers, the officers found Joe carried a loaded .25 caliber automatic pistol, while Jesus packed a .38 caliber pistol. On the front seat were an M-1 carbine and some marijuana; there were also two .45 caliber pistols. Facing his collar, Joe protested, "I'm being railroaded. The federal government has betrayed me. The federal government has proved to be as treacherous as the Mafia." He was there as a federal agent performing undercover race relations "to help restore law and order in the West End," he said.

Later that Saturday, Joe, in a sort of homecoming, stood before a judge in New Bedford District Court. At the Boston FBI office's urging, the district attorney dropped the firearms, narcotics, and assault charges against the duo, using as a fig leaf the fact that the arraignment had lacked a lawyer. This undeserved favor caused a minor uproar—but, facing a host of other charges, Joe remained incarcerated while his cousin skipped. Finally, two thousand years after the Crucifixion, the thief and murderer with a name beginning with the letter "B" remained in custody, while Jesus walked—covering his face with a hat to defend it from the awaiting photographers.

33

CONFEDERACY OF DUNCES

"You're no bargain, Joe, neither of us are."
— William Geraway, in a letter to Joe Barboza

The governments—municipal, county, state, and federal—joined forces to cope with Joe's about-face. The FBI immediately swatted down Joe's claim of being an "emissary." Easy enough. But when Anthony Stathopolous signaled he was ready to recant, the state's cases seemed about to buckle.

On July 21, 1970, the state parole board returned Joe to his alma mater, MCI Walpole. Until his parole term expired in October, his new lodgings would be in the block 10 isolation unit. This was a satellite building, comprising a series of steel doors, cells, hallways, and gates designed to destroy the prisoner utterly in body and spirit, as one occupant explained. A main corridor, blocked with a monster iron gate, linked the block to the main building like a central vein. Here resided the most openly antisocial and violent men of New England.

A prisoner's cell offered a solid steel bunk and table, both riveted to the wall, a pillow, and a thin mattress. Rules forbade conversation between guards and prisoners. Whistling at any time, or speaking after hours could mean fifteen days of total isolation and the loss of the few privileges prisoners were given. Predictably, the first year after block 10 opened up for business, one inmate managed to kill himself. Over time, other prisoners became catatonic and were shunted off to Bridgewater. One demented wretch landed in a mental facility; rather than return to block 10, he hanged himself with a toilet's flush chain. One solace there was friendship, real or imagined, and during the 8 A.M. to 8 P.M. period, prisoners chatted freely in low, intimate tones.

Block 10 was also the current address of convicted murderer and forger Billy Geraway, doing a snitch's time. He remained a prison lawyer and schemer—doing anything to redeem his living death. (Geraway, allegedly, had informed on his own father, who subsequently was convicted of some crime and died in Walpole.)

On July 20, 1970, a guard came by Billy's cell and, heraldlike, announced Joe was in a first-floor unit being searched. The grate at the corridor entrance opened, and Joe walked inside arrayed only in jockey shorts, and carrying his prison sneakers and dungarees. He was in "superb" shape and sported a small goatee, Geraway noted.

He saw Billy and said, "You're doing a bum beef, kid."

"I know, Joe," said Billy, who had resided with Joe twice. The first time had been at the Concord Reformatory in the 1950s; the second, in Walpole in 1963. Billy claimed he knew something of Joe's reputation as a vicious sexual "Animal" in prison. Geraway was wary of Joe's violence, but he was also a fearless opportunist.

Now Joe asked for cell 49, the one next to Billy's. The informants and other weaklings on the floor considered Joe a frightening "symbol of aggression." On the other hand, the men in the corridor behind Billy on block 10 were "primarily psychopathic types": they naturally venerated the Animal. One jailhouse gangster-pervert remembered the Animal from reform school and called out, "Joe, what are you doing on that side, that's for PCs [protective custodies]?"

Silence. Then Joe said, "What in the fuck do you think I'm doing on this side, I'm a rat, ain't I?"

During their first day as neighbors, Billy and Joe bonded with
a ten-hour conversation. Joe even copied out his poem, "City of
Forgotten Men," and rededicated it to Geraway:

> Written in 1958, and now in 1970 and 30 lives later, Bill Ger-
> awy [sic] accepts this poem also having lived many lives himself
> and struggling to maintain his own concepts instead of conforming
> and being part of the masses whose main concept is hipocracy [sic].

> Your Ace
> Joseph Barboza Baron
> July 22, 1970

Geraway realized that by "Ace," Joe meant someone who had
more than five kills to his credit—like a World War II pilot. Joe
then dubbed himself "Billy's Ace."

During the next ten weeks, Geraway and his ace chatted nonstop,
sometimes fifteen hours a day. Topics included poetry, torture,
and murder—although, for his part, Joe claimed their talks were
"mostly about the girls," including Dee Mancini and Paulette Ramos. Joe confessed to twenty killings, including Clayton's—that
was a "great thrill, the best I ever had, to kill this guy and then lay
his wife after she watched me do it." Wilson's burial provided Joe
great peace and comfort, as minus corpus delicti, he was uncharge-
able. He would prefer to bury all future victims. The stolen bonds
still required disposition—counterfeiter Billy explained Joe could
use them as collateral for 60 percent of their face value. But, blue-
collar thug Joe couldn't understand this trick of the white-collar
criminal caste.

The two also played chess, calling out their moves. As with boxing, Joe demonstrated some innate craft, mixing his aggression with defensiveness, Billy noted. Unable to defeat Geraway, over time, Joe's tantrums at losing made the game intolerable. Another solace for the two was exchanging letters. Billy noted Joe's excellent handwriting contrasted with his poor spelling and mispronunciations, for example, The Animal mispronounced "detrimental" as "deprimental." (Wanting to become a writer, Joe had, on the street, made five or six attempts to attend night school, without success.) Now, Joe turned to Billy for grammar and spelling guidance, asking him to spell "fulfill" at least twenty-seven times. Billy quickly abandoned correcting Joe's errors—he didn't want to die in the exercise yard enforcing spelling niceties.

In person and in print, Joe was a master actor, Billy noted. During one court appearance on block 10, Joe managed tears in front of reporters. Knowing the feds read all his epistles, sometimes Joe wrote letters under the name "Claire Wilson" to flaunt Clayton's murder. In one missive, Joe told Claire how much she meant to him. She replied, "Don't give me that horseshit, the only time you turn to us is when you need us or want to use us."

In response, Joe, out loud, called Claire a few "choice names," after which he calmed himself enough to write. To psyche Claire out, Joe created large stains on the letter with water drops, and then showed the missive to Billy. He said, "She'll think I was crying and go easy in the letters. And the feds will think I was crying." In his "more lucid moments," Joe admitted Claire was "crazy" if she didn't divorce him.

To prevent the guards from eavesdropping on them, Geraway or Joe would whistle while the other spoke. They also used a private code or language, sharing phrases such as "Willy's Ace," "Willy's base," or "Willy's case." Joe also discussed his future strategies, which included blowing up Richard "the Pig" DeVincent, then in Walpole. Joe wanted revenge for the Pig's killing of either Rocco DiSeglio or Chico Amico. Once released, Joe would use a pillow to suffocate the Oinker's elderly mother. DeVincent would receive a bereavement furlough, and Joe would plant time bombs in the funeral home. He'd obliterate the victim instantly—with the other mourners. Billy suggested using a radio controller to trigger the bomb.

"You mean I can set off an explosive, without actually being near it? Why, I could have planted explosives all over the North End and then blown up all the Italians in the city!"

Another plot was to simultaneously kidnap Jerry Angiulo's ancient mother and the young Raymond Patriarca Jr. Joe would ransom the hostages for $1 million apiece and retire to a fortress in California, surrounded by bodyguards. He'd use Billy as the middleman; when done, he'd kill all the other conspirators, except Billy, of course. Joe expected Billy's imminent departure— Geraway had enlisted a charitable Yale law professor to file a murder-conviction appeal (on a minor conflict-of-interest technicality). Joe repeatedly urged Billy, after he hit the outside, to secure the cars and motorcycles needed to impersonate the police for the kidnapping plot. Eventually, Billy signed on to the demented enterprise, just to appease Joe.

As literary amateurs, the convicts also recited poetry to each other. After Geraway performed by rote the grim "Ballad of Reading Gaol," Joe said, "That memory of yours is going to get you killed one of these days, Billy." Then the incident that left Chappaquiddick with the nickname of the "Kennedy carwash" drove another wedge betwixt the odd twain. The two argued fiercely, with Joe taking the side of the district attorney, who'd handled Edward Kennedy with some lenience.

After throwing his food tray against the wall, Joe yelled, "You motherfucker, the toughest guys in the country don't argue with me. . . . I'll kill you, you sonofabitch, I'll bite your fuckin' jugular vein out in the exercise yard, you punk motherfucker." Then Joe spoke in earnest, "Choose your words carefully, Mr. Geraway, choose your words carefully, you may say something you can never take back."

"Joe, fuck your mother."

Then Joe recited his favorite poem, "Death Be Not Proud," before discussing his wife and children (he also had a son by now).

As always, the New England criminal world was in a space as compressed as Fenway Park. As proof: Joe's second-floor room stood over death row—and so also the cells of Henry Tameleo, Peter Limone, Ronnie Cassesso, and Lou Greco. Joe and Geraway awkwardly passed through this mafia corridor each day to reach the exercise yard. The Deegan convicts knew somehow Joe was in jail to free them, and wanted no evidence to the contrary. Despite a veneer of civility, there was tension: Greco wouldn't speak to Joe, and Henry was reticent to talk publicly at all. Limone remained in his cell whenever Joe was in the exercise area—so the Animal screamed abuses at him publicly.

As group spokesman, Ronnie did the communicating with Joe. Once, while heading to the exercise yard, Joe and Billy stopped by the grate of bars blocking death row. Henry was there, looking out, recovering from a recent surgery. Joe requested an audience: Henry bent slightly and watched silently. Joe placed his left hand over his heart and raised his right hand to make an oath.

"Henry, the government brainwashed me into testifying against you," a teary-eyed Joe said. "I can't sleep nights thinking of what I did to you, you were like a father to me and I am sorry I lied about you. Henry, I swear on my two children I'm going to make this right. I'm going to tell the truth and take the lie tests, I promise. If I don't tell the truth, Henry, kill my brother Donald."

Henry offered no response. But when in the exercise yard, Billy said, "Joe, you've put them in a bind, they might take you up on it and kill Donald if you do not follow through."

"Fuck Donald, he's an asshole," the Animal replied. "Every time he comes to Boston he costs me money; the last time he borrowed six hundred dollars and never paid it back."

Under Bailey's prod, on July 28, Joe signed a statement explaining his desire to "recant certain portions" of his testimony. In Suffolk Superior Court, Joseph Balliro filed a petition for a new trial for Henry, with Joe's affidavit attached. Soon after, lawyers for the other Deegan condemned followed suit. Attorney Charles Curran also used the affidavit in a motion to clear Raymond, Henry, and Ronnie in the Marfeo case.

To avoid the perjury rap, under Billy's tutelage Joe restated his intention. Joe now claimed he hadn't actually meant to "recant" the Deegan testimony. Rather, as Joe said, "I mean recount. What do I know with a seventh-grade education? My testimony at the trial was the gosipal [gospel] truth."

But this legal nest, so violently disturbed, yielded hornets. From all sides, back and forth flew lies, accusations, false assurances, threats, and innuendos. During this messy wrangle, Bailey interviewed Joe several times in Walpole. In one meeting, Joe "had no hesitation at all about describing the most cold-blooded, ruthless killings." He claimed more than twenty kills, mostly in the Irish feud, "as if he were eating a piece of apple pie."

Raymond had a trusted ally, the Frenchman, in Walpole, who passed messages to Henry, and so on to Joe. A Federal Hill stalwart, the Frenchman regularly attended chapel so he could conduct whisper-chats with Henry. As Joe prepared to finalize his recantation, mysteriously, the Bear began attending services. Through the Frenchman, Raymond asked for an affidavit, from Joe, to clear him.

The Bear appeared agitated by this. He then went to the chaplain's office and hurled a metal nameplate at the Frenchman. The Frenchman then went at Flemmi with a pair of scissors, hoping to slash his throat. The Bear fled, and the Frenchman decided to retrieve his hidden knives and kill him.

But soon after, the feds transferred the Frenchman out of Walpole. Raymond's man credited that to the Flemmi-FBI connection.

Before Joe's slated release, District Attorney Garrett Byrne revoked his probation and slated hearings to reconsider the length of his jail term. Even with the marijuana smuggled in to him, Joe's disposition wasn't improving. Once Billy had to talk him out of biting out another inmate's throat. He also realized Joe's angry moods signaled he was due a soul-cleansing, orgasmic murder to relax him. Anxious, the Animal exploded at everyone—including Bailey.

"You motherfucker, you've got a $400 suit and a lead penny for a heart," Joe once yelled at the attorney. The mismatched counselor and client screamed from the visiting room at each other so loudly Billy heard them in his cell. "Open your briefcase, I bet there's $2,000 worth of bugging stuff in it," Joe bellowed. At times, it appeared an act: During these tirades, Joe repeatedly winked at Bailey. Given Bailey's knowledge of his affairs, Joe told Billy the attorney's wife was now a candidate for kidnapping, too.

Pointlessly, the Suffolk County Superior Court approved the polygraph, slated for August 31. After retaining the "dean" of polygraph examiners, Bailey even wrote to Joe Balliro, claiming the Animal had "felt for some time that he should make a direct effort to right the injustice which his testimony had caused." In his recantation, Joe had exonerated Tameleo, Limone, and Greco; to others, he'd even placed Jimmy Flemmi in Romeo's backseat. Bailey continued: "Although my sympathies are of course primarily and directly with the victims of your affair, I must give Baron either full representation or none at all and I cannot ask him to put in the hands of hostile counsel testimony which could result in very severe penalties to him."

On August 27, Joe broke down sobbing during a court cross-examination, and needed a recess. Then, on August 31, Joe begged off from the polygraph test, claiming the Deegan convicts would also take them that day. "I'm too upset to take one right now, plus if I did later, it would prove affirmative that I was talking the truth," he told Bailey.

"Liar," Bailey said.

"Who [is] a liar? You're the liar, Bailey." The feisty attorney threatened a perjury prosecution and swore "he'd make sure I never got out," Joe claimed.

The slowdown in proceedings became ominous. Each day, Billy left his cell to mop and sweep around block 10 until 2:30 P.M., when he returned to his cell. This job took him near the Deegan convicts downstairs, whom he befriended, somewhat. Billy soon noted they were starting to wonder what exactly was afoot.

The reality was, Joe was publicly making glorious fools of everyone: the government, the mob, and himself. The double, triple, and quadruple crosses commenced now on the other side of the bars. Lawrence Hughes and Herbie Jesus visited Jerry Angiulo, possibly at gunpoint. They informed him of Joe's activities—including the stolen bonds. In September, Lawrence Hughes also regularly contacted Boston detective John Doyle to update him about the bonds (some of which he had photocopied).

During a particularly hot August, Joe's relations with Billy worsened, with the duo arguing every six to eight hours. During exercise, Joe quickly snapped at Geraway's side with his teeth. Joe's prehistoric-class choppers penetrated Billy's thick gray sweatshirt and left a bloody moon-shaped wound. One night, to ease the unbearable heat in Walpole, Billy stood near the front of his cell to enjoy whatever night coolness was available. Joe stood next to him and stuck his big left hand in front of the bars, and opened and closed his fingers four times: It was his victim count, as Billy knew.

On the evening of September 1, a young man in a brown business suit stopped at Joe's cell, holding a six-by-nine manila envelope. "This is a letter from Mr. Bailey," he announced. "You are to show it to no one."

Joe announced he couldn't let Billy read the letter, "as it would break the attorney-client privilege with Bailey." Billy relaxed—he already knew enough about Joe's crimes to be on the Barboza Hit Parade, a few times over. But then Joe slipped the letter into his cell—Billy pushed it back through the bars. Joe held out a note that said, "Read this letter and tell me what to do." Now Billy took and examined Bailey's ten-page, single-spaced typed document, which summarized Joe's and Bailey's conversations, citing details of murder and false testimony.

"Innocent men's lives have been destroyed by your testimony." Joe should "come forth for once . . . and tell the truth, just because it's right . . . helping little people along the way, it all comes back to you someday." After reading this missive, Joe complained that Bailey had falsely accused him of Punchy's murder. He then sealed up the letter, and put Bailey himself on his ever-changing list of future victims.

Already argumentative, Joe soured even more a few days later when he demanded Billy play chess. Joe promised Billy he'd behave, and the two arrayed their pieces on the boards. Billy, playing white, checkmated Joe in fifteen moves.

"You motherfucker, my queen is on 66 and I take your queen, that's that!" Joe yelled.

"Joe, go fuck yourself; the game has ended, we'll never play

again and I won." Joe threw the chessboard against the wall, rat-
tled the bars, and asked if Billy wanted "to do something about it
in the corridor the next day."

"Joe, all you know how to do is shoot your friends and then take
the guns apart and throw them away."

"I never killed my friends," he screamed.

"What about Romeo Martin, Joe?"

"I hated that sonofabitch, he wasn't my friend."

"Horseshit. You killed all your friends. Not this one, Joe; I'd
never make the mistake of getting in a car with you."

"Don't forget, you have something I don't care about," Joe said,
still screaming.

"What's that?"

"A family."

"I have been messing with firearms since I was nine years old;
you wouldn't have a chance if we were both armed and I knew you
were after me," Billy warned. They calmed, and after Billy opened a
book to read, Joe invited him to the bars. After whispering for
Geraway to whistle, Joe said, "Billy, if you ever think anyone is going to move on you, take out one of their family."

One block 10 guard came on duty for the 3 P.M. to 11 P.M. shift,
and asked, "Is everybody happy?"

"You think I can be happy in here?" Joe screamed. "You think
it's funny to be locked up like an animal?"

Joe went calm and repeated his remarks while pointing to a
calendar on his wall. "I get out in sixteen days," Joe said. "Then, up
pops the devil. Do you know what I MEAN, sir?" His finger and
thumb extended to resemble a pistol. A few days later, Joe told
Billy that when he hit the street, he would disguise himself in a
goatee and Afro wig, and then visit the guard's house, and kill
him. Joe already had the address.

By now, Billy and Joe's relationship appeared stable. Then Joe returned from a visit seeming uncommonly cheerful but saying nothing until he summoned Billy to the bars. Joe then handed him a scrap of paper with a phone number on it. He explained it was the unlisted phone number of Billy's sister, Louise. Then, on his bed, Joe whistled, something he typically did when he'd made a particularly good point. Billy realized Joe was playing smug cat to his helpless mouse.

By now, Billy believed it was he and his family or Joe—even if attacking a high-profile witness provoked the authorities to block his appeal. The next day, Billy told Ronnie he was going to bury the Animal. Ronnie feared Joe would "do something bizarre," and the Deegan crew would take the blame. Also, Joe might light up on block 10 and make "their lives miserable." Relenting, Billy promised to give Joe a head start. The next day, Joe gave Billy an envelope full of marijuana to hold while he received a visitor. In case of a sudden search, Joe didn't want it found while he was out. Billy emptied some of the weed into his folder of legal materials for safe-keeping. Billy the Mouse could use this catnip to frustrate Joe the Feline. Two days later, Joe left the prison, shook Billy's hand, and promised he'd see him again.

34

CORNERED

On September 4, 1970, Bailey filed a motion to withdraw as Joe's counsel, prompting the Animal to threaten the attorney's family. As Joe knew, his parole-violation term was ending September 23, and he'd be free to start hurting people. But on the twenty-third, guards led Joe into Bristol county superior court in Taunton. The day before, a special grand jury had indicted him and Herbie Jesus for possessing drugs and firearms.

In the Taunton courthouse, Joe appeared in the bohemian-messianic form popular at the time, with long, unkempt hair and a beard. He resembled no more the well-groomed mob enforcer of the early 1960s but a homeless vagrant. Were he a comic strip character, undoubtedly flies would have been buzzing around his massive head. Before entering the court, he read a prepared press statement, claiming there was "a conspiracy between F. Lee Bailey and Bristol County authorities to get me on gun charges." An un-impressed judge held Joe on $100,000 bail, so his next stop was, once again, the Barnstable County House of Corrections.

"All I ask is for a fair break for my family," he said. "I pray for the indulgence of the court as a compensation for what I gave to the government and the people of New England for breaking the backbone of the Mafia."

He was still broke: His wife was taking a college class, and he wanted to bank something for his young son. In a September 28 letter, he revealed his desperation to Edward Harrington and acknowledged that in the past, he'd abused people unreasonably with his temper tantrums. Joe said he didn't "want to reach for stars anymore" as he'd endured the worst "torture agony & mental anguish" of his life. His newborn son was growing up not knowing him, his daughter was "acting horrible," and Claire's spirits were at their "lowest ebb."

He reminded Harrington of their private deal—presumably which meant a job for him. He asked how long the cash he'd taken from "those creeps" from the Office would last. He claimed Bailey had threatened Joe would come running to him at last—Joe vowed he wouldn't. He just wanted his job and a new location—and he'd be out of Harrington's hair completely. He'd work twelve hours a day, if need be. Joe gave his word—and he claimed he'd never broken it to him or Denny Condon—the men who now were his "hope & only hope." He admitted feeling weak, and to a "terrible persistent mood of depression, loneliness & longing for my wife." Once again, he was facing the worst agitation and mental torture of his life. "All I think of is that insidious bastard [Bailey] plotted different ways to bury me deeper, & I won't take it."

On October 1, a cocked hammer fell when Santa Rosa's police chief opened a letter from William Geraway. It fingered a "former Boston loan shark and 'hit' man from the Mafia" who "murdered a man and buried the body with the help of a female."

The devoutly egotistical Billy Geraway may have been a ruthless clown, but he was also a thorough one. Billy gave the authorities a diagram of the Wilson house, the identities of the witnesses, descriptions of their vehicles, and the names of the Wilsons' two children. Geraway detailed the color of the last pair of pants Clay wore, and the pet dog's name, "Chiang." The Santa Rosa police called the Massachusetts State Police, which promised to administer a polygraph to Geraway. Golden State lawmen traveled to Boston to interview the career informants (working with Geraway was another snitch who'd conspired with Joe). Billy now turned Joe's marijuana stash over to the Norfolk County district attorney. Then Billy started talking to the Deegan convicts, who promised him anything he wanted, as they assumed he was nailing Joe.

Then, suddenly, Lawrence Hughes "popped up like a mushroom" and volunteered to tell Santa Rosa authorities all about Joe. "You know, it is a little odd to get a letter from a prisoner, [a] convicted murderer, saying, I want to freely tell you about a conversation another murderer had with him," said a Santa Rosa investigator. This was clearly the Mafia's doing, he decided, and it was marvelous in his eyes.

On October 12, Sonoma County investigators visited eighteen-year-old Paulette Ramos at the track where she groomed horses. Immediately, she admitted her role in burying the body and led the police to the hornet-infested hillside-crypt that housed Clay's body. It took three investigators to remove the stump covering the remains. Although they found the decomposed body unidentifiable, the shirt pocket contained a piece of paper that said "Clay Wilson." There were also two spent bullets near the actual murder site.

Subsequently, at the Baron home two police investigators found Joe's odd collection of wigs and disguises—and a gun that proved a match for the spent slugs at Clay's murder scene. Under police questioning, Dee Wilson quickly broke down and confessed, and she and Paulette went into protective custody.

———

Joe realized his now-desperate situation. From Barnstable, Joe called (initially collect) the Sonoma County district attorney, Kiernan Hyland, on a "fishing expedition" to find out what Hyland had on him. Then Joe informed the Boston FBI "he had a good relationship with Clay Wilson and that he was being 'framed.'" But on October 16, Bay State authorities announced that Sonoma County had issued a warrant charging Joe with murder. A teary-eyed Henry walked to Ronnie and shook hands. In Boston, Angiulo shared a bottle of wine with Cassesso's father. In November, Billy signed an affidavit alleging Joe's perjury. Now, some people in Walpole dubbed Billy a rat who'd "nailed poor Joe Baron." Geraway even ran into a group of inmates standing in the corridor, waiting for the chapel to open.

"That bastard, Geraway, it looks like Joe is in trouble," someone said.

A nearby Peter Limone put his face into the grumbler's and said, "Let the sonofabitch get a taste of his own medicine, do you hear?" After that, no one dared to show Joe open sympathy.

A hard-drinking Massachusetts State police lieutenant detective contacted Geraway for a chat. This "Lieutenant Bill" (as Geraway styled him) seemed honest. "Let the chips fall where they may, just tell the truth," the lieutenant assured Geraway.

In November, Billy also announced he'd undergo a polygraph to prove Joe had confessed he'd killed Jack Francione, Raymond DiStasio, and Carlton Eaton. "The cases smell so badly that their odor is beginning to reach even the most secluded public nostrils," he wrote to the district attorney.

Although he didn't know it, the guards had their eyes intently focused on Billy. There was a special official file on him (with choice tidbits about his family), containing copies of his outgoing letters, and secret transcripts of his cell conversations. Additionally, Lt. Bill's manipulations and discussions were done in cahoots with top authorities. The trooper planted hostile seeds in Geraway's mind about the Deegan convicts. He even claimed Walter Bennett's body had passed "through a chicken feeder on Greco's farm." But, the lieutenant assured Billy that if he cooperated and buried the Deegan defendants forever, he'd walk. "It was an awesome temptation, one I yielded to without giving it a second thought," Geraway admitted. Still, the Office was more than generous to him. So happy was Jerry to see his former tormentor's torment, he gave Billy a $400 Dior watch.

The Office also delivered two beautiful typewriters, $2,000 in cash, and a pint of Chivas. Billy spent hours daily talking to Ronnie at the end of death row or near the room where he sorted laundry for block 10. Only, Ronnie didn't know the authorities were listening. At one point, Greco, Billy, Ronnie, and Henry sat down with Lt. Bill, thinking the lawman was on their side. And Henry "never sat down willingly with a cop in his life unless it was to arrange a payoff," as Billy put it.

Simultaneously, early in 1971, California attempted to retrieve its wayward adopted son Joe Baron. From jail, pugilist Joe fought the rendition, crafting his own writ, which claimed he'd not had a proper extradition hearing. No go: In February, Massachusetts green-lighted Joe's return west. After Harrington mounted a final unsuccessful defense, Joe yielded voluntarily and boarded a chartered plane to Santa Rosa. Although a spell of rough Midwestern weather kept the aircraft grounded briefly, Joe reached California to play out one last act.

35.

THE GOLDEN STATE

"I think we rolled 7's and 11's in that case."
—Defense attorney Marteen Miller

Once in California, Joe arrived for his arraignment (held securely in the county pen) in white jail overalls, a thick shock of black hair covering his forehead. He remained visibly emotionless as the judge read the first-degree murder charges. Now, before the court, a man who once commanded the best legal talent in Boston admitted he was broke.

The state then appointed him Marteen Miller, a seasoned attorney whose trained eye saw that his client's prospects were poor. There were two eyewitnesses (Dee and Ramos); another witness (Geraway), whose facts were correct; a body; and a client with a gory past. "I did not have too much hope at the beginning of the trial, but sometimes things go poorly for you and sometimes they break for you," Miller said.

During legal meetings meant to keep him from the gas chamber, the Animal constantly joked, performing antics and "banging things around"—including the defense team. Once, Joe interrupted Miller's young investigator, then discussing the case, by reaching over, grabbing him, and lifting him into the air. "Another word out of you and you are finished," he warned, joking.

But Joe fretted, too. "The newspapers & T.V. got everybody down here believing I am guilty," he wrote Harrington. "I got a fight on my hands because of them."

When Miller flew east to research the case, not surprisingly, he found Rico and Condon very helpful. Condon offered Miller directions to MCI Walpole, ensured his access to witnesses, and even helped him find lodgings. On the other hand, a Sonoma County investigator found the two Fibbies unresponsive. The many phone calls to them went unreturned. One day, before leaving his Boston motel, the investigator put his papers in the hotel safe, and fixed a hair on his briefcase. When he returned, the strand was gone, and it was an open question whether the Mafia or the FBI had opened the case.

Hoping to limit the damage, Harrington visited his onetime partner in the county jail. However, the day after the tryst, the prison authorities stuck the Animal upstairs in solitary, as he noted in a March 27 rant. He claimed he didn't do nothing wrong and was barred from TV, playing cards, and exercising in the yard—all things that kept his mind occupied. Believing this was done from "spite & savage amusement," he decided to sue the sheriff for cruel and unusual punishment. Even the cops back east on the take had more class than this sheriff. He ended the letter by saying: "If I still have my sanity by the time the trial comes around I'll see you."

When the Animal appeared in court, arrayed in bell-bottom jeans and loafers, the judge asked if Joe Bentley were his "true name."

In a "deep guttural voice," he said, "Yes."

"Are you also known as Joseph Barboza and Joseph Baron?"

"Those are legal names."

"Are you also known as Joseph Barboza Baron?"

He shook his head, and mumbled, "I don't know about that."

In April 1971, using Geraway's affidavits, from Atlanta, Raymond again sought a motion to vacate his conviction. In response, state police Lieutenant Bill told Geraway to secure $10,000 from Ronnie, which Billy would claim was a perjury bribe. The trooper said, "We'll just hold the ten grand until they come with their appeals, then we'll 'croak' them." He also boasted: "These bastards are going to the chair and I'd like to be the one to pull the switch."

During a chat with Ronnie, Billy requested $10,000 for legal, personal, and family expenses. Ronnie agreed, and Geraway introduced Ronnie to his sister Louise (back from California), explaining she was the designated go-between for the cash. On April 29, after a body search, police also fitted Louise with a wire. At a Boston hotel, Louise then met Ronnie's aunt, who gave her $10,000, and then returned, with Ronnie's father, to Somerville. Immediately, Louise turned the cash over to Norfolk County officials, who urged her to say Jerry Angiulo himself had delivered it.

But authorities squeezed Geraway ever more tightly, and in a fit of anger, he gave the mob's $2,000 gift to the trooper. Then he swore Joe's enemies had bribed him to testify to Joe's Deegan perjury.

Learning of Geraway's new affidavits, a publicly humiliated Raymond withdrew his motion for retrial. Billy realized that it wasn't a "spy game I was involved in with a television script and set guidelines; it was a life and death struggle by men under conviction for things they did not do—powerful and vindictive men." While the death row contingent knew Billy had retreated, they were unaware of just how much he'd sold them out.

Finally, although a self-admitted "immoral bastard," Billy realized that even if the Deegan four weren't his friends, they deserved better. "Ronnie, I have some bad news for you," he soon announced at the death row grate. The grim Ronnie flashed a half grin. "No, don't laugh. I'm serious." He told him about the $12,000 in bribe money he'd handed over to the state. Shocked, Ronnie asked if Billy would straighten out that which he'd made crooked. Billy agreed and gave up the official game plan.

Now Billy began frequenting death row, socializing with Henry, whose mind was active, despite his age. Henry enjoyed talking about his friendships across the continent. He shared various schemes so that Billy would "never have to cash checks again." There "were too many other ways to make a dishonest dollar." One scheme involved baking flawed diamonds in near-alchemical solutions to make them look perfect.

That July, authorities denied Billy's request for a retrial.

At the request of the Golden State, Geraway embarked west on his revenge pilgrimage to help put the Animal down permanently. After his arrival in California, authorities confiscated his goods, snapped his mug shot, and deposited him in the Santa Rosa jail's infirmary. Billy's cell contained restraints, reserved for drying alcoholics and crashing drug addicts.

"Boy, you must be fucking well hard up in California for state witnesses if this is the best you have to offer them," Billy told the deputy sheriff.

On October 19, the Wilson trial started. The state charged Joe as only a second-degree murderer—which was, under the circumstances, lenient. The trial reunited old acquaintances, some for Joe, others, against him. Among the latter was a tense Dee Mancini, granted immunity and perhaps more credibility than she deserved. During the trial, she relaxed, and Joe and she exchanged mysterious smiles.

U.S. Attorney General Elliot Richardson appointed as special agent Harrington, then in private practice, to testify. Rico and Condon flew to California to speak on Joe's behalf, which surprised some. But in the middle of a discussion with Miller, Joe slammed his hand down and said, "They owe me and they better do it."

The presence of the multiple unimpeachable defense witnesses jammed in the collective craw of Sonoma County's law enforcement arm. As Detective Sergeant Jim Brown noted, "when those fellows finished their testimony, Mr. Barbosa [*sic*] was a national hero."

Ironically, career criminal Geraway found the Hall of Justice, with its flower decorations and interior water fountain, beautiful. Feeding Billy's own bloodlust was the sight of the "sad and lonely" Wilson couple. Mrs. Wilson sat in the court with her head bowed, tears rolling down from behind her dark glasses.

At first, Joe acted cheerfully, pretending his onetime friend Billy wouldn't testify. Billy wrote up discovery documents that were irrelevant to the case, but that would become part of the public record. In them, Billy accused Joe of many things— including prison sodomy—any one of which would land a person on the Animal's ever-expanding and re-prioritized death list. It required hours for the defense attorneys to calm Joe down between trial sessions. While in his holding cell, Joe would yell threats so loudly Billy heard him in the detox lockup. "If that's what he wants, I'll give it to him," Joe said. "I'll give it to him right in court!"

On November 18, Billy appeared on the stand, certain if he didn't put his former ace in the gas chamber, his own life was in future peril. To make the point stick, Billy dressed in black, Joe's favorite color for hits. Billy sat twenty feet from Joe, to the judge's right. He knew the Animal could quickly, albeit messily, dispatch him with fang or ballpoint pen before the guards interfered. In his simple blue suit, Joe displayed the "appearance of a human being," but his eyes flashed hate. Nevertheless, sometimes Billy taunted Joe directly with loud remarks, and Miller had to soothe his savage client. When the spectators laughed, Joe would glare around and, as if throwing a kill switch, silence everyone. "Joe had the whole courtroom terrorized," Billy said.

With so many hostile witnesses, it was only natural that Joe, being arguably his own worst enemy, also took the stand. Naturally, Joe blamed the trial on his refusal to recant his testimony. In Joe's version, the murder was self-defense—in which he'd used Clayton's own pistol to shoot him in the head—twice. After eight weeks of testimony, on December 13, at Miller's urging, Joe, claiming disgust, pled guilty to second-degree murder. The Animal even enjoyed the rare distinction of blaming the mob for things it hadn't done. Not for Joe were mere facts: "I was told by word that if I played ball with the Mafia I could get out of it," he claimed. "I still refused."

After the plea bargain, a judge gave Joe five years plus and parole; authorities also granted him a parole in Massachusetts. The diligent Miller arranged that Joe's sentences run concurrently.

On December 13, a disappointed Billy Geraway learned Joe wouldn't get the chamber. "I had done my best, and although I had not achieved the ultimate, the results weren't too shabby," he reflected. At least the Geraway family had time to hide. Of the Wilsons, he said, "They waited for justice. They will wait a long time."

Back in Walpole, a "demonic Disneyland," Billy's situation was dicey, to say the least. The prison was more unmanageable than before, with prisoners routinely using feces as a weapon against the guards. That wasn't so bad. Geraway saw men burned alive, disemboweled, stabbed, or castrated, their genitals stuffed into their mouths. The bitter Deegan convicts refused to speak to him, despite his efforts to nail the Animal. They felt Billy had failed to step forward and testify to get them out of jail when he had the chance.

In July 1972, Billy and Ronnie parted ways over the Office's unfulfilled promises. Moreover, the $10,000 bribe Billy had engineered from the Cassesso family resulted in indictments for Ronnie and his aunt. Someone declared an open contract on Billy. He started one day by hearing a radio news flash that a gun had been smuggled in to kill him. Although Billy had survived several murder attempts, if he stayed in Walpole, he was a dead man.

36

BACK INSIDE

The California authorities sent Joe to a facility in Vacaville, in which, like a drainpipe to a massive cesspool, all convicts were received for processing. "He [Joe] is extremely devoted to his wife and children claiming that he severed connections with the Mafia after his marriage because he wanted something different for his family than he had known before," according to a California corrections report.

By June 1972, Joe was in isolation in Folsom State Prison. He was also toiling, with a newly contracted ghostwriter, on his autobiography, *In and Outside the Family.* To assist, James Chalmas enlisted a stocky Finnish woman to convert Joe's longhand autobiography into typed pages. She was about thirty. However, Joe was "adamant" that she not read the "various trashy" parts of the book. The typist told Chalmas she wasn't squeamish, but the arrangement made Joe blush. In a letter, he apologized, "in respect towards your womanhood." He also expressed his "unbounded gratitude" that she'd turned his manuscript into a "work of art." He offered her an autographed copy to place on her shelf "amongst the ghouls, vampires and horror books."

Soon after the epistolary conversation began, Joe declared his love for "Green Eyes." He asked her if she (or Chalmas) realized that such a relationship would start, given she was typing about a dirty old man (Joe)? She had called him an "idiot" previously; he realized she didn't mean anything by it. "That is the method in my madness. . . . Elementary & deduction my dear Watson! Smile. Until later tonite my Princess."

He mused on the craziness of the modern world, and noted: "Patient + patience all we do all our lives is want for one thing or another." Given Joe was a southpaw, he called her his "left arm," not that it made that much of a difference given she owned both arms anyway. Generally swarthy, he tanned well and was dark enough to "integrate." He asked for her measurements, noted that fifteen people had commented on his weight loss and how, silently he felt good hearing that praise. She had divulged she was five feet four inches and 170 pounds. He admitted he was totally bald, had a glass eye and false teeth. "Now what do you think of that, reader teaser mine?" She was, apparently, mechanically inclined and learning how to rip out and rebuild a Corvette engine! In a letter, Joe offered a literary sigh, and noted it was so ridiculous that "my little flower is rebuilding Corvettes!" He decided she was absolutely the most intriguing woman he ever met, always blowing his mind. "I find now the secret to our love is we are both cuckoo!" He drew a smiley face in this letter (as he did on some of the others).

By now, he claimed sex wasn't the biggest draw for him. "Honey, forget the *Playboy* or *Penthouse* I am too old & might get too excited & get a heart attack." Instead, he asked for packages of cheese, sausages, and cookies. "My wife you fit so divine & well in my arms. . . . Never, never be sad or depressed, I want your promise."

Breaking his prison routine, on May 26, 1972, Joe appeared as a witness for a congressional committee hearing. Florida representative Claude Pepper chaired the body, whose ostensible goal was to uncover the hand of organized crime in professional sports. When Joe volunteered to testify, he intended to offer as a plum none other than Frank Sinatra—whose song "My Way" was his favorite. Joe bragged to other inmates that he'd be a public rat. Then Joe invited Partington to manage his security detail in Washington, D.C., for the testimony.

"Shit, Joe, you don't know nothing about Sinatra, you're just making that shit up!" Partington said.

Joe laughed. "It gets me out of the joint for a while, don't it?" Partington declined.

To bolster its star witness, the Pepper committee reached out to Billy Geraway. A congressional investigator asked Billy to testify how the Mafia had framed the Animal. Geraway sent Joe a letter, claiming he was considering it. "You're no bargain, Joe, neither of us are. . . . I don't expect that you are going to be too happy over me in any case, but I remember a couple of things you said in 1970 and 1971. Once you said to me that we had common enemies in these people." He said there were "14 double crosses" and "I'm disgusted with the whole thing, and there is nothing they can do to me." But Joe was aware some in his circle now regarded Geraway as a "monsterous genious."

This particular Geraway plot apparently went nowhere—but Billy did. His conviction appeal succeeded, and soon he hit the street. Thereafter, he promoted himself as a reformed-criminal celebrity, giving lectures and appearing on TV talk shows. He claimed there were two attempts on his life outside jail. Someone had even opened fire on him while he drove, forcing him into a canyon. But by then, the jailhouse atheist had converted to faith in God and married, and he had something to live for. He even published a book, *There's $50,000 on My Head,* in which he crucified Joe in print. He apparently never crossed paths with the Animal again—with whom he had much in common by now.

"I may be killed at any time," Geraway said. "The Mafia must destroy those who have offended it, otherwise they would cease to exist. It may be a few months or a year, but it will happen. But while I have something to say I will say it."

The Pepper hearings became a circus of mobsters, athletes, and celebrities. The farce perfected when the paunchy, disheveled "Portuguese Savage" (as *The New York Times* reporter dubbed him) appeared. Spectators in the audience stared at Joe, speechless, with one reporter claiming he was the "roughest, toughest-looking man I have ever seen—a great witness." Dark glasses hiding his eyes, Joe strode to the witness table, under heavy guard. Joe wore a running suit top over a turtleneck shirt, whose high collar almost disguised his stubbly double chin. From under his Fu Manchu mustache, a cigarette poked out.

"Do you solemnly swear to tell the truth, the whole truth and nothing but the truth?" the bailiff asked.

Leaving the cigarette in the corner of his mouth, Joe raised his hand and said: "I do." Joe's oath opened up a two-and-one-half-hour flood of blather. "Fierce looking" behind his large dark glasses, he discussed, in "a husky but relatively soft voice for a man of his reputation," beatings, murders, and his onetime greatness as a hood. For no particular reason, he discussed breaking up the Peppermint Lounge and pushing out the Cleveland mob's hand (he confessed to his ignorance of what the Lounge's resident black pimp wanted).

Joe did claim, somewhat truthfully, that Sinatra was Raymond's partner. Later, in a choked voice, Joe said, "Mr. Pepper, organized crime is probably the worst threat to the United States. . . . I don't want to leave this on my children."

Joe's intended KO swing at Sinatra and Raymond did guarantee another fifteen minutes of Animal fame. The Associated Press was present, and newspapers everywhere carried the story of the odd accusations, making Joe, briefly, a nightmarish household figure. The Animal was now a star in his own movie—one un-likely to have a sequel. At his testimony's conclusion, Pepper said: "Without excusing any illegal acts you may have committed I want to commend you."

On July 19, sixty-four-year-old Raymond, fresh from his Atlanta jail, appeared before the Pepper committee and pleaded the Fifth seventy-eight times. Nevertheless, Raymond was in good form, and in referring to his St. Patrick's Day birth, claimed he was, "A good Irishman for an Italian."

The committee wanted the skinny on his onetime racetrack Berkshire Downs (although it had been one of Raymond's major failures). Years before, wanting "to lend class" to the ailing track, a desperate Raymond had made Berkshire Downs directors out of Dean Martin and Frank Sinatra. Nevertheless, over time, Ray-mond watched, disgusted and powerless, as it slid into bankruptcy. "I don't want to hear of Berkshire Downs again," Raymond had once said, "because every time I talk about it I'm sick at the amount of money I've lost—not only for myself, but for my friends."

Now, before Pepper and his minions, Raymond said, "I read I had $215,000 in Berkshire Downs. I wish I had. I've never had $215,000 in my life." He denied meeting Sinatra in person, which may have been true. "The only place I've seen him is on television." As for Joe, Raymond said, "He's a nutcake. . . . I'm afraid of that man; he lied about me once. He is liable to say anything to keep himself out of prison."

With a smile, Raymond commented on a bestseller of the time, *The Godfather*: "In my opinion, it was a good book, but I got a short memory and can't remember no lines. Good solid people like to read it after all the publicity people like you give it. Maybe I can publish the *Patriarca Papers* and make a million dollars." He tried to lecture the congressmen. "If I didn't have my case coming up, I would like to come back with you gentlemen when this is over with and really lay the law down what is going on in this country. . . . It

was a lot of hoodwink you people were giving me for a long time. . . .
I would like to talk to you about the United States of America and
what is going on."

Joe learned of Raymond's statement and said, "The mealy mouth
liar. . . . The only thing he [is] afraid of is losing his money, the
greedy buzzard!"

There was a final word from Frank Sinatra himself. The current
pal of gangsters and former friend of the Kennedys appeared, belatedly, before the House crime committee. "This bum [Joe] went
running off at the mouth and I resent it. I'm not a second-class
citizen," said the chairman of the ever-unnamed board. Congress
defunded the commission.

Given his testimony, Joe's cover was again nonexistent. So, on October 30, 1972, the California prison authorities moved Joe (under
the name of Joseph Bentley) to the Deer Lodge penal camp in
Billings, Montana. It was a Nordic "country club," where snow
blanketed the ground nine months a year during harsh winters.
To compensate, Joe wore a warm fur-lined jacket over long johns.
"What do you think I feel like in here like a sitting duck not being
able to move," he wrote.

He instructed Chalmas the Greek to spend $900 to purchase a
diamond for a wedding ring on his behalf. To his far-off lover, Joe
wrote, "I have all your pictures where & everywhere I turn in my
cell I see my [Green Eyes]." On December 7, Joe received a card and
remembered it was the anniversary of Chico Amico's never-solved
murder. That Christmas was especially hard on Joe, but at least he
was headed for the ranch. "Could dig doing a little horseback riding
to round up cattle. Told you my reading cowboy books would prove
not in vain! Smile." He struck a positive note. "Yes, we'll decorate if
I am home next Xmas. . . . I know how you feel this year. What is
the sense of decorating if there is no happiness."

As a budding writer, Joe hungered for books and wanted her to send him up to six paperback Westerns at once—preferably new ones. His eclectic Montana jail reading list ran from *The Last Nights of Pompeii* to Westerns, including *Little Big Man*. He said he was pretty sure he wanted to go to writing school. He found writing came easy to him, although he didn't know how to type. He was developing a literary style, and in one letter he told her he was going to read for a while and think about Texas. There he'd break out of Yuma Prison to get his hidden $100,000 from the stagecoach payroll. A posse would be in "hot pursuit," but never get too close "because I am dead eye Joe quick on the draw & worse I come from Montana! Poor story, I am from Texas? Breaking out of Arizona? From Montana?"

Naturally, when he heard she was getting a weapon, he applauded her, recommending a .38 police special with a six-inch barrel. He also noted the value of a shotgun. "Shot guns you don't miss with! . . . The Astoria kid rides again."

On the outside, Frankie Salemme lived in New York City until December 14, 1972. On that day FBI Special Agent John Connolly made—as in recognized—Frankie in downtown Manhattan. They'd met years before in Southie's L Street Bathhouse. Over Frankie's denials, at gunpoint, Connolly and another agent arrested him—and took him away in a taxi. In transit to Boston to face trial, he thought, "I'd rather have been any place else than on that plane going back to the trial." When the bombing proceedings finished, "I got my 30 years," as Frankie put it.

The work of Rico, Stevie Flemmi, and Connolly resulted in three decades of incarceration for Frankie. Soon after, Frankie arrived in Walpole, where he could pal around with the Deegan convicts. Joe's "beloved Bear" was also there, now a middle-aged junkie, fat and bearded. Flemmi was disintegrating on every level.

Paranoid, he'd walk by Henry's cell in the prison flats whenever Frankie was talking to the Deegan convicts. After one conversation, the Bear followed Frankie into his third-tier cell. "What are you doing here?" Frankie asked.

"Were you talking about me?" Flemmi asked.

"Why, what's the matter?"

"You know, I had to do what I had to do. I had to protect myself, I had to do what I had to do. . . . and you shouldn't discuss my business and my brother's business with them." This was puzzling, as Frankie didn't even know Stevie was in Montreal. Becoming flighty, the Bear bounced against Frankie's bookcase, knocking tomes off. After Frankie grabbed him, the Bear began yelling; Salemme pushed him out of his cell and threw him against the rail. The next day the Bear apologized to Frankie. Flemmi kept at the needle and the paradise it could provide in the most terrible hells.

The year 1973 found Joe outside the wall at a pleasant medium-to-minimum-security compound. Regrettably for him, if not literature, he'd also lost his ghostwriter. He said, "DoubleDay & NY is screaming for it & two movie companies want it estimated at over $1,000,000 and better than the *Godfather*." He was already facing some literary fights. Following in Joe's footsteps, Vincent Teresa had turned state's witness and penned his own tome: *My Life in the Mafia*. (A more accurate title would have read, *My Life Around the Mafia*.)

Hearing about the book, Joe wrote: "From what I understand he said a lot of things about me. Yet he can't back one [story] up & they are all lies."

Joe's appeal ground on so long that he feared he'd undergo a new trial. Finally, Montana's parole board ruled against Joe's release. On September 1, 1973, he leaked his own identity. Probably by coincidence, just then someone also smuggled a weapon into his facility.

Joe blamed the Montana corrections department, claiming to be "shell shocked from [the] breech of security." He also said a newly freed prisoner had blown his cover, once outside, Joe was ready to sue the state for $1 million to remedy this situation.

In December 1973, fate intervened when a guard found marijuana in Joe's size 10 shoe. "That is just my luck," said Joe before throwing a left hook at the guard and breaking his jaw. Montana, sickened of Joe, disgorged him into the receptacle of the Golden State. By February 1974, he was in isolation in California's San Quentin State Prison. Later, in Folsom, he lived in something that was little more than a cage.

Despite his incarceration, eventually, inevitably, as he'd promised, Joe managed to collect a series of unconnected and often bizarre anecdotes about his life. He'd told some of these stories already in court or on the street. These tales he handed to a gullible ghostwriter named Hank Messick, who gave the tales a rough order. It was honest work, of sorts: Joe complained to Messick about getting a thumb callus from pencil pushing. Eventually, a publisher with a less than acute sense of smell released this as a crudely formed bound and printed book called *Barboza*.

The book's unimaginative title wasn't an alias, or even Joe's legal name, Baron. Possibly, Joe felt he could trade most successfully on his own reputation. *Barboza* is a bizarre odyssey of half-truths and lies, a paean to his brutality and celebrity status. In it, he loved, killed, and betrayed grandly—or as grandly as a jailhouse poet and raconteur could. But he claimed that if one person stood up to fight the mob because of *Barboza*, "my endeavorments [*sic*] will not entirely in the least be in vain!"

After the tome's publication, several women even called Messick, long distance, wanting to meet Joe. Messick told the jealous Green Eyes—she became upset about this. She was committed to the Animal, to the end.

As for Joe, he had to admit his "traitor friends" had ruined him. But no matter what they did to him, he was ahead, and always would be.

Its ending was far from happy for him, he admitted. "I've lost my wife and children and that is my biggest sorrow. But I look myself in the face in the mirror and I know I've been right in standing up for what I believe." Indeed, he had reinvented himself as an anti-Mafia crusader. His motives may not have been noble, but they were real. "At first it used to reach me, the informant and canary bit," he said in a TV interview in 1970. "It doesn't reach me anymore. Because I have a purpose in life. I have only one purpose . . . peace of mind."

His revenge had been total on both the innocent and guilty alike, and perhaps even on the world itself. As he put it in a poem:

I started and caused an Empire to crumble, so now I've been told,
Living with a still unsatisfied memory, and growing old.

As for himself, he accepted his fate—or so he claimed. He'd hurt the men that had betrayed him far more than they could ever hope to hurt him back. And as he told Congress: "They have a $300,000 contract out on me. I am not concerned about my life. I don't want to die but I am not concerned about it."

Joe's most powerful enemies were concerned, however. A government memo about the Animal, dated September 19, 1975, advised "subject was being paroled in California. The word on the street in Boston is that the bad guys know this . . . and they plan on publicly executing him."

"WHAT GOES AROUND . . ."

"When the last of the dons die, the Mafia, the real Mafia, will die too. What you have now is the new secret society or syndicate, and it's nothing but a goddamn bunch of vicious thieves."

—Vincent Teresa

Once, after a con man took him for money, Joe offered the fraudster this warning: "You didn't know me well so you beat me. But I found out and someday I'll return the favor, 'cause what goes around comes around." He always smiled at the man—eventually, he spiked his drink to give him diarrhea, and then let everyone know he'd done it. Joe knew what he was facing when he hit the street on October 30, 1975.

At first, Joe moved in with James The Greek Chalmas, who provided sustenance, as well as a .38 and a shotgun. Soon after, as "Joseph Donati," Joe took a $250-a-month two-bedroom apartment with thirty-two-year-old Maggie Delfel, whose surname he later borrowed. The "pad" was comfortable, with a Pacific Ocean view and a fireplace—a nice place to vanish into. Neighbors interacted with the pair only casually. The couple was quiet, and a "very polite" Joe appeared "just like everyone else" and was sociable enough to exchange regular pleasantries with a fifty-five-year-old neighbor. Although no one ever saw Joe work, he had money. Possibly, he'd been doing shakedowns. If so, Joe was taking a big risk—he'd even admitted in a letter "the government might find a way to 'whack me out' and blame it on the Mafia."

But secretly, Chalmas contacted a onetime jail colleague, J. R. Russo, the East Boston Mafioso. Russo possessed a noble Roman profile, with prominent nose and chin and delicate features. In November 1975, Russo flew to San Francisco for a surprise face-to-face meeting with Chalmas. Looking for details, Russo asked Chalmas when he'd be seeing Joe next and asked if he "would like to make some big bucks." Russo then offered him $25,000 to do the job himself—which wasn't quite the rumored $300,000 bounty for Joe's head.

Russo threw his hands up in the air and said, "That's 25 big ones and that's a lot of money." A wary Chalmas said he preferred a "neutral position." Angrily, Russo pointed out the red hot Joe was a "bum" who'd lied about "George" (Raymond) and other men, now on death row. Chalmas softened. "Can you handle it?" Russo asked.

Chalmas's aunt owned a restaurant—he suggested he could arrange a cook's job for Joe there. "That would be a good place to take care of business," said Russo. Chalmas later said he promised to look into it and see "where the interest laid." Russo calmed, and left with the warning, "Keep your mouth shut. Don't say anything to him [Baron] or anybody else."

Chalmas knew Joe probably didn't feel like dying prematurely, and found him unpredictable, violent, and frightening. But Russo scared Chalmas, too, and the pressure caused him a "severe drinking and drug problem." During subsequent and periodic phone calls, Russo would ask, "Is that lying bum still out there?" They discussed shooting Joe; Russo even promised to send Chalmas "tasteless, colorless, deadly poison."

"I can't handle it," Chalmas told Russo. "I'm in no position to take care of it." Taut nerves sent him to Miami, ostensibly for the 1976 Super Bowl. He hoped Joe would be murdered before he returned—it didn't happen, and the pressure mounted. At one point, while driving with Joe a few blocks from his San Francisco apartment, Chalmas saw what he thought was Russo. (Obviously, Joe didn't see what Chalmas did.) Later, Russo told Chalmas he hadn't been in San Francisco of late, and the Greek was "crazy" from drink and pills.

By February 11, 1976, Chalmas had apparently signed on to a plan. Joe met the Greek in San Francisco and lunched at a deli. He stopped off at Chalmas's apartment in the Sunset District on the corner of Noriega and Twenty-fifth Streets, and then he left to fill a prescription. As Chalmas waited in his apartment, Joe approached his light blue Thunderbird. As he inserted his key into the door lock, a white 1972 Ford van drove past slowly. The right-side door opened, and a gun muzzle protruded from an open window and flashed repeatedly. In his apartment, Chalmas heard two quick, loud explosions, followed by two more booms, not quite as noisy, from a different weapon.

The Greek waited five minutes, and then headed to Joe's parking spot. He saw fifteen people standing around Joe's body, which gushed blood from the hole in the right side, where three-aught shotgun slugs had penetrated. The hit was of such professional grace and execution, Joe himself might have been proud it. In fact, the man wielding the weapon was, according to Larry Baione, a "very brilliant guy. Smart as a whip. Stepped right out with a [fucking] carbine."

The police didn't initially understand why an assassin had gunned down a Joe Donati—until they lifted the corpse's prints and matched them to Joe Barboza Baron. There was little else, except speculation. The abandoned murder van yielded, from behind the driver's seat, a .30 caliber shell from a carbine; a broken piece of seat belt; and a shotgun—but acid had erased the identifying numbers.

All Joe's incarnations—Bentley, Donati, Baron, Barboza,

Farouk—were gone, and his passage was perhaps the one indisputable and sincere public act since his birth. Naturally, the news made front-page headlines back in Boston. Joe was famous again, but it wouldn't help his writing career. Certainly, the public's emotions were mixed. "With all due respect for my former client, I don't think society has suffered a great loss," said F. Lee Bailey.

"I know it sounds odd," said John Partington, "but I felt funny as soon as the phone rang, as though I knew just then, for no reason, that Joe was dead. I had a love hate feeling for the guy. He was a killer, but still, we had gotten close." Joe, who had once called Partington his brother, had explained the life, "There's one thing in this game. Either you kill me or I'm going to kill you. You don't live long in this business."

Joe's brother Donald retrieved the body and held the funeral, in New Bedford. "You're one tough son of a bitch," he told the corpse. "You always told me this is how it would end. At least you're at peace now."

While family matron Palmeda had already died, Joseph Barboza Sr. was around to make the send-off for his namesake. With Claire Baron and the children absent, in death Joe reverted into Catholicism. A handful of mourners gathered at the grave site in in Dartmouth. Donald Barboza asked the officiating priest to perform the eulogy in the tongue of his fathers, instead of English. As he explained, "My brother was Portuguese."

Not long before his murder, Joe had penned a poem about the future, noting how most people don't seem concerned about significant things in this world so full of hypocrisy. Rather, they tend to postpone worrying until tomorrow, while enjoying everything they can today:

And then, when old age approaches, pray for an upper instead of a lower berth.

Days after the murder, there was a "For Rent" sign on Joe Baron's apartment. At some point, unnoticed, Maggie Delfel had gone elsewhere.

The old order of the North End steadily died off—and mostly in bed. During spring 1972 in Providence, a still hawkish-looking and dapper sixty-four-year-old Raymond was tried a second time as an accessory in the Melei-Marfeo killings. In court, Raymond tearfully embraced an alcoholic priest who'd perjured himself to give Raymond an alibi. The priest, either lying or deranged, claimed the day Raymond had ordered the hit, he'd actually been with him, praying over Helen Patriarca's grave. In short order, the prosecution blew this alibi out of the water—but Raymond was acquitted.

No matter, the senescent Raymond was vulnerable. Indeed, by now Raymond faced enough indictments for a lifetime, with plenty left over for his namesake and son.

Given the role J. R. Russo played in the assassination, Larry Baione proposed the Young Turk for promotion to capo. This became difficult when Russo, a somewhat hot property, vanished for years awaiting Raymond's permission to come home. Aware the government was investigating Joe's murder, Larry broached the matter with Jerry in the Angiulo office. The two onetime rivals joked about facing the death penalty together—the outcome if the California authorities prosecuted them. While the FBI listened, (in the bureau's God-like silence), Larry told Jerry how the statute of limitations on murder in California exceeded five years.

"I just hope they don't give it to the state," Larry said. "That's a [fucking] gas chamber." Larry shouted, taunting Jerry, "Gas chamber."

"The who chamber?" Jerry asked.

"Gas."

"Where?"

"And they got two, two chairs, Jerry. We can hold hands to-gether," said Larry, now laughing.

"Oh, oh, oh, oh, oh, never, never."

"They've gone to double chairs," said Larry, laughing. "No [shit]. I won't go any other [fucking] way."

"We, we'll go separate. We'll toss a [fucking] coin."

"I love him," Larry yelled. "I love him."

"Just my luck," Jerry laughed.

"I love him and I want him with me," shouted Larry.

"[Fuck] that [shit]. Toss the coin. Sorry, Larry."

"Is that what you're gonna say? You shoulda been a lawyer."

"Sorry, Larry. You go first. Just your luck." Jerry joked about a last-minute reprieve. "Here comes the phone, ringing. You're walking out."

In the middle of his laughter, Larry said, "Reprieve."

"Too late, reprieve."

"I'll say, Jerry: You shoulda been a lawyer."

"A what?"

"Two lawyers"—he laughed—"too late."

It was just as well they laughed. Both men, like the rest of the Office's managers, were destined to return to jail, for a long, long time. In less than a decade, with Raymond dead, the family wouldn't need the government to persecute it. The members would shoot one another down like common punks or petty thieves. By then, the stakes were rather poor—honest contractors could make more money than mob soldiers, with less headache. The time of Joseph Lombardo's Mafia, with the obscure rites and codes of feudal Sicily, were long since departed. For Joe Barboza had been a tiny earthquake that made a tsunami. The New England Mafia became a walking corpse whose decay became more obvious every year.

This book's introduction ended on a sarcastic question from H. Paul Rico: "What do you want, tears?" Humanely speaking, there isn't a final response to it. But perhaps we can say this: the downfall of the classic Boston mob (a demise in which Rico, Joe Barboza, Robert Kennedy, and J. Edgar Hoover played such instrumental roles) is many things, but not, perhaps, a cause for tears.

SOURCE NOTES

This book is a work of nonfiction. There are no invented characters, dialogue, or scenes. Given the distance that has passed, I have tried to rely on the accounts that were the closest to the time it occured. The dialogue is pretty much as the eyewitnesses recalled it, with allowances made only for grammar or clarity.

So, how to make sense of the dozens of conflicting stories of the Charlestown–Winter Hill gang war? How to get to the final answers of the many murders that are, essentially, unsolvable? Excellent questions. Also, given the vested interests for both lawmen and criminals to protect their reputations, incomes, or loved ones (not to mention their freedom from prosecution), one must apply a certain Newtonian logic. One's honesty is maintained inversely to the degree one's private interest is at stake. The more someone has to gain or lose by the truth, the more he or she is likely to bend or sacrifice it. So let the writer beware.

As an example, the ongoing (as of 2013) back-and-forth in court and print between Stevie Flemmi and his former colleagues James Bulger and Frankie Salemme makes it almost impossible to tell exactly who is giving the most accurate record of their collaborative murders. They all seem to be approximately accurate. So the principles I have adhered to are: What makes the most sense? What is most likely? Does a given story support or destroy another set of reasonable facts? If a story was ridiculous or unlikely, I tried to find ways to pick it apart. For instance, the bizarre stories Joe told about the murders of Leo Lowry and Ronald Dermody I discarded quickly once I had better explanations than the ones he gave. Additionally, I had several living sources who were active in the underworld during the time period covered. At their request, they remain anonymous. The conclusions I draw, in many cases, are my own.

The biggest help by far was the enormous congressional report, *Everything Secret Degenerates: The FBI's Use of Murderers as Informants*. This includes extensive FBI reports, newspaper articles, government memorandums and forms, and even letters from Joe Barboza from jail to various contacts outside. The never-reticent Barboza also wrote his own autobiography, which offers a few insights but precious little truth. He was dishonest in his own accounting of his life, as he was with all else. More enlightening was William Geraway's version of events. Although no friend to Joe and a career criminal, his accounts sound true.

Also useful, if not completely trustworthy, was Frankie Salemme's testimony before Congress. I also have relied extensively on the FBI reports of the period. It's my opinion that although the informants had their own agendas, the agents corroborated their information with other sources. The informants never knew one another, so each one could contradict others with impunity. The agents—whom I realize were not always exemplary—at least had to satisfy minimum requirements of honesty. They had to answer to their boss, J. Edgar Hoover.

Talking to as many people as I could, I have heard stories that illuminated or expanded the existing stories. For instance, one eyewitness (a credible one) said he was at the initial party on Labor

Day weekend when Georgie McLaughlin received a beating. He personally saw Buddy McLean dish it out. Other sources confirmed that Georgie received two more beatings that day—the worst and final of which put him in the hospital. And thereby hangs a tale.

Many other people who were peripheral to the underworld have offered perspective, anecdotes, and helped confirm or deny existing stories. For instance, for background on the Bear, Vincent James Flemmi, I had the stories of my own father and uncle, who recalled him from the South End.

Also helpful were the Boston police's logs and reports on the shootings of Bernie and Punchy McLaughlin. Legal proceedings, such as appeals and transcripts, where available online and elsewhere, were also valuable. In particular, in the 1974 *Commonwealth vs. Flemmi* appeal, the summary of the Bear's assault on James Abbout was helpful. Georgie McLaughlin's appeal for his conviction in the William Sheridan killing was also quite illuminating.

SELECTED BIBLIOGRAPHY

Newspapers

I used extensive newspaper articles from dailies and weeklies in Somerville, Canton, Dedham, Norwood, Westwood, and other Boston-area towns and cities. A brief list of the newspapers and articles follows.

Associated Press
The Boston Globe
The Boston Herald
The Boston Record American
The Boston Sunday Advertiser
The Boston Traveler
The Hartford Courant
The Lowell Sun
The New Bedford Standard-Times
The Newport Daily News
The Patriot Ledger

The Providence Journal-Bulletin
The New York Times
The San Francisco Chronicle
The San Francisco Examiner
The Somerville Journal

Magazine and Journal Articles

Davidson, Bill. "The Mafia: How It Bleeds New England." *Saturday Evening Post*, Nov. 18, 1967: 27–31. Print.

Goodwin, Jan. "Justice Delayed: The Exoneration of Joseph Salvati." *Reader's Digest*, Mar. 2008. Web.

Grinnell, Charles W. "I Spied on the Mafia for the FBI." *Saturday Evening Post*, Apr. 6, 1968: 21–69. Print.

Hunt, Thomas. "Raymond Patriarca: 'The Man.'" *Informer: The History of American Crime and Law Enforcement*, Oct. 2011: 34–50. Web.

Maher, Steven R. "Worcester Mafia Boss Frank Iaconi's War with the Providence Mob." *InCity Times*, Oct. 8, 2008. Web. <http://incitytimesworcester.org/2008/10/08/worcester-mafia-boss-frank-iaconi%E2%80%99s-war-with-the-providence-mob/>.

Russell, Francis. "The Knave of Boston." *American Heritage*, Aug. 1976. Web. <http://www.americanheritage.com/content/knave-boston>.

Stolley, Richard B. "Crime U.S." *Life*, Feb. 24, 1967: 23–29. Print.

Warner, Richard N. "Gaspare Messina and the Rise of the Mafia in Boston." *Informer: The History of American Crime and Law Enforcement*, Oct. 2011: 5–19. Web.

Books

Atkinson, Jay. *Legends of Winter Hill: Cops, Con Men, and Joe McCain, the Last Real Detective.* New York: Crown, 2005. Print.

Bailey, F. Lee. *The Defense Never Rests.* 1971. New York: New Amer. Lib., 1972. Print.

Barboza, Joseph, with Hank Messick. *Barboza.* New York: Dell, 1976. Print.

Beatty, Jack. *The Rascal King: The Life and Times of James Michael Curley.* 1992. Da Capo, 2000. Print.

Behn, Noel. *Big Stick-up at Brink's!* 1977. New York: Warner, 1978. Print.

Capote, Truman. *In Cold Blood.* 1965. New York: Random House, 1994. Print.

Carr, Howie. *The Brothers Bulger.* New York: Warner, 2006. Print.

————. *Hitman: The Untold Story of Johnny Martorano.* New York: Forge, 2011. Print.

————. *Rifleman: The Untold Story of Stevie Flemmi.* Frandel, 2013. Print.

Cianci, Vincent Albert, with David Fisher. *Politics and Pasta: How I Prosecuted Mobsters, Rebuilt a Dying City, Dined with Sinatra, Spent Five Years in a Federally Funded Gated Community, and Lived to Tell the Tale.* New York: St. Martin's, 2011. Print.

Clemente, Gerald W., with Kevin Stevens. *The Cops Are Robbers: A Convicted Cop's True Story of Police Corruption.* Boston: Quinlan, 1987. Print.

Connolly, Matthew. *Don't Embarrass the Family: The Trial of Whitey Bulger's Handler, FBI Special Agent John Connolly.* Dedham: Rock Hill, 2012. Print.

Connor, Myles J., Jr. *The Art of the Heist: Confessions of a Master Thief.* New York: HarperCollins, 2009. Print.

Cressey, Donald. *Theft of the Nation: The Structure and Operations of Organized Crime in America.* New York: Harper & Row, 1969. Print.

DeSario, Frank M. *Badge Number 1: Memoirs of a Boston Cop.* Desario, 2006. Print.

Earley, Pete, and Gerald Shur. *WITSEC: Inside the Federal Witness Protection Program.* New York: Bantam, 2002. Print.

English, T. J. *Paddy Whacked: The Untold Story of the Irish Gangster.* New York: HarperCollins, 2005. Print.

Foley, Thomas J., and Tom Sedgwick. *Most Wanted: Pursuing Whitey Bulger, the Murderous Mob Chief the FBI Secretly Protected.* New York: Simon & Schuster, 2012. Print.

Fopiano, Willie, and John Harney. *The Godson: A True Life Account of 20 Years Inside the Mob.* New York: St. Martin's, 1998. Print.

Ford, Beverly, and Stephanie Schorow. *The Boston Mob Guide: Hit Men, Hoodlums, and Hideouts.* Charleston: History, 2011. Print.

Frank, Gerold. *The Boston Strangler.* New York: New Amer. Lib., 1966. Print.

Georgianna, Daniel. *The Strike of '28.* New Bedford: Spinner, 1993. Print.

Geraway, William R. *There's $50,000 on My Head.* Hicksville: Exposition, 1976. Print.

Giancana, Sam. *Mafia: United States Treasury Department Bureau of Narcotics.* New York: HarperCollins, 2007. Print.

Goddard, Donald. *The Insider: The FBI's Undercover Wiseguy Goes Public.* New York: Pocket, 1992. Print.

Junger, Sebastian. *A Death in Belmont.* New York: Norton, 2006. Print.

Kelly, Susan. *The Boston Stranglers.* 1995. New York: Kensington, 2002. Print.

Lukas, J. Anthony. *Common Ground: A Turbulent Decade in the Lives of Three American Families.* New York: Random House, 1985. Print.

Maas, Peter. *The Valachi Papers*. New York: Putnam, 1968. Print.

Martini, Bobby, and Elayne Keratsis. *Citizen Somerville: Growing Up with the Winter Hill Gang*. North Reading: Powder House, 2010. Print.

McLean, Michael. *The Irish King of Winter Hill: The True Story of James J. "Buddy" McLean*. Houston: Strategic Book Publishing and Rights Co., 2013. Print.

Mollenhoff, Clark R. *Strike Force: Organized Crime and the Government*. Englewood Cliffs: Prentice-Hall, 1972. Print.

Nasaw, David. *The Patriarch: The Remarkable Life and Turbulent Times of Joseph P. Kennedy*. New York: Penguin, 2012. Print.

Nee, Patrick. *A Criminal and an Irishman: The Inside Story of the Boston Mob–IRA Connection*. Hanover: Steerforth, 2006. Print.

O'Connor, Thomas H. *Bibles, Brahmins, and Bosses: A Short History of Boston*. Trustees of the Boston Public Lib., 1991. Print.

———. *The Boston Irish: A Political History*. Boston: Back Bay, 1995. Print.

O'Neill, Gerard. *Rogues and Redeemers: When Politics Was King in Irish Boston*. New York: Random House, 2012. Print.

O'Neill, Gerard, and Dick Lehr. *Black Mass: The True Story of an Unholy Alliance Between the FBI and Irish Mob*. 2000. New York: HarperCollins, 2001. Print.

———. *The Underboss: The Rise and Fall of a Mafia Family*. 1989. New York: PublicAffairs, 2002. Print.

———. *Whitey: The Life of America's Most Notorious Mob Boss*. New York: Random House, 2013. Print.

Ouimette, Gerard T. *What Price Providence*. Lexington, 2010. Print.

Partington, John, with Arlene Violet. *The Mob and Me: Wiseguys and the Witness Protection Program*. New York: Simon & Schuster, 2010. Print.

Puleo, Stephen. *The Boston Italians: A Story of Pride, Perseverance, and Paesani, from the Years of the Great Immigration to the Present Day.* Boston: Beacon, 2007. Print.

Raab, Selwyn. *Five Families: The Rise, Decline, and Resurgence of America's Most Powerful Mafia Empires.* 2005. New York: St. Martin's, 2006. Print.

Ranalli, Ralph. *Deadly Alliance: The FBI's Secret Partnership with the Mob.* New York: HarperCollins, 2001. Print.

Reid, Ed. *The Grim Reapers: The Anatomy of Organized Crime in America.* Chicago: Regnery, 1969. Print.

Russell, Francis. *Tragedy in Dedham: The Story of the Sacco-Vanzetti Case.* 1961. New York: McGraw-Hill, 1971. Print.

———. *Sacco and Vanzetti: The Case Resolved.* New York: Harper & Row, 1986. Print.

Schorow, Stephanie. *The Crime of the Century: How the Brink's Robbers Stole Millions and the Hearts of Boston.* Beverly: Commonwealth, 2008. Print.

Sherman, Casey. *Animal: The Bloody Rise and Fall of the Mob's Most Feared Assassin.* Boston: Northeastern UP, 2013. Print.

Smith, John L. *The Animal in Hollywood: Anthony Fiato's Life in the Mafia.* New York: Barricade, 1998. Print.

Songini, Marc. *The Lost Fleet: A Yankee Whaler's Struggle Against the Confederate Navy and Arctic Disaster.* New York: St. Martin's, 2007. Print.

Stanton, Mike. *The Prince of Providence: The Rise and Fall of Buddy Cianci, America's Most Notorious Mayor.* 2003. New York: Random House, 2004. Print.

Sweeney, Emily. *Images of America: Boston Organized Crime.* Charleston: Arcadia, 2012. Print.

Teresa, Vincent Charles, and Thomas Renner. *My Life in the Mafia.* Garden City: Doubleday, 1973. Print.

———, with Thomas Renner. *Vincent Teresa's Mafia.* Garden City: Doubleday, 1975. Print.

Wallace, Brian P., and Bill Crowley. *Final Confession: The Unsolved Crimes of Phil Cresta*. Boston: Northeastern UP, 2000. Print.

Weeks, Kevin, and Phyllis Karas. *Brutal*. New York: Harper-Collins, 2006. Print.

Wolfinger, Joe, and Chris Kerr. *Rico: How Politicians, Prosecutors, and the Mob Destroyed One of the FBI's Finest Special Agents*. Wolfinger, 2012. Print.

Government Documents

United States. Cong. House. Committee on Government Reform. *Everything Secret Degenerates: The FBI's Use of Murderers as Informants*. Report. 108th Cong., 2nd sess. (Washington: GPO, 2004. Web. <https://www.fas.org/irp/congress/2003_rpt/fbi1.pdf>); (<https://www.fas.org/irp/congress/2003_rpt/fbi2.pdf>).
—————. Senate. Special Committee to Investigate Organized Crime in Interstate Commerce. Hearings. Part 2, U.S. Senate, 81st Congress, 2nd sess. Washington: GPO, 1950. Virgil Peterson testimony. Web. Published on the *American Mafia* Web site. <http://www.onewal.com/kef/kefp2.html>.

Web Pages

Olde Webster: History and Founding. <http://www.oldewebster.com/history/boatssold.htm.> Webster town Web site, contains unidentified newspaper accounts of Raymond's arrest for the United Optical Plant robbery.

The JFK Assassination. Mary Ferrell Foundation. <http://www.maryferrell.org/wiki/index.php/JFK_Assassination>. Contains thousands of declassified FBI reports and other documents about the New England Mafia, including accounts that shed light on the Kennedy assassination.

DVD

The Green Square Mile: The Story of the Charlestown Irish. Charlestown Historical Soc., 2007. DVD.

INDEX